MAXIMIZE YOUR WRITING

3

Maximize Your Writing 3

Pearson Education, Inc., 221 River Street, Hoboken, NJ 07030 USA

Staff credits: The people who made up the **Maximize Your Writing** team are Pietro Alongi, Rhea Banker, Tracey Munz Cataldo, Mindy DePalma, Gina DiLillo, Niki Lee, Amy McCormick, Lindsay Richman, and Paula Van Ells.

Text composition: MPS North America LLC
Design: EMC Design Ltd
Photo credit: Cover, PHOTOCREO Michal Bednarek / Shutterstock

ISBN-13: 978-0-13-466141-4   ISBN-10: 0-13-466141-9

Printed in the United States of America
2   16

pearsonelt.com/maximizeyourwriting

CONTENTS

Writing Level 3 – Intermediate to High Intermediate

PRE-TEST

Pre-Test 1

In the timed Pre-Test 1, you will demonstrate how well you understand sentence structure, grammar, punctuation, mechanics, and organization. You have 50 minutes to complete the test. Circle the letter of the correct answer.

1 I read _____ amazing book last month. _____ book was called *The Kite Runner*.

    a the / The
    b a / An
    c an / A
    d an / The

2 She doesn't like fancy gowns and prefers a _____ dress for her wedding.

    a simpler
    b simplier
    c simplest
    d more simpler

3 I don't have enough time to study for all my exams. I'll study for the one that is the _____ for my grade.

    a most important
    b importantest
    c more important
    d most importantly

4 It's clear that Jennifer is getting over the flu, because she is _____ she was last week.

    a as pale as
    b not as pale as
    c just as pale as
    d not much pale as

5 Rachel _____ to learn Farsi _____ to marry Ibrahim.

    a has / if she decided
    b had / if she decides
    c will have / if she decides
    d is going to have / she will decide

6 We were grateful to the doctors for _____ our father's life.

    a having saved
    b was saving
    c has saved
    d had saved

7 Jack pretended to be sick so that he _____ to school.

    a would to go
    b wouldn't have to go
    c doesn't have to go
    d will have to go

8 If I miss the bus, _____ to work?

    a must you drive me

    b you drive me

    c will you drive me

    d ought you to drive

9 John promised _____ me borrow his car.

    a to letting

    b he lets

    c letting

    d to let

10 She is usually busy in the mornings, but she _____ time to call you.

    a may have

    b must have

    c can't have

    d couldn't have

11 I'm looking for the medical imaging office in this building. What floor _____ to?

    a ought to I go

    b might I go

    c had I better go

    d should I go

12 When the kitten was born, he _____ his eyes, but now he _____ just fine.

    a wasn't able to open / could see

    b isn't able to open / can see

    c couldn't open / can see

    d can't see / could see

13 Semitic languages, such as Hebrew and Arabic, _____ from right to left.

    a is wrote

    b are written

    c is writing

    d have written

14 The house is still dirty! What _____ while I was at work?

    a were you doing

    b are you doing

    c have you done

    d you did

15 Can you believe they still _____ their grandmother in the nursing home?

    a had not visit

    b didn't visit

    c weren't visiting

    d haven't visited

16 We _____ to Greece last year for a family vacation.

   a go

   b went

   c were going

   d have gone

17 If I _____ you, I _____ to New York because the city is too crowded.

   a is; will not move

   b was; did not not

   c were; wouldn't move

   d will be; wouldn't move

18 Restaurant servers work hard, and _____ depend on tips from _____ customers for a decent wage.

   a they / their

   b they / there

   c she / her

   d he / his

19 _____ Diego Rivera's murals depicts one or more aspects of Mexican life.

   a Every

   b Most of

   c Each of

   d Most

20 Circle the letter of the correct form of reported speech for the original quote.

"Are we there yet?" asked the cranky child.

   a The cranky child asks if we were there yet.

   b The cranky child has asked if are we there yet.

   c The cranky child asked if are we there yet.

   d The cranky child asked if we were there yet.

21 Although my younger son liked all his school subjects, mathematics _____ his favorite.

   a is

   b are

   c was

   d were

22 Which sentence is written correctly?

   a Mandy got up stumbled to the kitchen started the coffee maker laid on the couch and then went back to sleep.

   b Mandy got up; stumbled to the kitchen; started the coffee maker; laid on the couch and then went back to sleep.

   c Mandy got up stumbled to the kitchen, started the coffee maker, laid on the couch and then went back to sleep.

   d Mandy got up, stumbled to the kitchen, started the coffee maker, laid on the couch, and then went back to sleep.

23 Which sentence is written correctly?

a My subscription to *Reader's Digest* expired while I was in the mountains of Kentucky last summer.

b my subscription to *reader's digest* expired while i was in the mountains of kentucky last summer.

c My Subscription to *Reader's Digest* expired while I was in the Mountains of Kentucky last summer.

d My subscription to *Reader's digest* expired while I was in the Mountains of Kentucky last summer.

24 Which sentence is written correctly?

a "This is my first day", said lost and confused student "I don't know where to find the admissions office."

b "This is my first day," said the lost and confused student. "I don't know where to find the admissions office."

c This is my first day, the lost and confused student said, I don't know where to find the admissions office.

d "This is my first day" the lost and confused student said "I don't know where to find the admissions office."

25 Which part of the sentence is an appositive phrase?

My parents are always yelling about my bedroom, the messiest one in the house.

a always

b about my bedroom

c the messiest one in the house

d in the house

26 Mr. Gonzalez is looking for the person _____ is blocking his in the parking lot.

a which car

b whose car

c who their car

d that car

27 During the Great Depression _____ many Americans migrated to different parts of the country to find a job.

a , when money was scarce,

b , where money were scarce,

c when money was scarce

d for which money was scarce

28 In many religions, people wash their hands, feet, and sometimes their entire bodies _____ they pray.

a before

b , once

c during

d , as soon as

29 Since he said he was coming to the performance, we waited to take our seats _____ the bell rang.

  a unless

  b after

  c before

  d until

30 What kind of phrase or clause is the underlined part of this sentence?

My son and his friends happily went out to play soccer <u>despite the rain</u>.

  a Prepositional phrase

  b Adjective (dependent) clause

  c Adverb (dependent) clause

  d Independent or main clause

31 What kind of phrase or clause is the underlined part of this sentence?

The car door shut <u>as she was getting out</u>.

  a Prepositional phrase

  b Adjective (dependent) clause

  c Adverb (dependent) clause

  d Independent or main clause

32 I can walk to work most of the time _____ my office is downtown.

  a so

  b and

  c because

  d yet

33 Fran needs a new computer, _____ she can't afford to buy one right now.

  a and

  b nor

  c but

  d because

34 Which label describes the sentence?

On graduation day a ceremony that includes speeches, awards, and music.

  a Fragment

  b Run-on

  c Comma Splice

  d Correct

35 Which sentence is written incorrectly?

  a People probably began to believe that umbrellas were bad luck in the house because, when they opened them, many accidents happened.

  b Since so many accidents happened when people opened umbrellas in the house, people probably began to believe that they were the cause of bad luck.

  c People probably began to believe in bad luck when people opened umbrellas in the house there were so many accidents.

  d Because of the many accidents that happened when people opened umbrellas in the house, many people probably began to believe that they were bad luck.

36 Which label describes the sentence?

Most of the world loves soccer, Americans still prefer other sports like football.

   a Fragment

   b Run-on

   c Comma Splice

   d Correct

37 What pattern describes the sentence?

A lot of my friends posted to Facebook and sent me cards on my birthday.

   a Subject Verb Phrase

   b Compound Subject Verb Phrase

   c Subject Compound Verb Phrase

   d This is not a sentence.

38 Which sentence is written incorrectly?

   a My friend moved to Austin last year, and she gave me all of her things.

   b My friend moved to Austin last year after she gave me all of her things.

   c My friend moved to Austin last year, she gave me all of her things.

   d My friend moved to Austin last year. So, she gave me all of her things.

39 Which sentence is written incorrectly?

   a Many people refuse to believe in climate change, though the earth's temperature continues to rise.

   b Many people refuse to believe in climate change though the earth's temperature continues to rise.

   c Many people refuse to believe in climate change, despite the fact that the earth's temperature continues to rise.

   d Many people refuse to believe in climate change, even though the earth's temperature continues to rise.

40 When I was a child, I was always picked last for sports. I loved it when the gym teacher let me be the _____ because that was the only time I got to be first.

   a select

   b selective

   c selector

   d selection

41 The students enjoyed the lecture. They thought it was quite _____ .

   a instructive

   b instruct

   c instruction

   d instructor

Which outline best describes the overall organization of the following paragraph? Circle the letter of the correct answer.

Sudoku is a numerical puzzle that originated in Japan. Sudoku, like the crossword puzzle, is often printed in newspapers and magazines for readers' enjoyment. It's not a word puzzle, however. The puzzle is a partially completed table with nine rows down and nine columns across. The table is further sub-divided into 9 squares. Each square is three rows down and three columns across. In order to solve the puzzle, a person has to complete each row, column, and square with the numbers 1–9. The same number cannot appear more than once in any row, column, or square. The Sudoku puzzle can be solved using the process of elimination. If a row already contains the number, for instance, then no other cell in that row can contain that number. Sudoku has become quite popular, first in Britain, and now in the United States. To sum up, Sudoku is a popular Japanese brainteaser that uses numbers.

42 a Numerical Puzzles
   1. Historical overview
   2. What it looks like
   3. How to play

b Japanese Puzzles
   1. Description
   2. How to play
   3. Popularity

c Sudoku
   1. Description
   2. How to play
   3. Popularity

Pre-Test 2

Paragraph

In the timed Pre-Test 2 Paragraph, you will demonstrate how well you can write about a topic. Pay attention to sentence structure, grammar, punctuation, mechanics, organization, and vocabulary.

Write about the following topic or the topic your teacher assigns.

You have 30 minutes to complete the test.

> Write a paragraph to express your opinion on the following topic: At what age should young people move out of their parents' homes? Support your idea with specific reasons and examples.

_____

_____

_____

_____

_____

_____

_____

_____

Essay

In the timed Pre-Test 2 Essay, you will demonstrate how well you can write about a topic. Pay attention to sentence structure, grammar, punctuation, mechanics, organization, and vocabulary.

Write about the following topic or the topic your teacher assigns.

You have 50 minutes to complete the test.

> Write an essay to express your opinion on the following topic: At what age should young people move out of their parents' homes? Support your idea with specific reasons and examples.

_____

_____

_____

_____

_____

_____

_____

_____

_____

_____

_____

_____

_____

_____

_____

_____

_____

PUNCTUATION AND MECHANICS

Periods and Question Marks

Periods and Question Marks

When to Use Periods

Use at the end of a statement, command, or sentence:
Don't wash your hair tonight. There isn't any hot water.

Use as a decimal point in numbers:
The average American family has 2.5 children.

Use with initials in people's names:
J.K. Rowling wrote the Harry Potter books.

Use with personal titles before people's names:
Mr. and Mrs. Johnson opened a new bank account.

Use with abbreviations that use lowercase letters or end in lowercase letters. Don't use periods with abbreviations that use all capital letters:
Dr. Jones worked at a clinic on Sunset Blvd. when he studied at UCLA.

Do not use a period at the end of a line in an address unless it ends with an abbreviation that requires a period:
Ms. Caroline Brown, CEO
Rainbow Media, Inc.
10 Green St.
Chicago, IL 60602

When to Use Question Marks

Use with a direct question:
Where are you going?

Use at the end of a tag question:
We are going to the movies, aren't we?

Use with polite requests:
Do you mind taking your papers off my desk?

Use after a series of questions, even if they do not constitute complete sentences:
Which places have you visited in Europe? London? Paris? Madrid?

Practice 1

Read each pair of sentences. Circle the letter of the answer that uses periods and question marks correctly.

Example:

1 **(a)** *I made a reservation for 9 P.M. at the restaurant.*
   b *I made a reservation for 9 P.M. at the restaurant?*

2 **a** I usually take my son to soccer practice every Saturday morning.
   b I usually take my son to soccer practice every Saturday morning?

3 **a** You submitted your application on time, didn't you.
   b You submitted your application on time, didn't you?

4 **a** Let's meet on Sun., the 5th, at 10:00 A.M.
   b Let's meet on Sun, the 5th, at 10:00 A.M.

5 **a** Do you know where the post office is.
   b Do you know where the post office is?

6 **a** Mrs. Haines asked if we were going to the party?
   b Mrs. Haines asked if we were going to the party.

7 **a** What other languages do you speak? German? Spanish? French?
   b What other languages do you speak? German. Spanish. French.

8 **a** F. Scott Fitzgerald wrote *The Great Gatsby*.
   b F Scott Fitzgerald wrote *The Great Gatsby*.

9 **a** It's cold in here. Do you mind closing the door?
   b It's cold in here. Do you mind closing the door.

10 **a** Tomatoes are on sale for $1,49 a pound.
   b Tomatoes are on sale for $1.49 a pound.

Practice 2

Read the letter below. Write either a period or a question mark in the blanks provided.

April 10, 2014

1 Ms _____ Karen Ruiz, Manager

ABC Electric Co

2 100 W _____ Bolton St _____

Des Moines, IA 50302

3 Dear Ms _____ Ruiz:

I am interested in working with your company and would like to know if you have any

4 positions available _____ I have been working as a certified electrician for two years _____

5 I completed my apprenticeship in Washington, DC, in September of 2011, and I received my

6 certification from the National Association of Electricians the following year _____

7 I have attached a résumé for your review _____ May I call you to discuss job

opportunities and to answer any questions you may have about my skills and experience _____

8 If so, what would be a convenient time for me to call _____

9

10 Thank you for your consideration _____

Sincerely,
John Nguyen, Jr.

APOSTROPHES

Apostrophes

Rules	Examples
Use an apostrophe (') with contractions in informal writing. It is not common to use contractions in formal, academic, and business writing.	The boy **can't** finish his homework tonight.
	I'll help you with homework after dinner.
Use an apostrophe (') before or after an *s* to show ownership. The 's can be attached to nouns or pronouns and to irregular nouns. If the noun ends in *s* because it is plural, add an apostrophe to the final *s*.	I borrowed the woman**'s** laptop.
	Is this anybody**'s** purse? I found it on the seat.
	I can hear the children**'s** laughter.
	The girls**'** shoes are filled with sand.
If you are showing possession with a proper noun (someone's name), and it ends in *s*, add an apostrophe + *s* ('s).	Henry James**'s** novels make some people yawn.
	Carson McCullers**'s** novels are lyrical.
Apostrophe + *s* ('s) goes at the end of a compound noun. It also goes at the end of the prepositional phrase attached to some nouns.	My father-in-law**'s** book
	The Duke of Windsor**'s** party
Use an apostrophe with the last noun if something is jointly owned. Use an apostrophe on both nouns if something is separately owned.	The party is at Sherri and Ricardo**'s** house.
	Both Ling**'s** and Jerry**'s** cars need to have the oil changed.
Use 's to make letters of the alphabet plural. Don't use an apostrophe to make abbreviations plural.	He pronounces his **h's**.
	Each year, the college awards a lot of AA**s**.
Do not confuse *it's* and *its*: it's = *it is* its = possessive of *it*	**It's** my brother's car. **Its** bumper is dented.

Common Contractions

Be	I am (not) = I'm (not)	it is (not) = it's (not), it isn't	they are (not) = they're (not), they aren't
Will	there will (not) be = there'll be, there won't be		
Have	we have (not) = we've (not), we haven't	he has (not) = he's (not), he hasn't	
Had	I had = I'd	I had not = I hadn't	
Would	I would = I'd	I would not = I wouldn't	
Can	he cannot / he can not = he can't		

Practice 1

Rewrite each item as a possessive phrase using an apostrophe or an apostrophe + *s*.

Prepositional Phrase with *of*

1 The speeches of politicians
2 The room of the mother and father
3 The surface of the table
4 The play area of the children
5 The husband of my sister-in-law
6 The diameter of Earth
7 The schedules of Mrs. Allen and Mrs. Ellis
8 The policy of the UN
9 The home of the Queen of England
10 The responsibility of nobody
11 The roles of the actresses

Possessive with Apostrophe

The politicians' speeches
_____
_____
_____
_____
_____
_____
_____
_____
_____
_____

Practice 2

Circle the letter of the answer that correctly uses or leaves out an apostrophe.

Example:

1 _____ a beautiful day.

   a *Its*
   b *It's*

2 The breads are delicious, because _____ baked daily.

   a they're
   b the'yre

3 My two best _____ birthdays are on the same day.

   a friends'
   b friend's

4 Surprisingly, both _____ applications were rejected.

   a Tim and George's
   b Tim's and George's

5 _____ make a promise you know you _____ keep.

   a Don't, can't
   b Do'nt, ca'nt

6 Tonight _____ having dinner at _____ house.

   a we're, Tom and Rosie's
   b were, Tom's and Rosie's

7 That _____ my cell phone. It must be _____.

   a isn't, Terry's
   b is'nt, Terrys'

8 Always proofread your essays, or _____ be full of mistakes.

   a they'll
   b the'yll

9 _____ have fish and _____ for dinner tonight!

   a Lets, chip's
   b Let's, chips

10 You _____ use other _____ credit cards.

   a shouldnt, peoples'
   b shouldn't, people's

CAPITALIZATION

Capitalization

Rules	Examples
Capitalize the first word of a sentence.	**D**o not swim here.
Capitalize proper nouns, months, days of the week, holidays, languages, religions, geographical areas, many physical structures, and historical events.	My brother **L**arry lives in **T**aiwan.
	I was born in **N**ovember.
	My children are fluent in both **E**nglish and **P**olish.
	World **W**ar II ended in 1945.
Capitalize the most important words of textual titles. Do not capitalize articles and prepositions in titles unless they begin the title.	Is *Of Mice and Men* a good novel?
	Here's a fascinating article: *The Therapeutic Misconception and Bioethical Frameworks.*
Capitalize the first word in direct quotations anywhere in a sentence.	My mother said, "**C**lean your room."
Capitalize personal and professional titles when they are part of a person's name.	The dinner was hosted by **V**ice **P**resident Anderson.
	Mr. Frank Welfin, **S**upervisor
Capitalize greetings and closings in letters, personal titles, and names.	**D**ear David, This is Mr. Smith writing. Mrs. Smith and I would like to have you to dinner. **S**incerely, Mr. Smith
Capitalize the first-person singular pronoun (*I*).	**I** believe **I** am qualified because **I** am committed.
Capitalize cardinal directions when naming a region or identifying where something is.	He's from the **S**outh.
Do not capitalize *black* and *white* when they refer to skin color.	The black and white populations lived on opposite sides of the river.
Do not capitalize the word *god* in non-monotheistic religions.	Ganesh is one god among many.
Do not capitalize cardinal directions when indicating in which direction to go.	Go west and find your fortune.
Do not capitalize the names of the seasons.	winter, summer, spring, fall / autumn

Practice 1

Underline the words that should be capitalized.

1 dear Ms. andres,

last friday, i dropped off my application for employment, but, unfortunately, it contained an error. attached is the corrected copy. please replace the old copy with this one. thank you.

sincerely,

Lorena cardozo

2 *the Old Man and the sea* is one of Ernest hemingway's more famous novels. the story is about santiago, a fisherman who hasn't caught any fish in months. when he goes out to fish, he has a desperate struggle to bring a giant fish home. he wants to sell the fish and make money for his village.

Practice 2

Underline 12 words in the résumé that contain errors in capitalization.

Lorena Cardozo

401 Second Avenue north

Hollywood, California 90049

Objective:

To obtain a position as a Teaching Intern

Experience:

Teaching Assistant, psychology 101, 2012

Spanish Tutor, 2008 to present

camp Counselor, Roxbury park 2006–2008

Education:

University of California, riverside: ma, Education, 2014

California State university, northridge: BA, spanish, 2012

Skills:

Spanish (fluent), Computers, typing (50 wpm)

References:

Available Upon Request

COLONS

Presentation

Colons

Rules	Examples
Use a colon to introduce a series of items.	I have visited many places this year: San Francisco, Philadelphia, New York, and Miami.
Use a colon to separate hours from minutes.	The appointment is at **5:30** p.m. tomorrow.
Use a colon at the end of a formal letter greeting.	Dear Dr. Espinoza:
Use a colon to connect an independent clause to a direct quotation.	Hiram reflected on his father's favorite saying: "A bird in the hand is worth two in the bush."
Use a colon to separate a title from a subtitle.	One of my favorite thrillers, *X-Files: I Want to Believe*, came out in 2008.
The information that follows a colon must be connected to a word or phrase before the colon in the sentence.	I saw many things on my trip: tigers and bears, birds and bees.
A colon usually follows an independent clause, not a phrase. If you feel you can logically put a period after the clause, then a colon can go there, too. You may also use *the following* or *as follows* before a colon.	He gave apples, oranges, and pears. > He gave the following: apples, oranges, and pears.
	I've been to many places this year: New York, Paris, and Tokyo. > I have been to the following places this year: New York, Paris, and Tokyo.

Practice 1

Read the text below. For each numbered blank, choose the letter of the answer that correctly punctuates the letter.

April (1) _____

Dear (2) _____

I am pleased (3) _____ will be able to chaperone our class camping trip this year.

You and your son will need to bring the following (4) _____ tent, sleeping bags, sturdy hiking shoes, and warm clothing. As a parent chaperone, you will also (5) _____ of the weekend schedule, a list of the students' names, and a leader badge. I have included these items in the letter. In addition, I have (6) _____ of the manual, "Snow Valley (7) _____Rules and Responsibilities." Please note your most important (8) _____ assist during activities and to report any misbehavior.

The school bus will leave from the school parking lot on Friday morning at (9) _____
A.M. Please arrive 30 minutes before departure. We will return to the school on Sunday evening at
(10) _____ P.M. (11) _____

Ms. Karen Teal, Teacher

Snow Valley Elementary School

1 **a** 21: 2014
   b 21 2014
   c 21, 2014

2 **a** Mr. Kifle:
   b Mr. Kifle
   c Mr. Kifle;

3 **a** that: you
   b that, you
   c that you

4 **a** supplies, a
   b supplies: a
   c supplies a

5 **a** need: a copy
   b need a copy
   c need; a copy

6 **a** included: a copy
   b included a copy
   c included, a copy

7 **a** Elementary Chaperone;
   b Elementary Chaperone
   c Elementary: Chaperone

8 **a** duties: to
   b duties to
   c duties, to

9 **a** 8:45
   b 8.45
   c 8 45

10 **a** 6:30
    b 6.30
    c 6 30

11 **a** Sincerely;
    b Sincerely:
    c Sincerely,

Practice 2

Circle the letter of the sentence with correct punctuation.

1 a These are three foods I refuse to eat liver, spinach, and oysters.
  b These are three foods I refuse to eat: liver, spinach, and oysters.

2 a At the restaurant last evening, I ordered: a salad, a steak, and a flan.
  b At the restaurant last evening, I ordered a salad, a steak, and a flan.

3 a Jan looked up and greeted the audience: "I am so pleased to have this opportunity to speak to you today."
  b Jan looked up and greeted the audience "I am so pleased to have this opportunity to speak to you today."

4 a Attending the class were only four people, Anna, Tom, Trisha, and Toshi.
  b Attending the class were only four people: Anna, Tom, Trisha, and Toshi.

5 a There are three countries in North America: Canada, Mexico, and the United States.
  b There are three countries in North America, Canada, Mexico, and the United States.

6 a On a cruise to Alaska, be sure to take along: a deck of cards, a camera, and a raincoat!
  b On a cruise to Alaska, be sure to take along a deck of cards, a camera, and a raincoat!

7 a I highly recommend the book *Learning English: One Woman's Struggle to Conquer the Language*.
  b I highly recommend the book *Learning English, One Woman's Struggle to Conquer the Language*.

8 a The doors will open to the public at exactly 2:00 P.M.
  b The doors will open to the public at exactly 2.00 P.M.

PARENTHESES

Rules	Examples
Use parentheses when you need to include extra information or additional comments connected to the main idea of the sentence.	Some animals that hibernate **(**mainly bears and rodents**)** will sleep for months during the winter.
Use parentheses when you use letters or numbers in lists within a sentence.	The priorities for our party's budget are **(1)** food, **(2)** music, **(3)** decorations, and **(4)** prizes, in that order.
Put periods and commas outside the parentheses for words and phrases.	Thank you in advance for reviewing my application **(**attached**)**, and please contact me at your earliest convenience.
Put periods and commas inside the parentheses for complete sentences.	Thank you in advance for reviewing my application. **(**I have attached it.**)**

Practice 1

Underline the words and phrases that should be in parentheses.

1

As we read, we often come across words we don't understand. Here's a useful strategy to help you figure out the meaning of unfamiliar words: a read the sentence the word appears in; b decide what part of speech the word is noun, verb, adjective, etc.; c determine if the word contains any letters before it or after it that give hints to its meaning prefixes, suffixes; d look for important words, phrases, and sentences around the unfamiliar word that might also give hints to its meaning context clues; e think of other words or phrases that could be used in place of the word synonyms.

2

Dear Azhar,

I can't wait to see you and your family at the company's annual picnic next Sunday afternoon. Your husband and son will be attending, too, I hope! My daughters, Leah and Yameena, are so big now eight and ten years old. I'm sure your son, Nabil, has grown a lot, too. My girls are looking forward to the picnic and to seeing and playing with him again.

It's been a long time since we've seen each other. When I moved to our office in the East something I wasn't happy about at first, I didn't think we'd lose touch for so long time flies, though. You still live in Venice Beach, right? I was wondering if you'd like to carpool to the picnic? We've got plenty of room in our car. I rented an SUV that seats seven comfortably! Give me a call at (205) 555–6573.

See you on Sunday,

Jamie

Practice 2

Use the phrases in the word boxes to arrange the sentence in the order that uses parentheses correctly.

Example:

1

| *Jerusalem* | *is a holy city* | *for three major religions* | *(* | *Judaism, Christianity, and Islam* | *)* | *.* |

2

| . | (| The famous actor |) | It was a gift from his father when he was 18 years old | owned a Porsche, a Mercedes, and a 1968 Volkswagen Beetle. |

_____

3

| i.e., put water in his bowl, give him food, and take him for a walk | Danny– | Please remember |) | the dog before you leave | . | to take care of | (|

_____

4

| if you keep them inside a paper bag | . | will ripen faster | (|) | peaches, avocados, plums, apricots, etc. | Some fruits |

_____

5

August 10, 1962	)	My grandparents	this year.	(	are celebrating their 50th wedding anniversary

6

.	He was having a temper tantrum.	(	picked up the box of toys	)	The child	and dumped it on the floor

7

after the car accident.	$3,000.00	paid us three thousand dollars	The insurance company	(	)

8

)	1809–1865	Abraham Lincoln	of the United States.	(	was the 16th president

9

8:00 A.M. to 6:00 P.M.	working in the garden.	We	spent all day Saturday	(	)

10

near Seattle to enjoy nature.	Mt. Rainier, Olympic National Forest, North Cascades	)	Every year,	hikers head to one of the many national parks	(

11

it is important to	(1)	(2)	choose copying options.	enter your code and	To use the copier in this office,

SEMICOLONS

Semicolons

Rules	Examples
Use a semicolon between independent clauses if there is a clear relationship between the two.	Sunrise is usually at about 6 a.m.; sunset is at about 6 p.m.
Use a semicolon with a transition word or phrase and a comma to form a compound sentence. The same sentence can also be divided by a period.	There is a huge danger of forest fires in the summer; **as a result**, many parks do not allow camping fires.
	There is a huge danger of forest fires in the summer. **As a result**, many parks do not allow camping fires.
	There is a huge danger of forest fires in the summer. Many parks, **as a result**, do not allow camping fires.
Use semicolons for items in a list that already includes commas.	I need to pick up a few things at Madison Market, which has the best organic vegetables; at the pharmacy where my doctor sent the prescription; and at Mudbay, which has my cat's food.

Practice 1

On each blank, write either a comma or a semicolon to punctuate the paragraph correctly.

Example:

The children left the back door open again _____;_____ *the kitchen is full of flies.*

An eclectic room tells a lot about a person _____ in fact, it tells more about a person than any other type of decor. Take, for example _____ my living room. It has an old Victorian sofa and armchair, which my grandmother gave me _____ a Turkish carpet I bought on a trip to Istanbul last year _____ a coffee table crafted from recycled wood _____ and a modern floor lamp, which I found for five dollars at a yard sale last week! My living room tells you a lot about me _____ it tells you that I cherish family heirlooms _____ enjoy traveling _____ care for the environment _____ and love a good bargain!

Practice 2

Read each sentence. Decide whether it requires a comma or a semicolon. Then circle the letter of the correct answer.

1 Some people use email to communicate _____ others prefer to talk on the phone.

   a ;

   b ,

2 Dog owners have been very good about keeping their dogs on leashes _____ as a result, fewer dogs have run away.

   a ;

   b ,

3 You will want to bring many items for the camping trip _____ for example, sleeping bags, pans, and warm clothing will make the trip better.

   a ;

   b ,

4 If I am able to go _____ I will definitely be at the party.

   a ;

   b ,

5 This conference has people who have come from Budapest, Hungary _____ Madrid, Spain; United Kingdom _____ and Mexico.

   a ; ;

   b , ,

6 I have paid my dues _____ therefore, my membership should be current.

   a ;

   b ,

7 Besides hiking and horseback riding _____ this camp offers swimming, gymnastics, and archery.

   a ;

   b ,

COMMAS

Presentation

Commas

Rules	Examples
Use commas to separate independent clauses in compound sentences.	Bill took the car to the mechanic, and his wife picked the kids up.
	My brother went to law school, but he quit to become a teacher.
A comma should separate a conjunctive adverb at the beginning, middle, or end of a clause.	My brother went to law school. **However**, he quit to become a teacher.
	My brother went to law school. He quit to become a teacher, **however**.
	My brother went to law school. He quit, **however**, to become a teacher.
Use a comma to separate a dependent clause when it comes first in a complex sentence. Do not use a comma if the independent clause comes first.	**When Angela went to New York**, she visited her grandmother.
	Angela visited her grandmother when she went to New York.
Use a comma to separate prepositional phrases, time expressions, and other sentence openers.	**Because of the cold weather**, we have decided to go to a movie.
	Last week, the couple left for a family trip down the Oregon coast.
Use a comma to separate items in a list of three or more.	The Midwest is the biggest producer of **corn, wheat, soybeans, and cattle** in the United States.
Use a comma to separate unnecessary (nonessential) adjective clauses and appositives.	Providence Hospital, **where I was born**, is closing next year.
	Carl Sagan, **a famous American scientist**, wrote the novel *Contact*.
Use a comma to separate a direct quote before or after the reporting phrase.	"Be careful," **Ann said**, "when you go out tonight."
Use a comma to separate the month and day from the year in dates.	September 17, 2014
Use a comma to separate the street, apartment, city, and state in addresses if written as a string. Use a comma to separate the street and apartment and the city and state if the address is written on separate lines.	301 Main St., Apt. 6, Seattle, WA 98103
	301 Main St., Apt. 6 Seattle, WA 98103
A comma separates the last from the first name. Do not use a comma if the first name comes first.	Smith, Jonas
	Jonas Smith
A comma separates numbers in multiples of three.	$1,000,000,000.00
	55,500 people
A comma follows the greeting and closing in an informal letter.	Dear John,
	Sincerely, Lamar Jones

Practice 1

Circle the letter of the answer that uses commas correctly.

Example:

1 *I bought* _____ *a melon at the supermarket.*

    a *apples, bananas, carrots and*

    (b) *apples, bananas, carrots, and*

2 This lamp _____ is more than a hundred years old.

    a , which I bought at a garage sale,

    b which I bought at a garage sale

    c , which I bought at a garage sale

3 A main difference between a harpsichord and a piano is in the use of their strings. Hammers are used to strike the strings of a _____ the strings of a harpsichord are plucked.

    a piano, However

    b piano, however,

    c piano; however,

4 Mrs. Carlin _____ "Can you can babysit Friday evening?"

    a called and asked me

    b called and asked me,

    c called, and asked me,

5 My brother-in-law Tim _____ is looking for a job with a major law firm.

    a who graduated from law school in May

    b , who graduated from law school in May,

    c , who graduated from law school in May

6 The president of the United States lives and works in the White _____ in _____.

    a House; his residence / Washington D.C.

    b House, his residence / Washington, D.C.

    c House his residence / Washington. D.C.

7 As she was driving home from _____ was stopped and got a ticket for speeding.

    a work. Nancy

    b work, Nancy

    c work Nancy

8 _____ the young woman
_____ .

   a Running to board the train. / slipped, and broke her arm

   b Running to board the train, / slipped and broke her arm

   c Running to board the train / slipped and broke, her arm

9 I've been living with my parents for the past _____ I'm remodeling my kitchen.

   a month, because,

   b month because

   c month, because

Practice 2

Circle the underlined part that uses commas correctly.

1 Alligators are native to only two countries in the world: the United States and China. In the United States, / the United States they live in the southeastern part of the country especially / country, especially in Florida and Louisiana. Both states claim to have more than one million alligators living in the wild in freshwater environments such as marshes, rivers, wetlands and swamps / wetlands, and swamps.

2 In China, alligators / China alligators live in the Yangtze River. However they / However, they are nearly extinct, and fewer / extinct and fewer than 500 are left in the wild. Most Chinese alligators live in zoos around the world, where / world where scientists are working hard to preserve the species. One zoo in Florida, for example, / Florida for example, has successfully reproduced Chinese alligators and has released / alligators, and has released some of their offspring back to the wild in China.

3 CREDIT CARD APPLICATION

Name (last, first): Smith, Ron / Smith Ron,

Date of birth: May, 7 1975 / May 7, 1975

Address: 3482 Rodeo Drive

City/State/Zip Code: Beverly Hills CA, 90210 / Beverly Hills, CA 90210

Occupation: Investment Banker

Annual salary: $55,000.00 / $55,000,00

QUOTATIONS

Presentation

Quotations

Rules	Examples
Use quotations to write the exact words from a source (a lecture, book, or radio program).	Barack Obama coined the famous saying "Yes, we can" in his speech at Knox College on June 4, 2005.
Use quotations for titles of songs, poems, speeches, or works that are found in compilations or complete works. Use italics for complete works.	I love the song "Something to Believe In" by the Steve Miller Band. It's on *The Joker* album.
	One of my favorite short stories is "Speech Sounds" from *Bloodchild and Other Stories*, a book by Octavia Butler.
To write direct quotations, use a subject + reporting verb phrase before, in the middle, or after to introduce the quote. Put commas, periods, and question marks inside a closed quote.	Tan said, "I'm sure I passed my test." "I'm sure I passed my test," Tan said. "I'm sure," Tan said, "that I passed my test."
It's possible to use other phrases without a reporting verb to introduce a quote.	My student Tan is optimistic. **In his words**, "I'm sure I passed my test."

Practice 1

Circle the letter of the answer that uses quotation marks correctly.

Example:

1 *I wasn't sure how to respond when Lara asked,* _____

   a *"Are you going to the party tomorrow?"*
   b *"Are you going to the party tomorrow"?*

2 Martin Luther King, Jr. argued for the rights of African Americans in his 1963 _____ speech.

   a "I Have a Dream"
   b I Have a Dream

3 We enjoyed the piano recital last night. As Tom said, _____

   a "it was awesome!"
   b "It was awesome!"

4 "If it rains _____ she asked, _____

   a tomorrow," / "will we still go to the beach?"
   b tomorrow"? / "Will we still go to the beach?"
   c tomorrow." / "will we still go to the beach?"

5 One of my favorite poems is _____
by Dylan Thomas.

   a Do Not Go Gentle into That Good Night

   b "Do Not Go Gentle into That Good Night"

6 "I'm studying _____ Diane said _____ love working with animals."

   a to be a vet / . "Because I

   b to be a vet," / , "because I

Practice 2

Fill in the blanks in the paragraph with quotations from the following dialogue. Use quotation marks correctly.

Passenger: Where are you going?

Me: To Portland.

Passenger: Me, too. Are you going for business or pleasure?

Me: For pleasure. One of my old college friends lives there. She's getting married this weekend.

Passenger: How funny! I'm going to a wedding, too. What's your friend's name?

Me: Her name is Kindra Ramsay, and she's marrying her college boyfriend, Bill Mason.

Passenger: We're going to the same wedding! Bill is my brother!

The passenger sitting next to me at the airport asked, 1 _____ *"Where are you going?"* _____

2 _____ I answered. She said,

3 _____ Then she asked me if I was going

for business or pleasure. I told her for pleasure. "One of my old college friends

4 _____ I said, "and she's getting married

5 _____ "How funny," she said, "I'm going to

6 _____ Then she asked me what my friend's

name was. "Her name is 7 _____ I told her,

8 _____ her college boyfriend,

9 _____ I couldn't believe it when she said,

10 _____ to the same wedding.

11 _____

PARAGRAPH FORMAT

Paragraph Format

Review the guidelines for formatting academic writing.

Features	Rules
Heading	If required, include your full name, class name, and date at the top left-hand corner of the page.
Title	If you include a paragraph title, center it on the line just after your heading.
Indentation	Skip a line after the title to start your handwritten paragraph. Then indent the first line of a handwritten paragraph five letter spaces.
	Start your typed paragraph on the line after the title. Use the Tab key to indent the first line of a typed paragraph ½ inch.
Line spacing	Typed paragraphs should be double-spaced. Set line spacing to 2.0.
	Skip a line after every written line for handwritten paragraphs.
Margins	Leave one-inch margins on the top, bottom, left, and right of the page.
	Set margins to 1 inch for typed paragraphs.
	The left margin should be straight. The right margin doesn't need to be straight.
	Use the margin lines on college-ruled paper for handwritten paragraphs.
Other considerations	Use 8.5-by-11-inch standard paper.
	Handwritten assignments should be in blue or black pen.
	Typed assignments should use appropriate font (e.g., Calibri, Arial, Times New Roman, Courier) and size (10–12 points).

Practice 1

Label the paragraph with the correct format features. For each blank line, write the word or phrase from the word box that matches that feature.

Indent	Heading	Uneven right margin
Even left margin	Title	

_____ Maria Lopez

ESOL 06

December 2, 2012

Our Financial Problem _____

_____ Last year, my husband and I had to borrow money because we

needed a new car. Now, I really need to get a job to help my husband

pay the money back, but I have a huge obstacle. Working will be

difficult, because I also have to take care of our children. My husband

and I have been discussing what to do. One solution is for me to work

part-time while my children are in school. Another solution is to ask _____

my mother to take care of the children so that I can get a full-time

job. Either way, my husband has agreed to help out more around the

house. We will all have to work together to solve our financial

troubles.

Practice 2

Draw a line to match each paragraph feature to its corresponding guideline.

Example:

1 *Heading* _____ *Upper left-hand corner*

2 Full name, Class, Date   2.0 or every other line

3 Paper   Center on the line after the heading

4 Date Format   10–12 points

5 Title   Month, Day, Year

6 Line Spacing   Heading

7 Margins   8½ by 11 (white or lined)

8 Font Style   ½ inch or 5 spaces

9 Font Size   1 inch on all sides

10 Indentation   Times New Roman

GRAMMAR

Simple Future

Presentation

Simple Future (*Will* and *Be Going To*)

We use *will* and *be going to* to talk about the future. These are the general rules for using *will* and *be going to*.

Rules	Examples
To form sentences with *will*, use subject + *will (not)* + verb. *Will* can be contracted to *'ll*. *Will not* can be contracted to *won't*.	**I will / I'll finish** the laundry.
	Joe will not / won't vacuum the rug.
To form sentences with *be going to*, use subject + *am, is, are (not)* + *going to* + verb. The verb *be* can be contracted.	**She is / She's going to sleep** at 10 p.m.
	We are not / We're not / We aren't going to take the trip anymore.
To form questions with *will*, use *Will* + subject + verb.	**Will you call** the bank today?
To form questions with *be going to*, use *Am, Is,* or *Are* + *subject* + *going to* + verb.	**Are you going to visit** your parents later?
Use *will* to make a prediction about the future.	I think the bus to Houston **will arrive** at the station at 6:00 p.m.
Use *will* to make an offer.	If you want, **I'll do** the dishes.
Use *will* to refuse to do something.	No, I **won't clean** my room.
Use *will* to make a request.	**Will** you **get** some eggs from the store?
Use *will* to make a promise.	I promise I **will go** to the store in the morning.
Use *be going to* to make a prediction about the immediate future based on something that is happening now.	Oh, look at those clouds. It**'s going to rain**.
Use *be going to* to state a plan or decision.	Jamal and his friends **aren't going to drive** to the soccer match together.
Use *be going to* to state an intention.	**I'm going to finish** my homework in the morning before work.

Practice 1

Circle the letter next to *the correct verb form* to complete the sentence.

1 What a warm day! We _____ to the pool after lunch.
  a will go
  b 're going to go

2 I can't open this jar. _____ help me?
  a Will you
  b Are you going to

3 No, I _____ buy that book for class. It's much too expensive!
  a won't
  b am not going to

4 Ana doesn't feel well. She _____ to the doctor.
  a 'll go
  b 's going to go

5 Her sons promise they _____ finish their homework before dinner.
  a will
  b are going to

6 **A:** What are your plans for the holiday?
  B: My family and I _____ spend the New Year in Portland.
  a will
  b are going to

7 **A:** I'd love a cup of cofee.
  B: OK, _____ make some.
  a I'll
  b I am going to

8 To be more connected with his friends, Tim _____ open a Facebook account tomorrow.
  a will
  b is going to

9 Look at the time. We _____ be late!
  a will
  b 're going to

10 If you need me, _____ be happy to help.
  a I'll
  b I'm going to

Practice 2

Write the correct form of *will* or *be going to* for each verb in parentheses to complete the sentence.

1 Sue is driving too fast. She _____ (get) a ticket.

2 It's a beautiful day today! I think I _____ (walk) to school.

3 Next week, the committee _____ (probably vote) to reduce the budget.

4 My friends and I _____ (travel) in Mexico and Honduras this summer.

5 Lee _____ (not apply) for that job. It doesn't pay enough money.

6 The reporter thinks Seattle _____ (be) sunny and clear this week.

7 The landlord assures us that he _____ (not raise) the rent this year.

8 Luis woke up late this morning, so I think he _____ (miss) his bus.

9 I forgot my wallet. That's OK. Sam promised that he _____ (pay) for lunch!

10 My boss _____ (not give) me the day off for my daughter's graduation. How unfair!

Articles

Articles: Indefinite and Definite

Articles come before nouns. We use them to show whether the noun is indefinite (*a, an*) or definite (*the*). Review the form, meaning, and use of indefinite and definite articles.

When to Use Indefinite Articles (a, an, Ø)

Use *a* or *an* for singular nouns and Ø (*no article*) for plural/noncount nouns for indefinite meanings.

Use *a/an* with singular count nouns that are not specific: *a truck*. Use *an* if the following noun starts with a vowel sound: *an orange*.

Place *a/an* before adjectives that modify nouns: *a great idea, an excellent solution*.

Do not use an article when referring to a class of things: *Ann wants me to bring Ø soda to the party.*

Ø Roses are quite diverse. There are many varieties.

Use *the* with singular count nouns, plural count nouns, and noncount nouns: *the boy, the trees*. Study the rules for using *the*.

Rules	Examples
Use *a* or *an* for singular nouns and Ø (**no article**) for plural/noncount nouns for indefinite meanings.	I bought **a car**. I planted **Ø flowers** in my garden. I bought **Ø milk**.
Use *a/an* with singular count nouns that are not specific. Use *an* if the following noun starts with a vowel.	I saw **a truck** pass by my house. Can I have **an orange**?
Place *a/an* before adjectives that modify nouns.	This is **a great idea**. I have **an excellent solution**.
Do not use an article when referring to a class of things or a group in general.	Ann wants me to bring **Ø soda** to the party. **Ø Roses** are quite diverse. There are many varieties.
Use *a/an* to introduce a person, place, or thing for the first time (the listener or reader does not know who, what, or where).	I got **Ø yogurt** from the store, but I had to take **the yogurt** back because it wasn't plain. I bought **a new laptop** yesterday. **The laptop** came with a protective case.
Use *the* with singular count nouns, plural count nouns, and noncount nouns that are used for the second time.	Yesterday I bought **a car**. **The car** has **a sun roof**. **The sun roof** needs repair.

Use *the* with people, places, or things that are unique (there is only one).	We had a meeting with **the president.**
	The moon is bright tonight.
Use *the* with nouns that are known to both the speaker and the listener.	I'm going to **the bank** at **the corner** of First and Main Streets.
Use *the* with ordinal numbers and superlatives.	On **the Fourth** of July, we go to the lake to watch fireworks. It's **the best place** to watch.
Use *the* with nouns with modifiers (e.g., adjectives, prepositional phrases, adjective clauses).	**The milk** that I just bought is sour.
	The house on the corner is for sale.
	The black dog belongs to Marcia.
Use *the* with some names.	**The** United States, **the** Statue of Liberty

Review of Article Usage

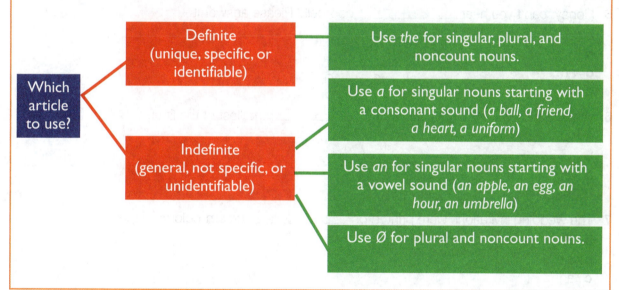

Practice 1

Circle the letter next to the correct indefinite or definite article (or no article) to complete each sentence.

Example:

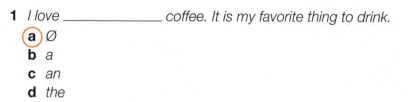

1 *I love _____ coffee. It is my favorite thing to drink.*
   a Ø
   b *a*
   c *an*
   d *the*

2 _____ lions at the local zoo seem quite tame.

   a Ø

   b A

   c An

   d The

3 Is _____ tomato a fruit or a vegetable?

   a Ø

   b a

   c an

   d the

4 I don't usually like dogs, but _____ dog next door is an exception.

   a Ø

   b a

   c an

   d the

5 Honey, can't you hear _____ doorbell? Please answer it.

   a Ø

   b a

   c an

   d the

6 When Sandy was a puppy, she was _____ smallest of the litter.

   a Ø

   b a

   c an

   d the

7 The wedding invitations were printed on _____ cream-colored paper.

   a Ø

   b a

   c an

   d the

8 We need _____ new doorbell. Ours isn't working.

   a Ø

   b a

   c an

   d the

9 Thank you for inviting me. It's quite _____ honor.

   a Ø

   b a

   c an

   d the

10 Katie needs _____ new sunglasses, but she doesn't have time to shop.

    a ∅

    b a

    c an

    d the

11 We finished planning the awards ceremony. Now we need to find _____ MC to host the show.

    a ∅

    b a

    c an

    d the

Practice 2

Circle the underlined indefinite or definite articles (or no article) that complete the sentences correctly.

Example:

I work for [(a)/ ∅ / an / the] car manufacturer, and I travel a lot on business.

Last week, I had an / a / ∅ / the amusing experience. There was a / an / ∅ / the group of basketball players on my flight to Chicago. The / A / An / ∅ players were all young, lean, and tall. The / A / An / ∅ tallest was nearly 7 feet; the / a / an / ∅ shortest was at least 6 feet 2. I am only 5 feet 8, and the / a / an / ∅ amusing thing was that I had a / an / ∅ / the seat on the / a / an / ∅ aisle, while two of the players had the middle seat and the window seat next to me. Unfortunately, the / a / an / ∅ plane was full, and there were no empty aisle seats for them to move to. I decided to offer my seat to one of the players. But which one? Both were equally uncomfortable. They discussed the / a / an / ∅ situation and decided that the / a / an / ∅ only fair solution was to flip a / an / ∅ / the coin. The / A / An / ∅ player with the window seat lost the toss. His friend moved to the aisle, I sat in the / a / an / ∅ middle, and the player who had the window seat spent most of the / a / an / ∅ flight to Chicago standing and walking up and down the / a / an / ∅ aisle.

Comparative and Superlative Adjectives

Comparative and Superlative Adjectives

Use **comparative adjectives** to compare two or more people, places, or actions.

When we compare the same kinds of words, phrases, or clauses, we use *than*.

Examples:

Barry is a **better** worker **than** Bill. (nouns)

Gabby eats **faster than** her brother does. (clauses)

Superlative adjectives are used to compare one person, thing, or place with a group of other people, things, or places. A superlative adjective tells us which person, place, thing, animal, or idea has the most or the least of something.

Superlative adjectives are preceded by the word *the*.

Follow these rules to form comparative and superlative adjectives.

Comparative Adjectives		
Rules	**Examples**	**Sentences**
Use adjective + *-er* to form comparatives with regular adjectives (1–2 syllables). If the adjective ends in vowel + consonant, then double the consonant.	small > small**er** cheap > cheap**er** hot > ho**tter** fat > fa**tter**	My new apartment is **smaller** than my old apartment.
Use adjective + *-ier* to form comparatives with two-syllable adjectives that end in y. Omit y.	sunny > sunn**ier** easy > eas**ier** funny > funn**ier** shy > shyer *(exception)*	I think Mark is **funnier** than anyone else I know.
Use *more* or *less* before adjectives that have two or more syllables.	convenient > **more / less** convenient	Driving to work is **more convenient** than taking the bus.
	beautiful > **more / less** beautiful	My town is **less beautiful** in the winter than it is in the summer.
Some adjectives with two syllables take *-er* or *more*.	friendly > friendl**ier** / **more** friendly	Some dog breeds are **friendlier / more friendly** toward children than others.

Good, bad, and *far* are irregular.	good > better	I'm much **better** at tennis than I used to be.
	bad > worse	
	far > farther	
Note that all adjectives take *less*.	smart > **less** smart	This chair is **less comfortable** than that chair.
	comfortable > **less** comfortable	

Superlative Adjectives		
Rules	**Examples**	**Sentences**
Use *the* + adjective + *-est* to form superlatives with one-syllable adjectives. If the adjective ends in vowel + consonant, then double the consonant.	strong > **the strongest**	My father is **the strongest** person I know.
	fat > **the fattest**	
Use *the* + adjective + *-iest* with two-syllable adjectives that end in *y*. Omit *y*.	easy > **the easiest**	In my opinion, Jerry Seinfeld is **the funniest** American comedian.
	shy > the shyest *(exception)*	
Use *the most* or *the least* before adjectives that have two or more syllables.	interesting > **the most** interesting	Many people think that Paris is **the most beautiful** city in the world. I disagree and think it is **the least beautiful** city.
	expensive > **the least** expensive	
Good, bad, and *far* are irregular.	good > the best	Buffalo, New York, has **the worst** winter weather in the United States.
	bad > the worst	
	far > the farthest	

Practice 1

Write the correct comparative and superlative forms of the adjectives in the table. Some adjectives can have more than one form.

Adjective	Comparative	Superlative
pure	purer	the purest
subtle		
far		
clever		
soft		
sad		
dirty		
athletic		

Practice 2

Read the passage. Write the correct comparative or superlative form of the adjective in parentheses. The symbols indicate a degree of comparison: + means "more or most," and – means "less or least."

Example:

1 My brothers are all _____older_____ (+old) than I am. I'm _____the youngest_____ (+young).

2 **A:** How did the apartment search go today?

   B: Fine. I saw three places I really liked.

   A: Really? Tell me about them.

   B: Well, they all have three bedrooms, but the first and third apartments have _____ (+ roomy) bedrooms than the second. The bedrooms in the second apartment are also the _____ (– attractive).

   A: What did you like about the second apartment?

   B: Well, the second apartment has _____ (+ beautiful) kitchen of the three apartments. The kitchen has a _____ (+ open) layout with stainless steel appliances. The kitchens in the other two apartments are _____ (+ narrow) and _____ (– spacious).

   A: How are the other rooms?

   B: Well, all three apartments have a bathroom, living room, and dining room, but the first apartment has _____ (+ tall) windows than the second apartment, and _____ (+ panoramic) views than the third apartment.

   A: Wow, it sounds like you have a tough choice. How will you decide which apartment to rent?

   B: Well, the first apartment is _____ (+ good), but it is also _____ (+ far) from my job, and I don't like to commute. I will probably choose the second one if I don't find anything better tomorrow.

Comparisons with as … as

Presentation

Comparisons with *as … as*

We use *as … as* and other phrases with *as* to say how two or more items are or are not equal. Review the rules for using *as … as* and these phrases.

Rules	Examples
as … as shows equality.	Picasso's paintings are **as disturbing as** Goya's.
just as … as adds emphasis to an equal comparison.	The sofa is **just as comfortable as** the bed.
not as … as negates an equation and denotes inequality.	A Volkswagen is not **as expensive as** a Mercedes.
the same … as is another way of denoting equality.	My mother bought **the same car as** my sister.
not the same … as denotes inequality.	This car is **not the same as** that car.
as much … as / as many … as compare numbers or amounts. *Much* is used with noncount nouns; *many* is used with count nouns.	The cake has **as much sugar as** the pie.
	Jake does not have **as many marbles as** Sally.
When comparing pronouns using *to be*, use the nominative case.	**She is** not as old **as I.**
	She is bigger **than he.**

Practice 1

Circle the correct phrase to complete each sentence.

1 My new cat is [as naughty as, just as naughty, naughty as] my old cat.

2 Mount St. Helens and Mount Rainier are both part of the Pacific Ring of Fire in the Cascade Mountains. Mount St. Helens, a volcano that last erupted in 1980, is a national monument. It is often compared to Mount Rainier because it is in [the same state as, as many state as, as much state as] Mount Rainier. Mount St. Helens is [not as tall as, not so tall, not tall] and [not as old as, not so old, not old] Mount Rainier, but it is [just as majestic as, so majestic, majestic] its cousin. Though it is still recovering from its last eruption, Mount St. Helens is [just as scenic as, the same scenic as, not as scenic as] Mount Rainier.

3 Mount Rainier is also a volcano, but it is [not as active as, just as active as, as much active as] Mount St. Helens. Mount Rainier doesn't get [as much attention as, the same attention as, as many attention as] Mount St. Helens, because it hasn't erupted in centuries. However, Mount Rainier gets [just as many visitors as, not the same visitors as, as much visitors as] Mount St. Helens since it is a popular place to hike, climb, and camp. Also, Mount Rainier is [not as far south as, just as far south as, as much far south as] Mount St. Helens. Mount St. Helens is [not as accessible as, as many accessible as, as accessible as] Mount Rainier for local Seattleites.

Practice 2

Read the passages. Write _as … as_, _not as … as_, _the same … as_, or _as much/many … as_ to complete each sentence. The symbols indicate a degree of comparison: = means "equal," ≠ means "not equal," and * means "emphasis."

Example:

1 *The train gets* _____as many passengers as_____ (= passengers) *the bus.*

2 Three popular family cars—the Volkswagen Passat, the Honda Accord, and the Ford Taurus— were compared by an independent car-testing company. Here is a summary of the test results. The car that got the highest overall rating was the Passat. It had a smoother ride than the other cars, although it was _____ (= noisy*) the other cars. Evaluators, however, said it was by far the most enjoyable to drive. The Passat was _____ (= comfortable) the Honda and the Taurus, but it was _____ (≠ cheap) the other two cars.

3 The Honda Accord, which was ranked second, received almost _____ (= points) the Passat. The two cars were similar in many ways. For example, the Honda was _____ (= safe*) the Passat. However, the other two cars ranked below the Honda in two categories: They didn't get _____ (= gas mileage) the Honda, and they were _____ (≠ aerodynamic) the Honda.

4 The Taurus, which came in third, had almost _____ (= number of options) the Honda, but it was _____ (≠ quiet) the Passat. Also, according to the testers, the Taurus was not as attractive as the other cars. In fact, in recent years, the Taurus has not sold _____ (= well) the other cars.

Conditional

FUTURE REAL CONDITIONAL

Presentation

Future Real Conditional

We use the **future real conditional** to discuss the result of a potential event or occurrence.

We use the future real conditional:

To make a prediction about what will happen after an event or condition

If the teacher doesn't come to class soon, the students will probably leave.

To make a promise about a potential event

I told my son, "If you don't get good grades, I'll take away your cell phone."

To make an agreement based on certain conditions

If the school receives extra money this year, the principal will reduce the computer lab fees.

Rules	Examples
To form statements, use *if* + simple present or *should* + subject + verb in the condition clause, followed by the simple future or a modal + verb in the result clause.	**If** you finish your homework, we **will go** for ice cream.
	Should they visit him, they **might find** him quite changed.
The result questions the condition in question statements. Turn the result clause into a question.	If it rains today, **what will you do?**
	If they shouldn't go on their trip, **what else might they do?**
The *if* clause can begin a sentence, or it can follow the result clause. Use a comma to separate the clauses when the *if* clause begins the sentence.	**If** you don't do your chores, you will not be allowed to watch TV.
	You will not be allowed to watch TV **if** you don't do your chores.

Practice 1

Circle the letter next to the answer that uses the future real conditional correctly.

Example:

1 *Larry will cook dinner if you _____ the dishes.*
   a *washes*   **c** *wash*
   b *washed*   **d** *will wash*

2 You _____ to see a doctor if you don't feel better by tomorrow.
   a would need   **c** needs
   b needed   **d** will need

3 Angie had a blood test yesterday. _____ her diet if her cholesterol level comes back high.

   a She'll have to change   **c** She has had to change

   b She would have to change   **d** She has to change

4 What will you say if your ex-wife _____ next week?

   a will call   **c** haven't called

   b calls   **d** didn't call

5 The late policy in the syllabus states, "_____ assignments late, the teacher might not accept them."

   a "Should students turn in ..."   **c** "If students would turn in ...."

   b "If students will turn in ..."   **d** "Could students turn in ..."

6 _____ more, we'll all be much healthier.

   a If we exercise   **c** If we had exercised

   b If we exercised   **d** If we would exercise

7 If your car breaks down, what _____

   a will you do?   **c** would you do?

   b did you do?   **d** you will do?

8 Should Juan have enough time _____ for a visit on Sunday.

   a , he might stop   **c** , he would stop

   b he will stop   **d** he might stop

9 You'll learn English faster _____ more.

   a if you practice   **c** if you'd practiced

   b , if you'd practice   **d** , if you practice

Practice 2

Write future conditional phrases using the words in parentheses to correctly complete the conversation. Use contractions for *I will, you will, do not,* etc.

MOTHER: Hurry up, Josh! It's 7:30! The bus is going to be here any second. If you _____ (not hurry) _____ (you / miss) it!

JOSH: If I _____ (not find) my history book, _____ (I / be able to leave). Where did you put it?

MOTHER: Me? I never even saw it! Listen, if you _____ (miss) the bus, _____ (I / not drive) you to school. You'll just have to walk!

JOSH: Walk? _____ (I / be) late for sure if I have to walk.

MOTHER: Your teacher says that if you're late again, _____ (she / lock) you out of the classroom!

JOSH: Ha! Ha! She's joking, of course, but I'll tell you what: If you _____ (take) me to school today, _____ (I / do) extra chores this weekend.

MOTHER: OK, but if you _____ (not wake up) by yourself tomorrow, _____ (I / dump) a bucket of water on your head!

PRESENT UNREAL CONDITIONAL

Presentation

Present Unreal Conditional

We use the present unreal conditional to talk about results of unlikely, untrue, or imaginary situations/conditions.

We use the present unreal conditional to

- Express a wish or desire. *If I **could** save some money, I **would** buy a car.* (I can't save some money.)
- Give advice. *If I **were** you, I'd get a haircut.* (I'm not you.)
- Talk about what would happen in an improbable scenario. *If I **won** the lottery, I **would** quit my job.* (I will probably not win the lottery.)

Rules	Examples
To form statements, use *if* + simple past in the condition clause and *would / could / might (not)* + verb in the result clause.	**If** you were smart, you **wouldn't go** to the park today.
	If I could call the president, I **might ask** him to fly me to the White House.
The result questions the condition in question statements. Turn the result clause into a question.	**What would you do** if you won a new car?
The *if* clause can begin a sentence, or it can follow the result clause. Use a comma to separate the clauses when the *if* clause begins the sentence.	**If** I won the lottery, I would travel all over the world.
	I would travel all over the world **if** I won the lottery.
The verb *be* is always *were*.	I would build a huge house if I **were** a rich man.

Practice 1

Circle the letter next to the answer that correctly uses the present unreal conditional.

Example:

1 *I don't get vacation at this job, but* _____ *I would visit my relatives in Nigeria.*

    a *if I did*

    b *if I can*

    c *if I do*

    d *if I could*

2 If Leon had a better job, he _____ to buy a house instead of renting an apartment.

   a could afford

   b can afford

   c should afford

   d afforded

3 I often sleep in on Sundays; however, I would go to the gym in the morning _____ _____ early.

   a if I woke up

   b if I will wake up

   c should I wake up

   d if I wake up

4 I wonder what she would do if she _____ the CEO of this company.

   a is

   b are

   c was

   d were

5 If Tom had enough time, he _____ my computer.

   a fixes

   b will fix

   c would fix

   d can fix

6 If Meggan _____ a U.S. citizen, she _____ a visa to study at an American university.

   a was / should not need

   b is / couldn't need

   c will be / would not need

   d were / would not need

7 How _____ different if you were not living in England?

   a could be your life

   b should your life is

   c will be your life

   d would your life be

8 Which sentence expresses the following?

The couple wants to travel, but they can't. They have to stay home with their children this summer.

   a We'll travel around the world this summer if we don't have to take care of the children.

   b We would travel around the world this summer if we didn't have to take care of the children.

   c We travel around the world in the summer if we don't have to take care of the children.

9 Which sentence is correct?

   a I'm telling you, if you are more honest with Mark, he will be less suspicious.

   b I'm telling you, if you are more honest with Mark, he is less suspicious.

   c I'm telling you, if you were more honest with Mark, he would be less suspicious.

10 Which sentence is true based on the following?

If I had enough money, I would go to China with you.

a The speaker has enough money and plans to go to China.

b The speaker has enough money but can't go to China.

c The speaker can't go to China, but he or she really wants to.

d The speaker can go to China, but he or she doesn't really want to.

11 Which sentence is true based on the following?

If the man had a car, he wouldn't need to take the bus to work.

a The man doesn't have a car, so he takes the bus.

b The man has a car, but he chooses to take the bus.

c The man plans to buy a car and stop taking the bus.

d The man doesn't want a car. He likes taking the bus.

Practice 2

Circle the correct word or words in brackets to complete each sentence in the present unreal conditional.

Example:

1 *If you (gave) / give / given me a dollar every time you said that, (I'd be) / I couldn't be / I were rich.*

2 A friend just told me that he lost his job. I was sorry to hear that because it's summer. If my friend [wasn't / hadn't been / isn't] unemployed, he [could take / he needn't take / he took] a vacation. However, since he's unemployed, he needs to be careful with his money. I told him, "If I [were / am / be] in your situation [I'd be / I would have be / I would to be] careful how I spend my money right now." He agreed, but decided he'd use the money he has to try to win more at the casino this weekend. I told him I thought that was a bad idea. "It [would be / would have be / would to be] OK to gamble if you [had / had you / had had] a job," I said, "but you [might not be able to pay / might have paid / might pay] your bills [if you lost / if you have lost / if you will lose] that money." He insisted it was worth the risk. "[If I won / If I have won / If I will win,]" he said, "I [wouldn't have to find / didn't have to find / have to find] a job for a long time."

I sure hope he wins!

Direct and Indirect Objects

Direct and Indirect Objects

Some verbs are followed by nouns and pronouns. These are objects of the verb. A direct object (DO) tells us who or what receives the action of a verb. Remember the formula: subject + verb + direct object (what or who). An indirect object (IO) is usually who or what receives the direct object. There has to be a direct object for an indirect object to exist.

The direct object (DO) always follows the verb. When a sentence has a direct object and an indirect object (IO), the indirect object can be placed in two positions. It can go before the direct object as a noun or pronoun or after the direct object as a prepositional phrase.

Examples:

My uncle gave **his wife** [IO: to whom he gave a watch] **a watch** [DO: what he gave].

My uncle gave **a watch** [DO: what he gave] **to his wife** [IO: to whom he gave the watch].

When using the indirect object in a prepositional phrase, we often use the prepositions **to** or **for**. We use *to* to describe the movement of something from one person or place to another. We often use *for* with requests:

Examples:

Give this newspaper *to me*, please.

Would you buy that toy *for me*?

For some verbs with a direct and indirect object, the IO can come only ***after*** the direct object:

Correct: I can't do it. You'll have to fix it for me.

Incorrect: You'll have to fix me it.

Review the list of common verbs that take an indirect object.

Rules	Examples
For some verbs, the indirect object can be placed before or after the direct object. Some of these verbs are *buy, do, find, get, give, make, order, promise offer, send, tell,* and *sell.*	I promised her the toy. I promised the toy to her.
	We sent Kate flowers. We sent flowers to Kate.
For some verbs, the indirect object must follow the direct object. It must be placed in a prepositional phrase. Some of these verbs are *change, close, describe, explain, fix, keep, prepare, repeat,* and *say.*	Can you change the channel for me? (~~Can you change me the channel?~~)
	I've described the whole situation to him. (~~I've described him the whole situation.~~)

Practice 1

Circle the letter next to the answer that uses a direct and an indirect object correctly.

Example:

1 *When my roommate graduated, she sold* _____ .
  (a) me her car
  b to me her car

2 Could you please make _____?
  a him a cup of tea
  b a cup of tea him

3 My husband cleaned the whole house _____ .
  a for me
  b to me

4 As soon as Sue opened the door, her daughter told _____ .
  a her the news
  b to her the news

5 Mr. Chin described _____ when he returned from London.
  a his trip to us
  b us his trip

6 Every year on my birthday, my mother cooks _____ .
  a all my favorite dishes for me
  b to me all my favorite dishes

7 All the students had to present _____ .
  a their reports to the class
  b to the class their reports

8 My boss asked me to read _____ before I mailed it to the customer.
  a the report to him
  b to him the report

9 Could you do _____?
  a me a big favor
  b a big favor to me

10 If you're going to the bank, could you please cash _____?
  a my check for me
  b me my check

11 Can you water _____ while I'm away?
  a my plants for me
  b me my plants

12 While Ann was away at college, her boyfriend sent _____ every day.
  a flowers to her
  b to her flowers

Practice 2

Part 1

Write an indirect object to complete each sentence.

1 **A:** Would you mind lending your car to _____ ?
   B: Why? Where's your car?
   A: It's at the shop. The mechanic's fixing it for _____ .
   B: OK, but you have to promise you'll bring it back to _____ with a full tank of gas.
   A: No problem. I can do that for _____ !

Part 2

Underline the direct object in each sentence.

1 She changed her clothes after school.

2 The electrician fixed the lights in the kitchen.

3 When did she learn to play the piano?

4 I always brush my teeth before I go to bed.

Gerunds and Infinitives

Presentation

Gerunds and Infinitives

Gerunds and infinitives can function as nouns. To form a gerund, use a verb + -*ing*. To form an infinitive, use *to* + the base form of the verb.

Examples:

Running (gerund)

To run (infinitive)

Rules	Examples
Gerunds and infinitives function the way nouns do (they can be subjects or objects). Don't confuse a gerund with the progressive tense, which also takes an -*ing* ending. Don't confuse the infinitive with *to* in a modal.	I like **cooking**. *(object)* / I am **cooking**. *(progressive tense)*
	He wants **to finish** school. *(object)* / He has **to finish** school. *(modal)*
Gerunds and infinitives can be a subject of a sentence.	**Reading** is an important skill to have.
	To be honest is an important value for some people.
Gerunds and infinitives can be an object complement. They follow the verb *be*.	The objective of this class is **improving** your grammar and writing skills.
	It is best **to be** honest.
Gerunds and infinitives can be an object of certain verbs.	Did you consider **not calling** him?
	I am hoping **to be** invited to the dance.
	I like **to play** at the park.
	I like **playing** at the park.
Gerunds and infinitives as subjects are always singular.	**Hiking** in the mountains **gives** me joy.
	To dance is the most amazing feeling in the world.
The negative *not* goes in front of the gerund or infinitive.	It's inconsiderate **not to thank** someone for help given.
	Not thanking people is very inconsiderate.
Many verbs take gerunds as objects. Some common examples include *admit, appreciate, avoid, complete, consider, discuss, dislike, enjoy, finish, keep, miss, mention, mind, practice, quit, recommend, risk, suggest,* and *understand*.	I avoid **eating** after 7 p.m.

Gerunds are often used with the verb *go* in expressions that describe recreational activities, such as *go skiing* and *go camping*.	We often **go camping** in the summer.
Gerunds are often used as objects of prepositions. Common combinations include the following: verb + preposition: *believe in, complain about/of, insist on, object to, talk about/of, take care of, think about/of* verb + noun/pronoun + preposition: *blame . . . for, discourage . . . from, forgive . . . for, keep . . . from, prohibit . . . from, protect . . . from, stop . . . from, thank . . . for* adjective + preposition: *capable of, excited about, good at, happy about, interested in, opposed to, responsible for, tired of, worried about* expressions: *feel like, in addition to, instead of, look forward to, used to*	I always **believe in being** honest.
	I've **forgiven Tom for not telling** me the truth.
	I'm strongly **opposed to turning** the park into a parking lot.
	I really don't **feel like working** today.
Many verbs take infinitives as objects. Some common examples include *afford, appear, ask, care, decide, expect, fail, hope, learn, manage, mean, need, offer, plan, prepare, promise, refuse, seem, threaten, wait, want,* and *wish.*	We can **afford to buy** a new car.
Some verbs are followed by noun/pronoun + an infinitive. Some common examples include *allow, cause, convince, encourage, force, instruct, order, permit, persuade, remind, require, teach, urge,* and *warn.*	I **persuaded my cousin to join** me on my trip to Europe.
Some verbs can be followed by an optional noun/pronoun + an infinitive, depending on the meaning. Examples include *ask, expect, need, want,* and *would like.*	We **expect to come** home on Tuesday. (We think we'll come home on Tuesday.)
	We **expect John to come** home on Tuesday. (We think John will come home on Tuesday.)
Some adjectives can be followed by infinitives. Common examples include *afraid, amazed, careful, certain, determined, difficult, excited, fortunate, glad, happy, important, likely, lucky, proud, relieved, reluctant, sorry, surprised, upset,* and *willing.*	I'm always **happy to visit** my grandparents.

Some verbs can be followed by either a gerund or an infinitive, with no change of meaning. Examples include *begin, can't stand, continue, hate, like, love, prefer,* and *start*.	I **love going** to the beach in the summer.
	I **love to go** to the beach in the summer.
Some verbs can be followed by either a gerund or an infinitive, with a change of meaning. Examples include *forget, go on, quit, regret, remember, stop,* and *try*.	I **tried putting** cold water on my burned finger. (I experimented with putting cold water on my finger.)
	I **tried to put** cold water on my burned finger. (I tried hard to put water on my finger.)
	I **remembered going** to the store. (I have a memory of going to the store.)
	I **remembered to go** to the store. (I didn't forget.)

Practice 1

Write the correct gerund or infinitive to complete each sentence.

1 I love _____ (travel), especially to faraway, exciting places.

2 What I don't love so much is _____ (pack) my suitcase!

3 I always worry about _____ (not take) everything I need.

4 My friends recommend _____ (look) on the Internet for good deals on hotels.

5 I prefer _____ (stay) in small pensions rather than large hotels.

6 I arrive at the airport early, because I hate _____ (wait) in long lines.

7 Once at my destination, I make every effort _____ (speak) in the language of the country.

8 I always take along a journal and keep _____ (write) in it throughout the trip.

9 I'm thinking about _____ (go) to India next summer.

10 Maybe I can persuade my best friend _____ (come) with me.

11 If I can afford _____ (pay) for her trip, I'll even do that!

12 Of course, I'll expect her _____ (return) the favor the following year!

Practice 2

Write a gerund or infinitive using the information from the first sentence and the words in parentheses to complete the second sentence.

Example:

1 *Tim's mother said, "You can play a video game." (allow / play) Tim's mother* __allowed him to play__ *a video game.*

2 The police officer told me, "Slow down!" (ordered / slow down) The police officer _____ .

3 I always have a good time when I go to the beach. (enjoy / go) I always _____ to the beach.

4 I drink a lot of milk, because I love its taste. (love / drink) I _____ milk.

5 I was happy that Melinda introduced me to her brother. (happy / meet) I was very _____ Melinda's brother.

6 I don't understand today's homework. I'm going to call my teacher about it. (ask / help) I'm going to _____ me with the homework.

7 I'm too tired to go out tonight. (not feel like / go out) I really _____ tonight.

8 Jerry said, "I'll come and help you move." (promised / help) Jerry _____ me move.

9 "You shouldn't drive in this weather," my brother said. (encouraged / not drive) My brother _____ in this weather.

10 I've been swimming since I was a little kid. (began / swim) I _____ when I was a little kid.

11 My mom said, "I'm so excited that my grandchildren are coming for a visit." (can't wait / see) My mom _____ her grandchildren.

Modals

ABILITY

Presentation

Modals: Ability

We use modals to give more information about a verb. Note the difference between these two sentences:

She **can** swim.

She **wants** to swim.

Both sentences are about swimming, but the first indicates ability. The second indicates desire.

Modals tell us about ability, necessity, possibility, or advisability. Modals can indicate degree and time. The modals we use for **ability** are *can*, *could*, and *be able to*.

Rules	Examples
Use modal + base form of the verb for affirmative statements.	The students **can study** all afternoon, since they don't have class.
Use modal + *not* + base form of the verb for negative statements. *Can not* (also written as *cannot*) contracts to *can't*. *Could not* contracts to *couldn't*.	That student **cannot / can not / can't** study because he has to work.
Use modal + subject + base form of the verb for *yes/no* questions.	**Can you come** tomorrow?
Use question word + modal + subject + base form of the verb for *wh-* questions.	When **can** you **come** over?
Use *can* to express what someone or something is or is not capable of in the present and future or to express general ability.	Who **can** drive the car? Simret **can** drive. He has his license.
Use *be able to* to express what someone or something is or is not capable of for all tenses.	Nguyen **is able to** come to the meeting at 4:00 p.m today.
	His friends **haven't been able to** visit him yet.
Use *be able to* to express completion in the past.	Olga **was able to** clean the house while her family was gone. (She finished the task.)
Use *be able to* to express possibility and ability (*may/might* + *be able to*).	Devon **might be able to** go with us on vacation. (It is possible that he can.)
Use *could* to express what someone or something was or was not capable of in the past.	When I was five years old, I **couldn't** ride a bike, but now I can.

Practice 1

Circle the letter next to the correct form of *can*, *could*, **or** *be able to* **to complete each sentence about ability.**

Example:

1 _____ chess? We play every Sunday afternoon.
   a *Do you can play*   **b** *You can play*   **c** *Can you play* (circled)

2 Raney has been studying French for three years. She _____ for your friend when he comes.
   a can translate   **b** be able to translate   **c** was able to translate

3 That exam was so hard. _____ answer the last question?
   a Can you   **b** Were you able to   **c** Couldn't you

4 I guess I have to buy bigger pants. I _____ the ones I have anymore.
   a couldn't button up   **b** may not button up   **c** can't button up

5 Recently, researchers _____ some possible causes for insomnia.
   a have been able to determine   **b** could determine   **c** can determine

6 The concert was canceled last week because the singer _____ .
   a cannot perform   **b** wasn't able to perform   **c** couldn't have performed

7 Javier has been working with a tutor for months. He _____ this class after all.
   a can be able to pass   **b** might be able to pass   **c** could be able to pass

8 Derrick had to stop playing basketball. After his knee injury, he _____ up and down the court.
   a couldn't run   **b** cannot run   **c** will not be able to run

9 Perry _____ all night when he was in college, but now he has to have at least five hours of sleep.
   a might be able to stay up   **b** can stay up   **c** could stay up

10 He _____ his house, because he can't pay the loan right now.
   a can keep   **b** might not be able to keep   **c** could keep

11 The lid on this jar is stuck! _____ it for me?
   a You could open   **b** You are able to open   **c** Can you open

Practice 2

Write the correct form of *can*, *could*, **or** *be able to* **to complete each sentence about ability.**

A: His mother used to _____ (watch) the kids, but now she _____ (not watch) them. She's getting older.

B: Right! Those two boys are really active. I bet you she _____ (keep up) with the boys just fine in the past.

A: Yeah! It wasn't a problem before. Nakenge says that she hasn't been feeling well. Perhaps, when she feels better, she might _____ (take care of) them again.

B: Maybe. What do you plan to do about the band in the meantime?

A: Well, our lead singer, Minnie, _____ (play) drums, but she _____(not sing).

B: Well, I _____ (not play) the drums, but I _____ (sing). Do you want me to fill in for a while?

A: What a great idea!

NECESSITY

Presentation

Modals: Necessity

The modals we use for **necessity** are *have to* and *must*.

Must is the more formal and less frequently used way of expressing necessity.

Rules	Examples
In affirmative statements, *have to* and *must* are followed by the base form of the verb.	You **have to eat** vegetables.
	You **must eat** vegetables.
In negative statements, *not* goes before *have to* and after *must*. You can use contractions with *have to*.	You do **not have to / don't have to** go swimming now.
	You **must not** go swimming now.
To form *yes/no* questions, use *do / does* + subject + *have to* + base form of the verb or *must* + subject + base form of the verb. (*Have to* is more common for questions than *must*.)	**Do you have to go** to school today?
	Must you go to school today?
To form *wh-* questions, use the question word + *do / does* + subject + *have to* + base form of the verb or question word + *must* + subject + base form of the verb.	**When do you have to go** to school?
	When must you go to school?
Use *have to* to say what is or is not required or necessary (less formal than *must*). Use *have to* for all tenses. *Have to* can also follow another modal.	What do you **have to** do today?
	We **have to** pick up some groceries. There is no food in the house.
	Last year, the government **had to** change the interest rate, but it **hasn't had to** raise taxes yet.
	I **may have to** work this weekend if I don't finish my project today.

Use *must* to say what is required or necessary. *Must* is stronger than *have to*. Use *must* only for present and future necessity.	Ana **must** learn to drive if she wants to work across town.
The meaning of the negative form of *must* (*must not* / *mustn't*) is not the same as the meaning of *not have to*. *Must not* indicates that something is not allowed.	You **must not** drive on this side of the road. (It is not allowed.)
	You **don't have to** drive on this side of the road. (You can, but it's not necessary.)

Practice 1

Circle the underlined forms of *have to* or *must* to correctly complete the sentences.

North Beach College

Student Code of Conduct

A primary goal of this college is that we learn together as an academic community. Discipline and honesty are essential values here. Over the years, the college has had to develop / must develop / has to develop a code of conduct that sets rules and guidelines on how students must behave / must to behave / have behave. New students will have to follow / had to follow / have had to follow these rules in order to be successful here. If a student violates the rules, he or she may have to leave /must leave / leave the college. All students must sign / has to sign / have sign the code of conduct before they can register. Please read all the rules, sign the code of conduct, and return the signed copy to the Admissions office.

a Students must be / mustn't be / don't have to be honest with teachers, administrators, and other students. If a student is witness to dishonest behavior, he or she has to report / must to report / have to report it.

b Students must not cheat / don't have to cheat / must cheat on assignments, tests, and other graded work. Teachers sometimes allow students to work together on projects. When this is the case, students will have to follow / have to follow / are having to follow the guidelines that the teacher might give for sharing work.

c Students have to cite / must to cite / has to cite outside sources (articles, books, documentaries, etc.) in their written reports and presentations. Failure to do this constitutes plagiarism. A student generally does not have to cite / must not cite / do not have to cite textbooks and other classroom material. Please follow the teacher's recommendations in this regard.

Practice 2

Write the correct form of *have to* or *must* and the verb in parentheses to complete each sentence.

Example:

1 *If a student wants to study in the United States, he or she* _____*has to have*_____ *(have) a student visa.*

2 You _____ (not speed) in a school zone. You'll get a ticket.

3 Lidia and her cousin have fair skin, so they _____ (use) sunblock when they go to the beach.

4 If you want to get good grades, you _____ (not be) late for school.

5 _____ anyone _____ (be) at home today for the package to be delivered?

6 To protect against identity theft, Tomoko _____ (install) software to protect her information online last week.

7 She _____ (not take) the bus to work. She can walk or ride her bike.

8 Bella's doctor explained that she _____ (eat) less and exercise more if she wants to lose weight.

9 A person _____ (not be) a U.S. citizen in order get a driver's license.

10 In many European cities, you _____ (not litter) in public places. Otherwise, you'll get a ticket.

11 How often _____ the children _____ (go) to the dentist last year?

POSSIBILITY

Presentation

Modals: Possibility

The modals we use for possibility are *can*, *could*, *may*, *might*, or *must*.

Rules	Examples
For affirmative statements, use subject + *can / could / may / might / must* + base form of the verb.	Jim didn't come to class. **He might be** sick.
For negative statements, use subject + *can / could / may / might / must* + *not* + base form of the verb. *Can* and *could* contract to *can't* and *couldn't*. *Might*, *may*, and *must* do not contract.	Leanne looks tired. **She may not come** out with us tonight.
For *yes/no* questions, use modal + subject + base form of the verb. For *wh-* questions, use the question word + modal + subject + base form of the verb.	Someone's at the door. **Could it be** John?
	I hear some noise upstairs. **What can it be**?
Use *could* to say there is a small possibility. Use *can't* (present) and *couldn't* (present or past) to say that something is impossible.	Is it likely to snow this winter? It hasn't snowed in the last couple of years, but it **could** snow.
	My car won't run. It **can't** be the engine; I just had it serviced.
	I just saw John leave. That **couldn't** be him again.

Use *might / may* to say there is a possibility (*may* is more possible than *might*). Use *might not / may not* to say there is a good possibility something won't happen.	Vladimir **may** visit his family this weekend, but he's not sure yet.
	He **might** visit us, but it's unlikely.
	Florence **might not** be working tomorrow, so we should find a replacement.
Use *must* to say there is a strong possibility in favor of something. Use *must not* to say there is a strong possibility against something.	The restaurant is so full. The food **must** be good.
	Janet **must not** be home. She didn't answer her phone.

Practice 1

Circle the letter next to the best answer.

Example:

1 *We* _____ *to cancel our trip if he doesn't feel better soon.*
   a *must need*
   b *couldn't need*
   (c) *may need*

2 You _____ mad that I didn't wash the dishes. That was last week.
   a can't still be
   b may not still be
   c must not still be

3 The cell phone isn't working, but it has already been charged. The battery _____ defective.
   a must be
   b couldn't be
   c can't be

4 They invited Carla to dinner, but she _____ . She has been busy lately and has not updated her calendar.
   a could not come
   b cannot come
   c might not come

5 I _____ your current debt if you were able to show me your receipts.
   a could reduce
   b may reduce
   c must reduce

6 Dinner _____ cold. I turned off the oven by accident.
   a can't be
   b must be
   c may be

7 **A:** Your friends are almost four hours late.

   B: I gave them the wrong directions, so they _____ lost.

   a must be

   b might not be

   c couldn't be

8 The watch got a little wet, but it _____ . Just let it dry first.

   a must still work

   b may still work

   c can't still work

9 The sky is so clear. It _____ today.

   a couldn't possibly rain

   b must not possibly rain

   c may not possibly rain

10 She hasn't slept in days, so she _____ tired.

   a might be

   b can be

   c must be

Practice 2

Circle the letter next to the correct modal to complete each sentence.

1 **A:** Someone's at the door. Do you think it's Jill?

   B: It _____ Jill. She's away on vacation until Monday.

   a must not be

   b could be

   c can't be

2 **A:** I gave the baby some cereal, but she didn't eat it. Then I gave her some fruit, but she didn't eat it either.

   B: She _____ hungry.

   a might not be

   b must not be

   c couldn't be

3 **A:** I don't think we can go to the beach tomorrow. It's supposed to rain.

   B: Don't lose hope. The forecast _____ wrong. They are never 100 percent accurate.

   a might be

   b must be

   c is

4 **A:** Do you know where Nadia is?

B: She _____ shopping. She said she needed a new pair of shoes.

a must be out

b is out

c can be out

5 **A:** I'm worried about Tom. He's always on time, but now he's more than an hour late.

B: Don't worry. There's construction on the bridge, so he _____ stuck in traffic.

a may be

b must not be

c can't be

6 **A:** The phone is ringing. Do you know who it is?

B: It _____ Irina. I recognize her phone number.

a might be

b could be

c must be

7 **A:** Is Isabella coming tonight?

B: I don't know. She's been very busy lately, so she _____.

a must not come

b might not come

c couldn't come

8 **A:** Do we have all the shifts covered for tomorrow?

B: Well, Brian _____ coming tomorrow, so we should find someone to cover his shift.

a must not be

b might not be

c could not be

9 **A:** Do you think you'll join us for a movie tonight?

B: I'm not sure. I have a report due tomorrow, so I _____ to stay at the office late to finish.

a must need

b might need

c could need

10 **A:** It's so cold here. Do you think the furnace is broken?

B: It _____ broken. We just had it inspected.

a might not be

b can't be

c must not be

ADVISABILITY

Presentation

Modals: Advisability

The modals we use for **advisability** are *should, ought to,* and *had better*.

Rules	Examples
For affirmative statements, use subject + *should / ought to / had better / 'd better* + base form of the verb.	This swimsuit has a hole in it. You **ought to / should / had better / 'd better get** a new one.
For negative statements, use subject + *should not / shouldn't / had better not / 'd better not / ought not* + base form of the verb. (*Ought to* is not common in the negative form.)	That boy is a bad influence. You **should not / shouldn't / had better not / 'd better not hang out** with him.
For *yes/no* questions, use *should* + subject + base form of the verb. For *wh-* questions, use the question word + *should* + subject + base form of the verb. (*Ought to* is not common in questions. *Had better* is not used in questions.)	**Should I get** a new car?
	What should we do about the house?
Use *should* and *ought to* to give an opinion, advice, or a suggestion. (*Should* is less formal than *ought to*.)	What **should** they do about the car? They **shouldn't** wait. They **should** get it fixed by a mechanic.
	Roland **ought not to** drive home. He looks sick.
Use *had better* to make a strong suggestion for doing something (implies that something bad will happen if the suggestion isn't followed). Use *had better not* to make a strong statement against doing something or something being the case.	I have been driving all day. I **had better** rest before I have an accident.
	Samantha **had better not** be at home. She is supposed to be taking a test.

Practice 1

Circle the letter next to the best answer.

Example:

1 **A:** *I don't understand this problem. Can I look at your worksheet?*

    B: *OK, but you* _____ *my answer.*

    a *should not copy*

    b *ought not to copy*

    (c) *had better not copy*

2 There is a dress code at that club. You _____ jeans.

    a ought to wear

    b shouldn't wear

    c had not better wear

3 Amanda already has a lot of debt. _____ those earrings on her credit card?

    a Should she put

    b Had she better to put

    c Ought she to put

4 Sam is always so careful. He _____ some risks.

    a should not take

    b had better take

    c ought to take

5 She hasn't practiced piano in a while. She _____ this weekend.

    a not ought to perform

    b ought not to perform

    c ought to not perform

6 The boys _____ all that candy. They'll get cavities.

    a had not better eat

    b have better to not eat

    c had better not eat

7 **A:** I am so bored.

    B: You _____ something to do then.

    a should find

    b had better to find

    c ought find to

8 If Mike has high blood pressure, he _____ in the sauna.

    a ought to not go

    b shouldn't go

    c had not better go

9 They can't decide what to do. _____ to the performance or attend the lecture?

    a Had they better go

    b Ought they to go

    c Should they go

10 Elise _____ for her history test, or she will fail.

    a had better study

    b should study

    c ought to study

Practice 2

Read the letter to an advice columnist in the newspaper. Write the correct form of *should*, *ought to*, or *had better* to complete the sentences.

1 Dear Abby:

My sister and I used to be very close, but now we hardly see or talk to each other. It all started last year when her husband died. She became depressed and began spending most of her time at home and in bed. I told her that she _____ (get out) of the house and do things that would distract and amuse her; otherwise, she'd go into a deeper depression. She got angry with me and said that I _____ (be) more sensitive to her feelings. Furthermore, she didn't think that I _____ (tell) her what to do.

My sister won't answer my telephone calls or respond to my emails. She even goes out of her way to avoid me at family gatherings. When I try to talk things over with her, she tells me that I _____ (not bother) her any more, or else she will never speak to me again! I'm sorry about this situation. How can I make things better between us? What _____ (I / do)?

Sorry in Orangeburg, South Carolina (SOS)

2 Dear SOS,

It seems that your sister was having a hard time dealing with the loss of her husband, and that she may have felt that you were not being supportive. That is probably why she got so angry.

Let me start by saying that you _____ (not give up) hope. You and your sister will resolve this conflict. I think you _____ (write) her a letter. Tell her that you are truly sorry that she feels you weren't sensitive to her feelings. Explain that you only meant to help her when you suggested that she _____ (get out) of the house and do things to distract and amuse herself. Assure her that, in the future, you will try to be more aware of her feelings. You _____ (end) the letter telling her how much you love her and miss her.

One lesson we can all learn from your experience is that we _____ (think) carefully about the advice we give to someone in his or her time of need. Otherwise, we will end up in a conflict like this.

Abby

Phrasal Verbs

Phrasal Verbs

A phrasal verb is a verb followed by a particle. Phrasal verbs are usually idiomatic expressions, and their meanings are not always obvious. Phrasal verbs cannot be understood based on the meaning of individual parts. Rather, all the parts need to be understood as a whole.

Example:

He always **brings** it **up** when we argue.

bring = verb that means to *carry*, *fetch*, or *transport*.

up = preposition that means *to*, *toward*, or *at an elevated place*.

bring up = to mention or introduce something.

Phrasal Verbs	Examples	Meanings
To put (original verb)	Please **put** the plates on the table for dinner.	to place something somewhere
To put on (verb + particle)	Why don't you **put on** the red dress?	to dress in something
To put down (verb + particle)	I don't like it when you say mean things and **put** me **down**.	to criticize someone
To put off (verb + particle)	They can't come to the appointment. They need to **put** it **off** until tomorrow.	to postpone until later
To put up with (verb + particle + preposition)	The dog is always making a mess, but we love him and **put up with** his bad behavior.	to accept / tolerate someone's behavior

Rules	Examples
Intransitive phrasal verbs have no object (subject + verb + particle only).	The **girls dress up** and go to parties on the weekend. *(dress up = to wear clothes of a certain style)*
Separable transitive phrasal verbs are followed by an object that can come before or after the particle. If the object is a pronoun, it can come only between the verb and the particle.	The company **laid 30 clerks off** last week. *(lay off = to fire someone)*
	The company **laid off 30** clerks last week.
	<u>Correct:</u> The company laid them off last week.
	<u>Incorrect:</u> The company laid off them last week.
Inseparable phrasal verbs cannot be split. The verb must stay with its particle. If inseparable phrasal verbs are followed by an object, that object goes after the particle.	She's absent from school today, because she **came down with** a cold. (come down with = *become ill with*)
	Her sister had the flu, and she **came down with** it, too.

Practice 1

Write the correct particle from the word box that follows the designated verb in each sentence.

after	off	on	over
back	off on	out	up

Take

1 After his knee injury, he took _____ walking instead of running.

2 The plane took _____ at 4 P.M. and arrived in Houston at 8 P.M.

3 She bought a jacket, but it didn't fit her. She decided to take it _____ .

4 Can you take the trash _____ tonight? I'm tired.

5 The baby has her father's features. She really takes _____ him.

6 The students weren't getting their project done. That's why the teacher took _____ .

Go

7 When her husband comes home late too often without calling, she goes _____ him.

8 Do you have time to go _____ this report?

9 Every weekend, the couple goes _____ to a movie.

10 I never get a chance to talk about my family. He goes _____ for hours about his.

11 Oh no, my son didn't bring his lunch. I'll have to go _____ home and get it.

Practice 2

Write the phrasal verbs from the word box in the blanks to complete the sentences. Each verb is used once. Include objects if they are provided. Pay attention to meaning, form, and tense.

call on	get together	stay up	throw away
dress up	keep on	take back	try on
drop in on	show up	take off	

1 In many cultures, it is customary for men to _____ (their hats) when they come indoors. In some religions, however, men _____ (them) all the time, even indoors.

2 In the United States, people used to _____ and go to cultural events, such as concerts or operas. These days, many people wear casual clothes on these occasions.

3 In the Philippines, people believe it is bad luck for a bride to _____ (her wedding dress) before the wedding.

4 In many cultures, it is common for friends and relatives to _____ (each other) frequently. In the United States, however, it is customary to check before you _____ (somebody).

5 To prepare for the coming New Year, people in many cultures clean their homes and _____ (anything old, broken, or useless). They _____ until midnight on New Year's Eve. On New Year's Day, families _____ and eat traditional foods.

6 In many small, rural places, it is traditional for everyone in town to come for weddings and other happy occasions. In large cities, however, it is rude to _____ without a formal invitation.

7 In the United States, if you purchase something and later decide you don't like it, you may _____ (it) to the store as long as you have a receipt.

The Past

THE SIMPLE PAST

Presentation

The Simple Past

We use the simple past to talk about an action that happened in the past once, never, or more than once. It is also used to talk about feelings and events that were completed before now. Below are the forms of the simple past. See the **Appendix** to review spelling rules for regular and irregular past tense endings.

Rules	Examples
To form affirmative statements with regular verbs, use subject + verb + -ed.	**Helen washed** her clothes late last night.
To form affirmative statements with the verb be, use subject + was / were.	**She was** excited to see the boys.
	They were tired and went to bed.
To form negative statements with regular verbs, use subject + did not / didn't + verb.	**Joe did not / didn't wash** his clothes last night.
To form negative statements with the verb be, use subject + was not / wasn't / were not / weren't.	**He was not / wasn't** in a good mood. **You were not / weren't** a very good friend.
To form yes/no questions, use did + subject + verb or Was / Were + subject.	**Did you wash** your clothes last night?
	Was he there last night?
To form wh- questions, use the question word + did + subject + verb or the question word + was / were + subject.	**When did you visit** Paris?
	How were the girls?
Some verbs are irregular. You need to memorize the past tense forms of these verbs.	become > became forget > forgot begin > began get > got break > broke go > went bring > brought have > had buy > bought hear > heard catch > caught keep > kept choose > chose mean > meant come > came meet > met do > did pay > paid drink > drank put > put drive > drove read > read eat > ate know > knew fall > fell leave > left find > found let > let fly > flew lose > lost

	make > made	take > took
	run > ran	teach > taught
	say > said	tell > told
	see > saw	think > thought
	send > sent	throw > threw
	sing > sang	understand >
	sit > sat	understood
	sleep > slept	wear > wore
	speak > spoke	win > won
	stand > stood	write > wrote
	swim > swam	
Use the simple past to talk about a completed event or situation in the past.	They **arrived** at Grand Central Station this morning. **Did** you meet them there?	
Use the simple past to talk about events that never happened or happened more than once.	I never **smoked** cigarettes. I **jogged** every day.	
Use the simple past to talk about past feelings that may or may not be true or valid now.	When my father died, I **felt** sad for months. I **was** devastated. (The emotions of sadness and devastation are no longer felt.)	
Use signal words that show when the event took place. Examples include *whenever, when, yesterday, today, last, ago, since in 2001, at 9 p.m,* and *on April 15th.*	We **went** on our family vacation **last July**.	

Practice 1

Write the correct simple past form of the verb in parentheses to complete the sentences.

1 Many years ago, when Jacques first _____ (come) to the United States, he _____ (attend) ESL classes every day. He _____ (want) to learn how to speak English well so that he could get a better job. After he _____ (learn) enough English, he _____ (not get) a job. He [_____] (decide) to enroll in college.

2 Yesterday morning, my mother _____ (call) me at 5:00 A.M. Of course I _____ (not answer) the phone, because I _____ (not be) home at that time, so she _____ (leave) a message. She _____ (want) to know what I was doing.

Practice 2

Write the correct simple past form of the verb in parentheses to complete the sentences.

1 **A:** What _____ (happen) to Chris?
   B: He _____ (yawn), and a fly _____ (fly) into his mouth. He _____ (be) so surprised that he _____ (swallow) it!

2 Yesterday afternoon Jessica _____ (sit) on her bed and _____ (read) a book. Suddenly she _____ (hear) loud noises. She _____ (get) up and _____ (look) out the window to see what they _____ (be). Some workers were cutting down a tree across the street.

THE PAST PROGRESSIVE

Presentation

The Past Progressive

We use the past progressive to talk about an action that happened over time in the past or about two actions that happened at the same time in the past. Below are the forms for past progressive. See the **Appendix** to review spelling rules for the **-ing** ending.

Rules	Examples
To form affirmative statements, use subject + *was / were* + verb + *-ing*.	**Adrienne was walking** in the park at 8 p.m. last night when she saw me.
To form negative statements, use subject + *was not / wasn't / were not / weren't* + verb + *-ing*.	**She wasn't working** on her final paper.
To form *yes/no* questions, use *Was / Were* + subject + verb + *-ing*.	**Was she walking** in the park alone after dark?
To form *wh-* questions, use the question word + *was / were* + subject + verb + *-ing*.	**What were you doing** when it happened?
Use the past progressive to talk about an event that continues for a period of time in the past.	I **was watching** that movie for three hours last night.
Use the past progressive to talk about a continued situation at a particular time in the past.	At 7 a.m., she **was getting** ready for work. (She prepared for work before and continued around 7 a.m.)
Use the past progressive to talk about two past events that happened at the same time.	Jack **was watching** TV while Jill **was learning** the dance.
Use the past progressive to talk about a past event that begins and continues when another event happens. The interrupting event is in the simple past.	The lid closed on the piano when I **was playing**. (I started on the piano and continued until the lid interrupted my playing.)
Use signal words to indicate an event in the past progressive. Examples include *when, while, for a period of time*, and *at that time*.	I was taking a bath **when** the phone rang.

Practice 1

Write the correct past progressive form of the verb in parentheses to complete each sentence.

1 What _____ (do) at this time yesterday?

2 My roommate _____ (look) for his keys when I got home.

3 Marie _____ (smile) all day yesterday after she received an A on her test.

4 Matt burned himself, because he _____ (not pay) attention while he _____ (take) the pan out of the oven.

5 When she called us, we _____ (not fix) our car in the garage. We _____ (clean) the basement.

6 Sorry, I didn't come. I _____ (finish) my test at noon last week.

7 The boys _____ (play) down the street when they heard their mother calling them. She asked them, "What _____ (you do)? Why didn't you come when I called?" "Why _____ (you shout)?" they replied, "We were just down the street."

Practice 2

Write the correct form of the verb in parentheses to complete each sentence. Use the simple past or the past progressive form.

1 The students in Ms. Baker's English grammar class _____ (wait) for almost ten minutes when she finally _____ (arrive). They asked her, "Where have you been? What _____ (you / do)?
Ms. Baker _____ (apologize) and _____ (explain) that she _____ (be) in a car accident while she _____ (drive) to work.
She _____ (wait) at a red light when a car _____ (hit) her from behind. Fortunately, she _____ (not be) hurt, but the other driver _____ (have) some injuries.

The Present Perfect

Presentation

The Present Perfect

We use the present perfect to talk about past events that are connected to the present tense. Below are the forms of the present perfect. See the **Appendix** to review spelling rules for regular and irregular past participle endings.

Rules	Examples
To form affirmative statements, use subject + *have / has* + past participle.	**Tonya has watched** this movie four times.
To form negative statements, use subject + *have not / haven't / has not / hasn't* + past participle.	**She hasn't traveled** to Germany.
To form *yes/no* questions, use *Have / Has* + subject + past participle.	**Have you eaten** yet?
To form *wh-* questions, use the question word + *have / has* + subject + past participle.	**What have you eaten** today?

Some verbs are irregular. You need to memorize the past participle forms of these verbs.	be > been
	become > become
	begin > begun
	break > broken
	bring > brought
	buy > bought
	catch > caught
	choose > chosen
	come > come
	do > done
	drink > drunk
	drive > driven
	eat > eaten
	fall > fallen
	find > found
	fly > flown
	forget > forgotten
	get > got/gotten
	go > gone
	have > had
	hear > heard
	keep > kept
	mean > meant
	meet > met
	pay > paid
	put > put know > known
	     leave > left
	     let > let
	     lose > lost
	     make > made
	     read > read
	     run > run
	     say > said
	     see > seen
	     send > sent
	     sing > sung
	     sit > sat
	     sleep > slept
	     speak > spoken
	     stand > stood
	     swim > swum
	     take > taken
	     teach > taught
	     tell > told
	     think > thought
	     throw > thrown
	     understand > understood
	     wear > worn
	     win > won
	     write > written

Use the present perfect to talk about events that happened at some undefined time in the past. In this case, it isn't important when the event occurred. It's only important that it occurred.	Many people **have lost** their jobs, and the economy is still struggling. (It happened in the past, but it doesn't matter when. It is affecting things now.)
Use the present perfect to talk about events that finished very recently.	**A:** Are you too tired to work in the garden? **B:** No, I've just **taken** a nap.
Use the present perfect to talk about events that began before and may still be true now.	She **has visited** her grandmother every summer since she was 11 years old. (It started in the past, but it is unclear if it just stopped or if it is still continuing.)
Use the present perfect to talk about how often an event occurred in the past.	For many years, I **have** always **cooked**, and my husband **has** always **done** the dishes. (This habit was true in the past. It may be true now, but it's possible things have changed.)
Use signal words with the present perfect, such as *just, recently, ever, never, yet, already since,* and *for.* (Use *since* for specific time events. Use *for* for an amount of time.)	I have come to this place **since** I was 5 years old.
	I have come to this place **for** 25 years.

Practice 1

Write the correct form of the present perfect to complete the sentences.

1 Are you mad at me? You _____ (not call) me in over a week!

2 People around the world _____ (sight) unidentified flying objects (UFOs) for many years, but the number of sightings _____ (increase) in recent months. Government investigators have been working overtime to check out all the reports, which _____ (pour) in from all parts of the globe.

People _____ (report) not only sightings but also actual physical contact with visitors from other planets. One man reported that he had actually been taken aboard a UFO, examined, and then released. Although government experts _____ (investigate) the incident since it happened, they _____ (not be able) to either prove or disprove it.

Government officials have been preparing a report on UFOs for several months, but they _____ (not complete) it, because they _____ (not solve) all of the sightings yet. As expected, all the sightings they _____ (inspect) until now _____ (have) perfectly logical explanations.

Practice 2

Complete each sentence with either the simple past or the present perfect.

Julia is getting married in August. She _____ (get) engaged last October, but she _____ (already plan) her wedding. Her mother _____ (help) her a lot since the very beginning. They _____ (not have) any problems so far. However, now, it is July, and Julia _____ (not find) a wedding dress she likes. She and her mother _____ (visit) all the stores in town without success.

Julia _____ (decide) to tell her fiancé about her problem.

"My mother and I _____ (plan) everything except for the wedding dress," she told him.

He _____ (respond), "Well, you know me. _____ (I / ever enjoy) wearing a suit? Why don't we get married in blue jeans?"

To which she replied, "I _____ (dream) of the perfect wedding all of my life, and I am not wearing jeans."

Subject-Verb Agreement

Subject-Verb Agreement

Verbs need to agree with the subject of the sentence. If the subject is singular, the verb must be singular. If it is plural, the verb must take a plural form. Singular subjects in the third person singular (*he, she,* and *it*) take a verb with an *–s* ending in the simple present. Other ones do not.

Examples:

His assistant **helps** him organize his schedule. (third-person singular subject)

The women **commute** by bicycle. (plural subject)

In a noun phrase, pay attention to the first word to determine whether the subject is singular or plural.

Examples:

Many **varieties** of food are grown in the Midwest. (subject = varieties)

The **list** of actors who have received parts is posted on my door. (subject = list)

Rules	Examples
The verbs *do, be,* and *have* must agree with their subjects.	**Gary doesn't** work.
	Do the **planes** always arrive on time here?
	The **buses haven't** left yet.
	His **wife is** skiing, and his children are playing in the snow.
	I was absent yesterday, but my **friends were** there.
Modals have one form for singular and plural.	The **river may** freeze.
	The **streams may** freeze.
Verbs in the simple past have one form for singular and plural.	We **walked** the dog.
	She **walked** by herself.
These words always take a singular verb: *something, someone, somebody, each, none, no one, nobody, nothing, everyone, everything, much, every;* school subjects, such as *physics, mathematics,* and so on.	**Something isn't** right here.
	Each student **has** a pencil.
	None of them **is** coming home.
	Everyone takes a piece of cake.
	How **much** milk **is** left?
	Every dog **has** a collar.
	Physics interests me.

Gerunds take a singular verb.	**Swimming is** something that I love.
	Learning how to speak Chinese **takes** a long time.
These words always take a plural verb: *many, both, few, several;* compound subjects.	**Many** people **don't** eat meat.
	Both of us **have** a cold.
	Few people **have** read the whole book.
	Several crabs **have** escaped.
	Omar and I have traveled all over the world.
Some quantifiers will be either singular or plural, depending on whether the noun is a count (plural) or noncount (singular) noun. Examples include *some, all, most,* and *a lot.*	**Some milk is** left over. *(noncount)*
	Some apples are rotten. *(count)*
	All of the milk is spoiled. *(noncount)*
	All of the apples are rotten. *(count)*
	Most air is polluted in some way. *(noncount)*
	Most rivers flow to the sea. *(count)*
	A lot of milk is spoiled. *(noncount)*
	A lot of the kids were absent. *(count)*
In sentences with *there is / there are*, the form of the verb *be* depends on the noun / pronoun subject.	There **is a cup** on the table.
	There **are bowls** in the cupboard.
	There **is a spoon** and forks in the sink.
The correlatives *either . . . or* and *neither . . . nor* take the singular or plural, depending on the subject.	**Either** the police officer or the firefighter **is** here.
	Neither the sheep nor the cows **are** visible.

Practice 1

Circle the letter next to the best answer.

1 Each of the children _____ a pencil and a notebook.

   a has

   b have

2 _____ there any more milk in the carton?

   a Is

   b Are

3 Both of my parents _____ born in Germany.

   a was

   b were

4 Mathematics _____ the most difficult course I am taking.

    a is

    b are

5 Bread and butter _____ always served at the beginning of the meal.

    a are

    b is

6 Some of the students _____ Spanish in Ms. Baker's class.

    a speak

    b speaks

7 Either Mr. Johnson or one of his sons _____ home to meet the service repairperson.

    a plan to stay

    b plans to stay

8 The firefighters _____ to the emergency yet.

    a hasn't responded

    b haven't responded

9 Every dish at those restaurants _____ a culinary masterpiece.

    a are

    b is

10 Most of the people in our small town _____ a living from farming.

    a doesn't make

    b don't make

Practice 2

Write the correct form of the verb to match the subject to complete each sentence.

Example:

1 *There _____are_____ several mistakes in the letter you wrote.*

2 The main export crop of many South American countries _____ (be) bananas.

3 Neither the Toyotas nor the Hondas _____ (come) with a built-in phone.

4 I have been studying hard, because getting good grades _____ (keep) my parents happy.

5 Angela feels that most of the advice from her friends _____ (not be) helpful recently.

6 _____ (be) somebody planning a surprise party for the president of the company?

7 Each piece of candy in the box _____ (have) special wrapping.

8 The doctors in that hospital, which caters exclusively to children, _____ (call) themselves pediatricians.

9 Sheep _____ (be) raised in Ireland for many years.

10 The noise from cars passing by my house _____ (make) it hard for me to concentrate.

11 Hair _____ (not grow) very fast.

The Passive Voice

Presentation

The Passive Voice

We use passive voice to emphasize what happened. We use it when it is not important or not known who or what is performing the action. In the passive voice, the object of an active sentence becomes the subject of the passive one. The subject of the active becomes the object of the passive or is dropped. Review the rules for using passive voice. See the **Appendix** for regular and irregular past participles.

Active voice:

The boy broke the window. (boy = agent / subject; window = thing that received the action / object)

Passive voice:

The window was broken. (agent is not named; window = thing that received the action / subject)

If the agent needs to be mentioned in the passive sentence, use *by* + noun/pronoun.

Example:

The window was broken **by the boy**.

Rules	Examples
To create a sentence in the passive voice, use *be* + past participle.	His arm **was broken**.
Use the passive voice to emphasize what happened, not who did it.	The Statue of Liberty **was dedicated** in 1886.
Use the passive voice when the agent is a thing—not a person.	My clothes **were destroyed** by the washing machine.
Use the passive voice to be objective and neutral and to avoid assigning blame.	A more influential novel **has not been written**.
	Has the rent **been paid?**
	Mistakes **were made**.
You can use the passive voice with all tenses.	Many cars **are made** in Detroit. (*simple present*)
	Many mistakes **were made** in the past. (*simple past*)
	This project **will be / is going to be completed** next year. (*future*)
	Many cars **are being built** in Detroit. (*present progressive*)
	Many children **were being raised** by strict parents. (*past progressive*)
	Dinner **has been served**. (*present perfect*)
	By the time I arrived, the meeting **had been adjourned**. (*past perfect*)

Practice 1

Rewrite the sentence by changing the active voice to the passive voice. Do not include the agent.

Example:

1 *The chair adjourns the meeting.*

The meeting ___is adjourned_____ .

2 *A tornado destroyed many homes.*

Many homes _____ .

3 *Every four or five years, we remodel the law office where I work.*

Every four or five years, the law office where I work _____ .

4 *We are remodeling it now.*

It _____ now.

5 *The office manager hired an interior decorator to plan and manage the work.*

An interior decorator _____ to plan and manage the work.

6 *A crew of workers started the physical labor last night.*

The physical labor _____ last night.

7 *By the time I arrived this morning, the workers had removed the old carpeting.*

By the time I arrived this morning, _____ .

8 *Painters were painting the manager's office.*

The manager's office _____ .

9 *Someone will deliver the new furniture later this week.*

The new furniture _____ later this week.

10 *They will finish the whole job by the end of the week.*

The whole job _____ by the end of the week.

11 *In the meantime, we have to deal with all the dust and noise.*

In the meantime, all the dust and noise _____ .

Practice 2

Write the correct form of the verb in parentheses, using the active or passive voice to complete each sentence. Pay attention to subject-verb agreement and verb tense.

Example:

1 *English, which ____is spoken____ (speak) around the world, ____uses____ (use) over 500,000 words.*

2 A two-year-old French poodle _____ (bite) in the leg yesterday. A man who _____ (wear) a Siamese cat costume _____ (see) running away. The man _____ (pick up) by the police after a neighbor _____ (report) the incident. The arrested man _____ (recently identify) as Felix Smythe, 36, of Rock Ridge. Apparently Smythe's Siamese cat _____ (chase / frequently) by the French poodle, and Smythe _____ (want) to get revenge. Mr. Smythe _____ (charge) with disturbing the peace, and the owner of the injured dog _____ (sue) him now.

Reported Speech

Presentation

Reported Speech

We use reported speech to paraphrase what others say, write, or think. You may have to change pronouns, possessives, time and location words, and verb tenses in the paraphrase. Review the rules for creating reported speech.

Rules	Examples
Begin the statement in reported speech with a reporting clause: subject + reporting verb (present or past) + *that*. Follow the reporting clause with a paraphrase (dependent clause).	The teacher says, "I am going to end this class early today." *(direct quote)*
	The teacher says that she is going to end this class early today. *(reporting clause in the present)*
	The teacher said that she was going to end that class early yesterday. *(reporting clause in the past)*
When you turn a direct quote into reported speech, change pronouns and possessive adjectives from first person to third person.	He says, "I always go to bed early." *(direct quote)*
	He says that he always goes to bed early. *(reported speech)*
When the reporting verb is in the past, you need to shift back the tense. present simple > past simple	David said, "I **clean** my house every day." > David said that he **cleaned** his house every day.
present progressive > past progressive	David said, "I**'m cleaning** my house." > David said that he **was cleaning** his house.
present perfect > past perfect	David said, "I**'ve cleaned** my house." > David said that he **had cleaned** his house.
present perfect progressive > past perfect progressive	David said, "We**'ve been driving** for hours." > David said that they **had been driving** for hours.
past simple > past perfect	David said, "I **cleaned** my house." > David said that he **had cleaned** his house.
past progressive > past perfect progressive	David said, "I **was watching** TV when you called." > David said that he **had been watching** TV when she had called.
past perfect > past perfect	David said, "I **had already painted** the room." > David said that he **had already painted** the room.

future simple *(will)* > *would*	David said, "I'll clean my house." > David said that he **would clean** his house.
The modals *should, ought to, might,* and *would* do not shift. The modal *may* changes to *might, must* changes to *had to,* and *can* changes to *could.*	Chris said to me, "You **should** call your parents." > Chris said that I **should** call my parents.
If the reporting verb is present or future tense, do not change the tense in the clause with the reported speech.	David says, "I **clean** my house every day." > David says that he **cleans** his house every day.
In some cases, you do not have to shift back the tense, even though the reporting verb is in the past (e.g., when the information is still true).	Laura said, "The sun **rises** in the east." > Laura said that the sun **rises** in the east.
When you turn a direct quote into reported speech, you might need to change time and location words. Examples include the following: *this (weekend)* > *that (weekend), today / this day* > *that day, these (days)* > *those (days), now* > *then, (a week) ago* > *(a week) before, last weekend* > *the weekend before / the previous weekend, here* > *there, next (week)* > *the following week, tomorrow* > *the next day / the following day.*	Mark said, "I'm going to visit my parents **today**." > Mark said that he was going to visit his parents **that day**.
	Yuko said, "I don't want to fail my test **next week**." > Yuko said that she didn't want to fail her test **the following week**.
You can drop *that* in the reporting clause.	Mark said, "I'm leaving for two weeks." > Mark said he was leaving for two weeks.
When you change *yes/no* questions into reported speech, use *if / whether* instead of *that*.	Linda asked, "Did you remember to close the door?" > Linda asked **if / whether** I had remembered to close the door.
When you change *wh-* questions into reported speech, use the question word. Keep the word order in the paraphrase.	Linda asked, "**What** time will you be back?" > Linda asked **what** time I would be back.
When you change an imperative into reported speech, use *to*.	Greg told his children, "Get out of there!" > Greg told his children **to** get out of there.
The reporting verbs can include *say, told, ask, explain, inquire, yelled,* and so on.	Mark **told** me, "I'm leaving for two weeks." > Mark **told** me that he was leaving for two weeks.
	Linda **inquired**, "Did you remember to close the door?" > Linda **inquired** if I had remembered to close the door.

Practice 1

Write each quote as reported speech using the same reporting verb with the correct use of reported speech. Pay attention to verb tense, pronouns, time expressions, and location phrases.

Example:

1 *"I have a stomachache."* She said that ____she had a stomachache____ .

2 "I may have to work tonight." Juan told us that _____ that night.

3 "Are the boys going to eat at this restaurant tomorrow?" Narayan wanted to know _____ the following day.

4 "Get down from that window!" I was really worried when I yelled at my cat _____ from the window.

5 "The ocean looks blue because it reflects the sky's color." The professor explains that _____ the sky's color.

6 "Does the study group meet at the library?" Our new study partner inquired _____ at the library.

7 "Fifty percent of marriages end in divorce in the United States." The article stated that 50 percent of _____ in the United States.

8 "Please call me again." The woman told her friend _____ again.

9 "Can I have the rest of your popcorn?" My boyfriend asked me _____ .

10 "You ought to call your mother." My husband suggested that _____ mother.

11 "Patient information is private and confidential." The nurse explained that _____ private and confidential.

Practice 2

Read the dialogue. Write the correct reported speech in the blanks on the next page to complete the paragraph.

(Doorbell rings)

A: Who is it?

B: It's your Uncle David.

A: I don't have an Uncle David.

B: What's your name? Who lives here?

A: My name is Andrew.

B: Oh, I think I have the wrong house.

A: Who are you looking for?

B: I'm looking for my niece, Yolanda. She has recently moved to this neighborhood.

A: Yolanda lives on this block. Just go to the yellow house at the end of the block.

B: Oh great. Thanks.

I was talking on the phone last week when the doorbell rang. I went to the door and asked _____ . The person told me _____ Uncle David. I was surprised. I explained that _____ an Uncle David. Then he inquired _____ and _____ . I told him that _____ Andrew. He thought that _____ the wrong house. I wanted to know _____ so I could help him. He answered that _____ , Yolanda. According to him, _____ the neighborhood, but he didn't know where. I knew Yolanda, so I told him _____ to the yellow house at the end of the block. He thanked me and left.

Pronoun Agreement

Pronoun Agreement

A pronoun must agree in number and gender with the noun it refers to.

Rules	Examples
A pronoun must match the number and gender of the word to which it refers.	**Angela** wants to be a doctor, so **she** is studying biology.
	I picked up **John** last night, and I took **him** to school in the morning.
	My friends and I rented a cabin. **Our** cabin was far from the lake.
	The **computer** wouldn't work. **It** just went blank.
	We need to repair the **buildings** and remodel **them**.
Indefinite pronouns (*anyone, nothing, somebody*) and some quantifiers (*none, each, one, neither, either, much, every, neither . . . nor, either . . . or, not only . . . but also*) use singular pronouns. We use *he or she* or *him or her* to include both genders and avoid gender bias.	Anyone can take that test, but **he or she** may not pass it.
	None of the workers wants **his or her** paycheck today.
	Can you call either John or Helen? We need **him or her** to come and work today.
Certain words (*all, none, most, some*) take singular or plural pronouns. It depends on whether the noun is count or noncount.	**All of the popcorn** is gone. The kids ate **it** fast. (Popcorn *is a noncount noun.*)
	We know **all of those children**. **They** go to our church. (Child *is a count noun.*)
You can use the words *people, you,* and *someone* to avoid gender bias.	We want **people** who can type. We need to hire **them**.
	We want **someone** who can type. We need to hire **you**.
	We need to hire **someone** who can type.

Practice 1

Write a pronoun or pronouns in the second sentence to replace the noun or nouns in the first sentence.

Example:

1   *My friend Hulio is going to buy a new car today.* _He_ *is going to buy a new car today.*

2   My mother does not want me to stay out late on weeknights. _____ does not want me to stay out late on weeknights.

3   Scientists have discovered new ways of curing diseases. _____ have discovered new ways of curing diseases.

4   Mira's brother said we could borrow his car if we were very careful. Mira's brother said we could borrow _____ if we were very careful.

5   My parents just bought a beautiful new house. _____ just bought a beautiful new house.

6   Astronomers use telescopes to look at the stars and planets. _____ use _____ to look at the stars and planets.

7   Maria bought her new shoes at the store downtown. _____ bought _____ at the store downtown.

8   My friend Paula and I asked Marta if we could borrow her math book. _____ asked Marta if we could borrow _____.

9   Can you give the apples to my mother? Can you give _____ to _____?

Practice 2

Write the correct pronoun in the blank to complete the sentences.

These days, security at airports is very strict. Now, all departing passengers are required to come to the airport three hours before their flights. Upon arrival, each passenger is required to have _____ luggage checked before _____ is allowed to enter the boarding area. If someone is carrying a gun or any kind of sharp object, security officers will question and possibly even arrest _____. In addition, passengers must pass through a metal detector and have their carry-on bags X-rayed. At this point, _____ must say good-bye to family and friends, because no one except passengers with tickets is allowed past the metal detectors. There is also a new procedure for picking up arriving passengers. _____ has changed. In the past, people could meet a passenger at the gate as soon as _____ got off the plane. Nowadays, _____ must meet passengers in the baggage-claim area. The new security measures are time-consuming and inconvenient. Nevertheless, most people cooperate with _____ , because everybody understands that these measures could save their life.

Quantifiers

Presentation

Quantifiers

We use quantity expressions with count nouns (singular and plural) and noncount nouns to indicate and modify the quantity of the noun.

Quantifiers	Examples
With singular count nouns, use *a, an, one, each, every, another, neither,* and *either.*	I bought **another** snake.
	Every person wants to be happy.
With plural count nouns, use *one of, each of, every one of, both, several, a number of, few (=not many), a few (=enough), many, a couple of,* and *none of the.*	Do you have **many** friends?
	Both lamps have nice shades.
	I can lend you money. I have **a few** dollars.
	I am so broke. I have **few** dollars.
With noncount nouns, use *a great deal of, a good deal of, a little (= enough), little (=not much), much, not much, a bit of,* and *no.*	She drank **a great deal of** water.
	We can make bread. We have **a little** flour.
	We need to go to the store first. We have **little** flour.
	You haven't had **much** experience.
	We have **no** milk left.
Some quantifiers can be used with both count and noncount nouns: *all of the, some, most of the, enough, a lot of, lots of, plenty of, a lack of.*	There are **some** trees behind my house.
	There was **some** dancing at my wedding.
The quantifier *much* is used in questions and negative statements unless it is combined with *of.*	**Much of** the milk is already gone.
	How **much** milk do we have?
The quantifier *most of* must include the article *the* when it modifies a specific noun (both count or noncount). Do not use *the* when you talk about a general plural noun.	**Most of the** milk is already gone.
	Most of the teachers at my school are young.
	Most colleges require an admission letter.

Practice 1

Write the correct quantifier from the word box in each blank to complete each sentence.

each	one of the	a little
some of	both of	a few

Example:

1 *The teacher collects* ___each___ *assignment, but she only corrects* _____ *them.*

2 Aria wants to take _____ children to the museum. She doesn't think she can handle _____ them.

3 You still have _____ time to study! There are _____ days left before the final exam.

plenty of	a number	many
a great deal of	much	

4 There will be _____ food. We bought a _____ corn and _____ of potatoes for the barbecue.

5 My parents didn't give me _____ advice before I left for college. However, after I left college, they made _____ suggestions about what I should do next.

Practice 2

Circle the correct quantifier in brackets to complete each sentence.

1 Recently, I took up a new hobby: gardening. I began by reading [a couple of / few / one] books about it, and I talked to [a great deal of / a number of / a few] my friends who are experienced gardeners.

2 I don't have [any / some / many] spare time, so my friends recommended [every / a few / a little] plants that would look nice and wouldn't require [much / many / a little] care.

3 It took me a couple of weeks to plant everything. Now, [much / both / several] months later, the plants are blooming and the vegetables are growing. It doesn't require [a number of / a lot of / several] effort to keep the garden going.

4 I spend [a few / a large amount / few] hours working there [every / both /every one of] weekend, and I make sure to give the plants [plenty of / many / most] water. I get [enough of/ a great deal of / a number of] pleasure from my beautiful garden.

SENTENCE STRUCTURE

Simple Sentences

Presentation

Simple Sentences

A simple sentence:

Begins with a capital letter and ends with a period, question mark, or exclamation point.

Has one subject + verb combination.

The *subject* tells *who* or *what* the sentence is about.

The *verb* expresses the action (*work, sing, dance*) or the condition of the sentence (*is, seem, feels*).

Is a complete idea that can stand alone.

Example:

> She (subject) is (verb) my mother.

Simple Sentence Patterns

one subject + one verb

Moses went to the library.

compound subject (two or more items) + one verb

Cats and dogs make great pets.

one subject + compound verb (two or more verbs)

The teacher walked into the room **and greeted** the class.

compound subject + compound verb

The managers and employees are taking the day off **and going** to the company picnic.

Practice 1

Circle the letter of the correct pattern for each sentence.

1 My dog likes to run in the park.
   a subject + verb
   b compound subject + verb
   c subject + compound verb
   d compound subject + compound verb

2 The Taj Mahal is one of the Seven Wonders of the World.
   a subject + verb
   b compound subject + verb
   c subject + compound verb
   d compound subject + compound verb

3 Seattle is foggy and cold in the morning.

   a subject + verb

   b compound subject + verb

   c subject + compound verb

   d compound subject + compound verb

4 Helen and her boyfriend visited Las Vegas last week.

   a subject + verb

   b compound subject + verb

   c subject + compound verb

   d compound subject + compound verb

5 Gina and her friends are singing and dancing to the music.

   a subject + verb

   b compound subject + verb

   c subject + compound verb

   d compound subject + compound verb

6 The police chased the thief through the park and finally caught him.

   a subject + verb

   b compound subject + verb

   c subject + compound verb

   d compound subject + compound verb

7 Marty and I drive to and from school together every day.

   a subject + verb

   b compound subject + verb

   c subject + compound verb

   d compound subject + compound verb

8 The cherry blossoms were beautiful this year.

   a subject + verb

   b compound subject + verb

   c subject + compound verb

   d compound subject + compound verb

9 All the lamps and chairs in my apartment are blue.

   a subject + verb

   b compound subject + verb

   c subject + compound verb

   d compound subject + compound verb

10 My coworkers and I often meet at the local coffee shop and have coffee before work.

   a subject + verb

   b compound subject + verb

   c subject + compound verb

   d compound subject + compound verb

11 Jorge shops and cooks for his mother every Saturday.

    a subject + verb

    b compound subject + verb

    c subject + compound verb

    d compound subject + compound verb

Practice 2

Circle the subject(s) and underline the verb(s) in each sentence.

Example:

1 *Wisconsin is known as the cheese state.*

    Subject: (Wisconsin)

    Verb: is known

2 The cat sat in the window all day.

3 All plants and animals need oxygen to live.

4 Paul went shopping and bought two new shirts.

5 My friends and I decided to go to a Saturday matinee.

6 Gun violence has risen steadily in the past few years.

7 My grandparents get up early every morning and take a brisk walk around the lake.

8 Trinidad and Barbados, two islands in the Caribbean, are five miles off the coast of Venezuela.

9 The recession has greatly increased the level of poverty in urban areas.

10 Susana and Jack like to drink coffee and listen to music at the coffee shop.

11 Experts on environmental pollution are currently studying its long-term effects on children.

Compound Sentences and Coordinating Conjunctions

Presentation

Compound Sentences and Coordinating Conjunctions (*and, but, so, or, yet, for, nor*)

A **compound sentence** combines two simple sentences using a comma and a coordinating conjunction between them.

Example:

The boys washed their hair, **and** I made lunch.

NOTE: We don't use a comma with coordinating conjunctions to combine two words or phrases.

Examples:

They walked through the fields slowly **and** carefully. (2 adverbs)

We walk around the lake in the morning **but not** in the evening. (2 prepositional phrases)

There are seven coordinating conjunctions (*For, And, Nor, But, Or, Yet, So*). Use the mnemonic **FANBOYS** to remember them. It is important to understand the meanings to use them correctly in sentences.

Rules	Examples
Use *and* or *nor* to indicate addition. Use *and* to combine similar ideas.	Gary has lived in Spain, **and** Joanne has lived in Japan.
Use *nor* to combine similar ideas that are negated. Do not use a negative verb phrase in the second clause with *nor*. Use the question word order in the second clause.	Gary hasn't lived in France, **nor** has Joanne lived in China.
Use *but* or *yet* to indicate contrast. Use *but* to combine opposite ideas.	I was working a lot, **but** I was still unable to pay the rent.
Use *yet* to combine surprisingly opposite ideas.	I didn't study at all, **yet** I passed the test.

Use *so* or *for* to indicate cause and effect. In sentences with *so*, the first clause is the cause, and *so* introduces the effect.	John didn't have any eggs to make an omelet, **so** he went to the store.
In sentences with *for*, the first clause is the result, and *for* introduces the cause.	I couldn't eat lunch, **for** I had left my wallet at home.
Use *or* to introduce a choice. The choice in each clause is equally possible.	We can go for a walk, **or** we can drive to my friend's party.

Practice 1

Read the paragraph. Choose the correct coordinating conjunction to complete each sentence; be sure to use each one at least once.

and	for	or	yet
but	nor	so	

Example:

1 *I don't have any eggs for the cake, __so__ I need to go to the store.*

2 My sister asked me to babysit my two nieces last Monday from 1:00 P.M. to 4:00 P.M., _____ I wasn't sure I wanted to (or could!) watch the girls for three hours. I love my nieces, _____ they're very close in age (4 and 2), _____ they're also very active! I knew I'd have to find a fun activity for us to do for those three hours. We had two choices—we could stay home and watch videos, _____ we could go to the park and play on the slide and swings. It wasn't a very nice day, _____ was the sun shining. I knew the girls loved books, _____ I decided we'd go to the library. I'm glad we did, _____ the storyteller arrived ten minutes after we did. She amused the children for the next hour and a half, _____ she amused me, too! I didn't want to babysit, _____ I had fun. I can't wait until the next time!

Practice 2

Complete each sentence with an appropriate coordinating conjunction from the box.

and	for	or	yet
but	nor	so	

Example:

1 *Helen went shopping, __and__ Kevin went skiing.*

2 Diabetes is a disease in which the body does not make insulin, _____ it does not use the insulin it does make effectively.

3 Insulin is important, _____ it helps glucose, a simple sugar, enter the body's cells, where it is converted into energy for muscles and tissues.

4 Too much sugar in the blood is dangerous, _____ it may eventually damage organs.

5 People with Type 1 diabetes produce no insulin at all, _____ they must take daily insulin injections to survive.

6 People with Type 2 diabetes do produce insulin, _____ they can often manage the disease with diet and exercise alone.

7 Type 1 diabetes usually develops in people under the age of 20, _____ it can occur at any age.

8 Type 2 diabetes usually develops in adults over 40, _____ it is now being diagnosed more and more in children and adolescents.

9 Type 1 diabetes is not easy to live with, _____ is Type 2 diabetes always easy to manage.

10 Both types of diabetes are serious lifelong diseases, _____ many people live with Type 2 diabetes for years without knowing they have it.

Complex Sentences

INDEPENDENT AND DEPENDENT CLAUSES

Presentation

Independent and Dependent Clauses

Complex sentences connect an independent clause to a dependent clause using a subordinating word.

Rules	Examples
A prepositional phrase does not have a subject or verb phrase. It is not necessary to the sentence. It adds extra information and can be removed.	**In the morning**, I go to the park to run. (*prepositional phrase*)
An independent clause has at least one subject and at least one verb phrase. It expresses a complete idea and can be used as a simple sentence.	**Jorge and his friends have been playing soccer**. (*Jorge and his friends = subject; have been playing = verb phrase*)
A dependent clause starts with a subordinating word. It has at least one subject and at least one verb phrase. It must be used with an independent clause to form a complete idea, and it cannot stand alone as a simple sentence.	**Wherever I go**, I bring my asthma medicine to be safe.
A dependent clause can begin a sentence, or it can follow an independent clause. If it begins a sentence, a comma must separate it from the independent clause. Do not use a comma if the independent clause comes first.	**Since I work from home**, my work hours are flexible.
	My hours are flexible **since I work from home**.

Practice 1

Circle the letter of the answer that tells what the underlined part of the sentence is.

Example:

1 *The woman <u>who works in the payroll department</u> gave me information about my benefits.*
  a *A phrase*   **(b)** *A dependent clause*   **c** *An independent clause*

2 My local grocery sells different fruits and vegetables <u>from around the world</u>.
  a A phrase   **b** A dependent clause   **c** An independent clause

3 <u>Mohsen and his friends had to walk to the barbecue</u> because his car wouldn't start.
  a A phrase   **b** A dependent clause   **c** An independent clause

4 <u>When I was in New York</u>, I went to a Van Gogh exhibit at the Metropolitan Museum of Art.
  a A phrase   **b** A dependent clause   **c** An independent clause

5 Every spring, <u>I plant vegetables</u> in the garden behind my mother's house.
  a A phrase   **b** A dependent clause   **c** An independent clause

6 Angela was the star player <u>of her high school basketball team</u>.
  a A phrase   **b** A dependent clause   **c** An independent clause

7 I loved the purse <u>that I found in San Francisco</u>.
  a A phrase   **b** A dependent clause   **c** An independent clause

8 The cat hid under the bed all night <u>because of the storm</u>.
  a A phrase   **b** A dependent clause   **c** An independent clause

9 <u>Since the library closed at 8:00 P.M.</u>, Jenny's study group met in the early afternoon.
  a A phrase   **b** A dependent clause   **c** An independent clause

10 <u>The neighborhood</u> where I grew up <u>has changed a lot</u>.
  a A phrase   **b** A dependent clause   **c** An independent clause

11 <u>After picking up his daughter</u>, Jose drove to the park to meet friends.
  a A phrase   **b** A dependent clause   **c** An independent clause

Practice 2

Underline the nine dependent clauses in the conversation.

SHARON: Jack's 21st birthday is on Saturday, and we're planning a surprise party for him. Let's decide how we're going to divide up the work.

MAX: What are the things that need to be done?

SHARON: We need to clean the apartment, send out invitations, buy food, and get the drinks. Oh, and we need to find someone who will bring Jack to the party.

MARTA: I can do that. I'm taking Jack to a movie that afternoon, and afterward, we're going to have dinner. While we're eating, the guests can come over and help set everything up. After eating, I'll say that I need to stop by your apartment to get my guitar. Then everybody will shout, "Surprise!"

SHARON: That's a great plan. OK, now let's decide what we're going to eat and drink. Of course, we need a cake.

MAX: I'll get that if you tell me where to buy it.

SHARON: Go to Sophie's mom's bakery. But go early in the morning so that you can find a parking place.

MAX: What about the drinks and food?

SHARON: I'll ask Sophie to bring juice and soft drinks. When I call the guests, I'll ask each of them to bring something. If people want anything else to drink, they can bring their own.

SUBORDINATING CONJUNCTIONS

Presentation

Subordinating Conjunctions

Complex sentences are formed with a dependent clause and an independent clause. One type of dependent clause is an adverb clause. An **adverb clause** starts with a **subordinating conjunction** that connects an adverb clause to an independent clause to form a complex sentence.

Use a comma to separate the clauses if the dependent clause begins a sentence. Do not use a comma if the independent clause is first.

Examples:

Since my parents wanted a better life, (adverb clause) they moved from the country to the city. (independent clause)

My parents moved from the country to the city (independent clause) **since** they wanted a better life. (adverb clause)

Study the subordinating conjunctions below.

Rules	Examples
To indicate **time,** use *after, as soon as, since, until, when,* or *while. After* refers to the period of time following an event.	The students met at the library **after** they finished their test. (They finished their test first. Then they met at the library.)
As soon as refers to the time immediately after an event.	**As soon as** I finish reading this book, I'll call her back. (I will finish reading this book. Then I'll call her immediately after that.)
Since refers to the period of time between an event in the past and the present.	They haven't seen each other **since** Susan had that party. (The last time they saw each other was at Susan's party.)
Until means "up to" a point in time.	We waited at the coffee shop **until** it was 5:30 P.M. (We didn't wait past 5:30 P.M.)
When means "during the time that."	**When** we ran out of gas, we were almost home. (Around the time we were home, we ran out of gas.)
While refers to an event that happens at the same time as another event.	**While** the children were walking, it began to snow. (At the same time as the children were walking, it began to snow.)
To indicate reasons for something, use *because* or *since*.	She's going to the party, **because** she wants to dance.
	Since she wants to dance, she's going to the party.
To indicate the meaning "for a reason," use *so that.*	I had to go home early **so that** I could get some sleep.
To indicate a condition, use *if* or *unless*. The independent clause tells us what the result will be because of the condition in the dependent clause. (*Unless* means "if not.")	**If** it rains, I will go home.
	I'll stay at the picnic **unless** it rains.
To indicate contrast, use *even though* or *although. Even though* is more emphatic than *though.*	**Even though** it was noisy, we had a good time.
	Although he had just won a prestigious award, he felt sad.
To introduce opposite situations, use *whereas* or *while.* Use a comma in both positions with these subordinating conjunctions.	I want to go to the beach for the long weekend, **whereas** my husband wants to go to the mountains.
	While I am a good singer, my sister is not.
	My sister is not a good singer, **while** I am.

Practice 1

Write the subordinating conjunctions to complete the sentences.

after	because	so that	whereas
although	if	until	
as soon as	since	when	

John and his best friend, Thomas, have been friends _since_ they started elementary school. Now, _____ they will both be graduating from high school next spring, they will be going separate ways. _____ both of them are excellent students, they have very different plans _____ they graduate. John wants to be an engineer, _____ Thomas wants to join the army. _____ John graduates, he plans to leave for a summer science program. Right _____ he finishes his summer science program, he plans to start college in New York. John wants to finish college as quickly as possible _____ he can start working at his father's engineering firm. Thomas, on the other hand, isn't as sure about his long-term plans. He thinks that _____ he serves in the army first, he can learn useful skills and figure out what he wants to study in college. He doesn't plan to start college _____ he is finished with basic training.

Practice 2

Rearrange the phrases to make a complex sentence with an adverb clause and a main clause.

Example:

1 [from the wall][,][we can hang the picture][.][the handyman moves the furniture][As soon as]
   As soon as the handyman moves the furniture from the wall, we can hang the picture.

2 [her twin, Yutaka, is quiet and business-minded][.][My friend Tomoko is creative and outgoing][whereas][,]

   _____

3 [approves][plans to accept the marriage proposal][if][Berhan][her father][.]

   _____

4 [send probes into space][so that][.][Scientists][other planets][they can study]

   _____

5 [everybody][,][Since][Starbucks][is very successful][.][loves coffee]

   _____

6 [finds a babysitter for his daughter][unless][My favorite pianist won't be able to play][.] [for my recital][he]

   _____

7   [,][.][Ann] [in Houston every year][was twelve years old][she has been going to visit her family] [Since]

_____

8   [opened with one turn of the key][.][the lock][Although][was rusty][,][the door]

_____

9   [they left][The boys][for Europe][.][stayed up all night packing][before]

_____

10   [Mike was mowing the lawn][was doing the dishes][.][,][his wife][While]

_____

11   [.][hire temporary workers][when][Companies][they][get too busy]

_____

ADJECTIVE CLAUSES AND RELATIVE PRONOUNS

Presentation

Adjective Clauses and Relative Pronouns

Complex sentences are formed with a **dependent clause** and an **independent clause**. One type of dependent clause is an adjective clause. An adjective clause starts with a **relative pronoun** (_who/whom, whose, which, that, when, where_) that connects an adjective clause to an independent clause to form a complex sentence. The adjective clause gives information about a noun or pronoun in the main clause. It most often appears after the noun it modifies. The noun can be the subject, the object, or the object of a preposition. There are two types of adjectives clauses: restrictive and non-restrictive.

Restrictive adjective clauses identify the noun or pronoun. A restrictive adjective clause makes the noun or pronoun essential, because it tells us which person, place, thing, or time the writer means. We do not use commas with restrictive adjective clauses.

Example:

    The movie **that my boyfriend and I saw last night** was very violent.

The adjective clause in the example identifies the noun _movie_ (the subject of the main clause).

Non-restrictive adjective clauses provide additional information about the noun or pronoun. Either the information is not essential to identifying the noun or pronoun, or the writer has already identified the person, place, thing, or time, so the additional information is not essential. We use commas with non-restrictive adjective clauses.

Example:

    John, **who is a student in my class**, works at Microsoft.

The subject of the adjective clause can be the relative pronoun. We use a comma with the adjective clause, because we already know who John is, or the information between commas is not essential to identifying him.

Functions	Rules	Examples
Subject	Use *who* or *that* (informal) for people in subject positions.	The man **who / that** lives next door is a doctor. *(restrictive)*
		I visited Grandpa Jim, **who** has been in the hospital. *(non-restrictive)*
	Use *which* or *that* for things in subject positions.	The books **which / that** came were cheap. *(restrictive)*
		We visited Machu Pichu, **which** is in Peru. *(non-restrictive)*
	That can be used only in restrictive clauses. Do not use *that* in non-restrictive clauses.	Correct: The book that I've just read was a present from Grandpa Jim. *(restrictive)*
		Correct: Grandpa Jim, who is my mother's father, gave me the book. *(non-restrictive)*
		Incorrect: Grandpa Jim, that is my mother's father, gave me the book.
Object	Use *whom* (formal), *who*, or *that* (informal) for people in object positions.	The man **whom / who / that** I love is a doctor. *(restrictive)*
		The manager called Sharon, **whom** she had just given a job. *(non-restrictive)*
	Use *which* or *that* for things in object positions.	The books **which / that** the teacher ordered were cheap. *(restrictive)*
	Do not use *that* in non-restrictive clauses.	Psychology, **which** many study in college, is the science of the mind. *(non-restrictive)*
	The relative pronoun can be omitted in restrictive clauses.	The man I love is a doctor. *(omitted relative pronoun in restrictive clause)*
Possessive	Use *whose* for people and things.	The office clerk **whose** report was lost is really upset. *(restrictive)*
		My roommate Tina, **whose** brother lives in Los Angeles, was just fired from her job. *(non-restrictive)*
		They climbed the mountain **whose** top was covered in snow. *(restrictive)*
		Mount Blanc, **whose** top is always covered in snow, is a difficult mountain to climb. *(non-restrictive)*
	Use *of which* for things in formal sentences.	They climbed the mountain the top **of which** was covered in snow.
Describing locations	Use *where* in adjective clauses that describe locations.	The house **where** I lived as a child has been sold.
Describing time	Use *when* in adjective clauses that describe timing of events.	The decade **when** the computer was invented was changed by new technology.

Practice 1

Circle the letter of the adjective clause that completes the sentence correctly.

Example:

1 *I'll never forget the moment* _____ .
   a *, when my child was born*
   (b) *when my child was born*
   c *where my child was born*

2 Maria and Dana are the only secretaries _____ .
   a that have been given the day off
   b whom have been given the day off
   c , that have been given the day off

3 The man _____ is over there.
   a , who bought your computer,
   b whom bought your computer
   c who bought your computer

4 Mrs. Lopez _____ refused to let her take the car.
   a who was furious with her daughter
   b , whom was furious with her daughter,
   c , who was furious with her daughter,

5 Jorge _____ has two children.
   a , who works at my office,
   b , that works at my office,
   c that works at my office

6 One of the people _____ is my grandmother.
   a , whom I admire the most,
   b whom I admire the most
   c to whom I admire the most

7 The University of Washington _____ is in North Seattle.
   a which has more than 10,000 students
   b , which has more than 10,000 students,
   c , that has more than 10,000 students,

8 This dictionary has a section _____ .
   a that contains grammar reference charts
   b , which contains grammar reference charts
   c , that contains grammar reference charts

9 I can't find the man _____ .
   a whose phone I borrowed
   b which phone I borrowed
   c , whose phone I borrowed

10 The United States celebrated its bicentennial the year _____ .

    a where I was born

    b , when I was born

    c when I was born

11 Boeing _____ is opening a factory in Kansas City.

    a , that makes airplanes,

    b which makes airplanes

    c , which makes airplanes,

Practice 2

Use the second sentence to write an adjective clause for the underlined noun.

Example:

1 *My father's* mother *, whose house is near the beach, swims in the ocean every day. (Her house is near the beach.)*

2 The student _____ is in one of my classes. (You just met her parents.)

3 In New York, there are thousands of people _____ . (They don't speak English.)

4 My neighbor Amy _____ is very strange. (Amy lives by herself and never talks to anyone.)

5 Our teacher _____ told us a very funny story. (She has a wonderful sense of humor.)

6 Mozart was born in Salzburg, Austria _____ . (Salzburg was a famous center for music.)

7 The students _____ raised their hands. (Their names were called.)

8 The girl _____ was very helpful. (She explained the homework to me.)

9 On our trip, we visited many areas of the United States _____ before. (We had never seen them.)

10 The place _____ to is beautiful!! (They're taking Bob to that place.)

11 Early morning is the time _____ . (I do my best work then.)

Word Forms

Word Forms

Many English words belong to **word families**. A family of **word forms** shares the same root meaning, but each form has a different meaning, depending on its function in a sentence. This function is called its **part of speech** (noun, verb, adjective, adverb). It's important to match the word form with the part of speech.

Verb	Noun	Adjective	Adverb
to devote	devotion	devoted	devotedly
—	happiness	happy	happily
to interrupt	interruption	interrupting	—

Practice 1

Complete the table with the correct word forms. Use a dictionary to help you.

Verb	Noun	Adjective	Adverb
succeed	success	successful	successfully
X	accuracy	_____	_____
commit	_____	committed, committable	X
X	_____	traditional	_____
identify	_____	identical	_____
_____	revolution	_____	X
presume	_____	presumable, presumptuous	_____
_____	prediction	_____	predictably
_____	_____	motivated, motivational	X
X	philosophy	_____	_____
interpret	_____	interpretive	interpretatively

Practice 2

Complete the paragraph with the correct form of the words in parentheses.

Example:

The farmer's market is a great place to get <u>natural</u> *(nature) healthy food.*

My three _____ (Canada) friends, Mark, Milt, and Marsha love

5-pin bowling. The game, a _____ (vary) on the more widely

known 10-pin game, is played only in Canada. In the game, players try to knock down

five _____ (relative) small pins, as compared to the larger

ones _____ (typical) used in 10-pin bowling. Also, the ball the players

use to knock the pins down is much smaller and lighter than the one used in the 10-pin game.

The 5-pin game was devised in the early 1900s by the owner of a bowling alley who had received

many _____ (complain) about the _____

(difficult) of playing the 10-pin game. He adapted, or changed, the game to make it easier for

people to play. His _____ (adapt) was a huge success! It made the

game _____ (access) to more people—especially children, who

could _____ (easy) lift and toss the lighter ball. To this day, 5-pin bowling

remains a popular form of _____ (entertain) for everyone in Canada—

including my three friends, whose first stop on a trip home is the bowling alley!

Appositives

> ### Presentation
>
> ### Appositives
>
> **Appositives** are noun phrases in which a noun follows another noun to rename or describe it in more detail. Like adjective clauses, appositives provide more information about a noun. Appositives most often appear after the nouns they modify.
>
> **Necessary (essential) appositives** identify the noun or pronoun. They tell which person, place, thing, or time the writer means. We do not use commas.
>
> **Example:**
>
> I read the book ***The Girl with the Dragon Tattoo*** last summer.
>
> The appositive in this example gives more information about the noun *the book*.
>
> **Unnecessary (non-essential) appositives** provide extra information about the noun or pronoun. The writer has already identified the person, place, thing, or time. We use commas.
>
> **Example:**
>
> We studied Charlie Parker, **a famous jazz musician**, in our music class.
>
> We use a comma with the adjective clause, because this is extra, non-essential information.

Practice 1

Underline the ten appositive phrases in the paragraphs.

Example:

The composer <u>*Wolfgang Amadeus Mozart*</u> *is regarded as one of the greatest musical geniuses who ever lived.*

Mozart was born in 1756 in the Austrian town of Salzburg, a stunningly beautiful city with a long musical history. Mozart's musical gifts became obvious almost immediately. By the age of four, he could already play the piano. He published his first compositions, four pieces for violin and harpsichord, before his eighth birthday.

Mozart's father, Leopold, had been a music teacher. However, he quit teaching to manage young Wolfgang's career. When Mozart was six, he began playing concerts with his sister, Nanerl, who was also a gifted musician. At the age of seven, Mozart was invited to Vienna, the capital of Austria, to play for the royal family. From there, his reputation as a genius spread all over Europe.

Mozart's first public performance took place in Munich, a city in southern Germany. In 1984, a mostly fictional account of Mozart's life was told in the film *Amadeus*. Much of the film focuses on Mozart's rivalry with another composer, Salieri. At the end of the movie, Salieri, who was jealous of Mozart's genius, poisons Mozart. In fact, the cause of Mozart's death at age 35 is not certain. It may have been a medical condition called uremia, a result of advanced kidney disease. Mozart died before completing his last masterpiece, his unforgettable "Requiem."

Practice 2

Use the second sentence to write an appositive for the underlined word or phrase.

Example:

1 *Pirates of the Caribbean: At World's End* , one of the most expensive U.S. movies, *cost $300 million to make. (One of the most expensive U.S. movies is **Pirates of the Caribbean: At World's End**.)*

2 Ethiopians eat a sourdough flatbread _____ with their meals. (The flatbread is called injera.)

3 We _____ plan to have a party after the game. (We are teammates.)

4 They painted the entire house their favorite color _____ . (Their favorite color is blue.)

5 The *Seattle Post Intelligencer* _____ moved to a solely online format in 2009 rather than go out of business. (The *Seattle Post Intelligencer* was a popular print newspaper in Seattle.)

6 The Oreo _____ celebrated its 100th birthday in 2012. (The Oreo is one of the bestselling cookies in the U.S.)

7 The defendant was represented by his mother-in-law _____ . (His mother-in-law is an attorney.)

8 In 2006, I bought a Kia Spectra _____ . (A Kia Spectra is a reliable Korean car.)

9 The White House is located in Washington, D.C. _____ . (Washington, D.C., is the capital of the United States.)

10 Saul _____ won an award for his research on HIV. (Saul is an excellent biologist.)

Fragments

Fragments

A **fragment** is an incomplete sentence. The sentence might be missing information or express an incomplete idea.

To fix a fragment, you can:

- Add missing subjects and verbs.
- Add the fragment to the sentence that comes before or after by combining sentences or clauses.

Solutions	Fragments	Revisions
Add subject.	Is nobody in the street.	**There** is nobody in the street.
Add verb or verb phrase.	The ship been sailing for twenty days in the Arctic Ocean.	The ship **has** been sailing for twenty days in the Arctic Ocean.
Combine two clauses.	I have seasonal allergies. Especially in the spring and the summer.	I have seasonal **allergies,** especially in the spring and the summer.

Practice 1

Underline the eleven fragments in the paragraphs.

Los Angeles is a multinational city with immigrants from all over the world. Many of these immigrants live in "ethnic" neighborhoods. For example, Chinatown. Is a unique community of approximately 14,000 people. Chinese culture dominates the area. Have Chinese restaurants, clothing stores, bakeries, banks, bookstores, gift shops, jewelers, markets, beauty salons, and more. Some of Chinatown's residents have lived there for 40 or 50 years, and they have never learned much English. Because they haven't needed it. Is possible to get almost any Chinese product or service in Chinatown. Without traveling to China.

Los Angeles is an enjoyable city to visit. If you have a car. If not, you will need to depend on public transportation. Which is neither fast nor convenient. Los Angeles has a new subway, but it does not travel to most of the popular tourist attractions. There is no system of elevated trains or streetcars. Only buses, and they can take a long time to go anywhere. Because traffic is very heavy. Especially in the early morning and late afternoon, when people are traveling to and from work.

Practice 2

Circle the letter of the complete sentence.

Example:

1 a *Many wildflowers that are edible.*
   b *Unless we find a babysitter, we can't go.*
   c *With the news that the work had been done.*

2 a My husband likes to run early in the morning.
   b Having heard the annoying sound of the alarm clock.
   c After he came face to face with a bear on the path.

3 a Salsa dancing is my favorite pastime.
   b Tim, Jackie, and I on Saturday evening.
   c To see a romantic movie this weekend.

4 a With so much traffic during rush hour.
   b Cars crawling along on the highway.
   c Commuting to and from work is not fun.

5 a If you could please hand me that book.
   b Reading an interesting biography of his life.
   c The author is a well-known biographer.

6 a The car broke down in the middle of the road.
   b Tomorrow, if the tow truck doesn't arrive soon.
   c Unless you have an idea of how to fix it.

7 a As soon as I leave for vacation in two weeks.
   b My neighbor will water my plants while I'm gone.
   c Spending time in a beautiful part of the world.

8 a Fluffy and her friends enjoying a cat nap.
   b Curled up next to the heater, they look so cozy.
   c Are three large but empty saucers under the table.

9 a The most beautiful cities are in New England.
   b Being on vacation in the best city in the world.
   c Many interesting places to visit this summer.

10 a On Monday, if it doesn't snow.
    b Friday is my dentist appointment.
    c Going to have a very busy week.

11 a All seven of us helping you today.
    b Thinking only of her dad, Jane raced home.
    c After I return from the movies this afternoon.

Run-On Sentences and Comma Splices

Run-on Sentences and Comma Splices

A **run-on sentence** is two or more independent clauses that have been incorrectly combined with missing or incorrect punctuation and/or connectors.

Example:

I am in Spain I am happy.

A **comma splice** is two or more independent clauses combined with a comma and no coordinating conjunction.

Example:

I am in Spain, I am happy.

To correct run-on sentences and comma splices:

- Use appropriate punctuation (check for correct use of periods, semicolons, and commas).
- Use coordinating conjunctions to combine equal, independent clauses.
- Use subordinating conjunctions to combine clauses if one is secondary and dependent.
- Use a transition signal to combine the clauses with a semicolon and comma.
- Use a transition signal and separate the clauses with a period.

There needs to be a comma between a subordinating clause and an independent clause if the subordinating clause starts the sentence. If the independent clause starts the sentence, no comma is necessary.

Examples:

If it rains, we will not go outside.

We will not go outside if it rains.

Run-on Sentences	Possible Revisions	Solutions
My name is Cristina I am from Brazil.	My name is Cristina, and I am from Brazil.	Add a comma + a coordinating conjunction *and*. (Adding just a comma does not fix the run-on sentence.)
	My name is Cristina. I am from Brazil.	Separate the run-on sentence into two sentences.

I will finish my homework, after I will go to bed.	I will finish my homework, and then I will go to bed.	Write a compound sentence.
	After I finish my homework, I will go to bed.	Write a time clause with *after*.
	I will finish my homework, after which I will go to bed.	Write a time clause with *after*.
I hate my apartment, I'm going to move.	I hate my apartment. I'm going to move.	Replace the comma with a period.
	I hate my apartment, so I'm going to move.	Add a coordinating conjunction.

Comma Splice	Possible Revisions	Solutions
Lisa came to the game, her roommate went to the library.	Lisa came to the game, but her roommate went to the library.	Use a coordinating conjunction.
	Lisa came to the game although her roommate went to the library	Use a subordinating conjunction.
	Lisa came to the game; however, her roommate went to the library.	Use a transition signal with a semicolon.
	Lisa came to the game. Her roommate, however, went to the library.	Separate clauses with a period, and use a transition signal.

Practice 1

Circle the letter of the answer that describes each sentence.

Example:

1 *On Sunday we worked in the garden, later we went to a baseball game.*
   a *Run-on Sentence*
   b *Comma Splice*
   c *Correct Sentence*

2 Broccoli is an ancient vegetable, it has been around for more than 2,000 years.
   a Run-on Sentence
   b Comma Splice
   c Correct Sentence

3 The word *broccoli* comes from the Italian word *brocco* it means "arm" or "branch."

    a Run-on Sentence

    b Comma Splice

    c Correct Sentence

4 It is one of the healthiest vegetables it is rich in vitamins and low in calories.

    a Run-on Sentence

    b Comma Splice

    c Correct Sentence

5 Surprisingly, it has as much calcium as does the same amount of milk.

    a Run-on Sentence

    b Comma Splice

    c Correct Sentence

6 Broccoli contains a special chemical substance called sulforaphane, it helps reduce the risk of cancer.

    a Run-on Sentence

    b Comma Splice

    c Correct Sentence

7 Broccoli usually grows best in cool climates; however, new varieties that grow well in mild and subtropical climates have recently been cultivated in Taiwan.

    a Run-on Sentence

    b Comma Splice

    c Correct Sentence

8 Most varieties of broccoli are green, however, there are a few that are purple.

    a Run-on Sentence

    b Comma Splice

    c Correct Sentence

9 Broccoli is one of the most popular vegetables in the United States not everyone likes it, however.

    a Run-on Sentence

    b Comma Splice

    c Correct Sentence

10 One famous person who disliked broccoli was George Bush he was president of the United States from 1989 to 1993.

    a Run-on Sentence

    b Comma Splice

    c Correct Sentence

Practice 2

Circle the letter of the sentence in each group that is correctly written.

Example:

1 **a** *I packed only light clothes for the camping trip, at night I was cold.*
    b *I packed only light clothes for the camping trip, so at night I was cold.*
    c *I packed only light clothes for the camping trip therefore at night I was cold.*

2 **a** The lead singer was sick, but the band still sounded great.
    b The lead singer was sick, however, the band still sounded great.
    c The lead singer was sick, the band still sounded great.

3 **a** It was very foggy we didn't take a drive down the coast.
    b It was very foggy, we didn't take a drive down the coast.
    c It was very foggy, so we didn't take a drive down the coast.

4 **a** We'll take the bus into town, or maybe we'll walk.
    b We'll take the bus into town, maybe we'll walk.
    c We'll take the bus into town maybe we'll walk.

5 **a** We decided to stay home yesterday, a big storm was heading our way.
    b We decided to stay home yesterday, for a big storm was heading our way.
    c We decided to stay home yesterday a big storm was heading our way.

6 **a** We were exhausted, we went out dancing after class.
    b We were exhausted, yet we went out dancing after class.
    c We went out dancing after class, we were exhausted.

7 **a** Summer heat is not always pleasant high temperatures are dangerous for some people.
    b Summer heat is not always pleasant and high temperatures are dangerous for some people.
    c Summer heat is not always pleasant; moreover, high temperatures are dangerous for some people.

8 **a** I'm going to Spain this summer; my friends are going to France.
    b I'm going to Spain this summer, my friends are going to France.
    c I'm going to Spain this summer but my friends are going to France.

9 **a** Our apartment building doesn't have a swimming pool, nor does it have a roof-top terrace.
    b Our apartment building doesn't have a swimming pool it doesn't have a roof-top terrace either.
    c Our apartment building doesn't have a swimming pool it doesn't have a roof-top terrace.

10 **a** My father was a kind and decent man and he was also my best friend.
    b My father was a kind and decent man, and he was also my best friend.
    c My father was a kind and decent man he was also my best friend.

Transition Signals

Transition Signals

Transition signals connect phrases, clauses, and sentences and create relationships between them. There are four types of transition signals: coordinating conjunctions, subordinating conjunctions, conjunctive adverbs, and prepositions. Each is governed by different grammatical rules. Review the charts for rules and the most common different transition signals organized by relationship and type.

Transition Signals	Rules	Examples
Coordinating conjunctions	Coordinating conjunctions combine two independent clauses. They are separated with a comma.	Rice is popular in Asia, **but** bread is popular in Europe.
Subordinating conjunctions	Subordinating conjunctions combine an independent clause with a dependent clause. A comma separates the clauses if the subordinating conjunction begins the sentence.	**Although** rice is popular in Asia, bread is popular in Europe.
Conjunctive adverbs	Conjunctive adverbs combine ideas in two sentences. They can begin a new sentence, but they must be followed by a comma.	Rice is popular in Asia. **However**, bread is popular in Europe.
	Conjunctive adverbs begin a clause following a semicolon. The adverb begins with a lower case letter and is followed by a comma.	Rice is popular in Asia; **however**, bread is popular in Europe.
	Conjunctive adverbs end a sentence following a comma.	Rice is popular in Asia. Bread is popular in Europe, **however**.
	Some conjunctive adverbs can be in the middle of a sentence and separated with commas.	Rice is popular in Asia. Bread, **however**, is popular in Europe.
Prepositions	Prepositions must be followed by nouns.	Rice is popular **in Asia** in spite of bread being popular **in Europe**.

Relationships	Coordinating Conjunctions	Subordinating Conjunctions	Conjunctive Adverbs	Prepositions
Addition	and, nor		also, in addition, moreover, furthermore	
Contrast	but, yet	although, while, whereas	nevertheless, however, by contrast	instead of, in spite of, despite
Cause or reason	for	because, since, as	for this reason	due to, because of, as a result of, in case
Effect or result	so	so that, in order that	therefore, as a result, consequently, thus	the cause of, the reason for
Choice	or		on the other hand, otherwise	
Condition		if, unless		
Time or logical order		before, after, when, while, since, as soon as	first of all, next, subsequently, then, after that, above all, more importantly	
Examples			for example, for instance	such as, an example of
Comparison	and	as	similarly, likewise	
Conclusion			finally, in conclusion, to conclude, for these reasons, last of all	it is clear that

Practice 1

Circle the letter of the appropriate transition signal for each sentence.

Example:

1 *Their new house has six bedrooms and five bathrooms. _____ , it has a huge swimming pool!*

   (a) *Moreover*　　　　**b** *However*　　　　**c** *Consequently*

2 Last night, Cindy spilled juice and didn't clean it up. _____ , she woke up this morning to an army of ants in her kitchen!

   a Moreover　　　　**b** However　　　　**c** As a result

3 Jon wants to buy a car. _____ , he wants to buy a new car.

    a As a result   **b** Consequently   **c** Moreover

4 Liz has a valuable collection of costume jewelry. One of the pieces she has, _____ , is worth more than $500!

    a however   **b** for example   **c** nevertheless

5 I'll either go to the party tonight, _____ I'll stay home and watch a video.

    a so   **b** or   **c** for

6 Hank and Ellen have been married for 20 years; _____ , Joe and Sue have been married that long, too.

    a likewise   **b** subsequently   **c** in contrast

7 Jeremy loves to play tennis, _____ his wife is not so crazy about the sport.

    a and   **b** for   **c** but

8 Let's go shopping today _____ we have everything we need for the week.

    a since   **b** so that   **c** while

9 He knows that he should eat less and exercise more, _____ he never does.

    a yet   **b** or   **c** for

10 _____ her interest in history, she has never read an historical novel.

    a Because of   **b** In addition to   **c** Despite

Practice 2

Choose the appropriate transition signals to complete the paragraph.

and	but	In addition	otherwise
so that	for	because of	First of all
Therefore	Moreover	It is clear that	

Many adults find it difficult to balance work, family, and school when they return to college. _____ , it is important for these students to develop good time-management skills _____ they can have an enjoyable and successful experience. _____ , students must be aware of the important dates for each class, such as those for assignments, quizzes, and tests, _____ they will need to take these into account when scheduling family and work-related events. _____ , college students must count on approximately two hours of study time for every hour of class time they have, _____ they need to include these study hours into their weekly schedules; _____ , the hours will easily be taken up by activities that are not school-related. _____ adult students can, _____ their responsibilities, face difficulties, _____ good time-management skills will help them overcome these difficulties. _____ , they will have fun in the process!

Paragraph Structure

Paragraph Structure

Paragraphs have three parts: a topic sentence, supporting sentences, and a concluding sentence.

The **topic sentence** states the subject of the paragraph and tells the reader what the writer wants to say about the subject.

Supporting sentences give important information (explanation, examples, facts, descriptions, personal accounts, expert opinions) in order to support the topic sentence. Supporting sentences are of two classes: sub-points and supporting details.

A **sub-point** is an idea related to the topic sentence that supports the writer's perspective on the topic sentence. **Supporting details** support the sub-point and make it clearer. A supporting detail can be a fact, an example, an explanation, or a reason.

A **concluding sentence** reviews the main point and the sub-points in a final sentence that also provides a final thought, opinion, suggestion, or prediction.

Example Paragraph

Topic Sentence:

The Mediterranean monk seal is one of the most endangered animals on Earth.

Sub-point #1:

At one time, thousands of these animals could be found on beaches and in caves all around the Mediterranean Sea, but now only an estimated 300 to 500 of them remain.

Supporting Detail:

The remaining seals live in two main colonies, one in the eastern Mediterranean and the other on the western coast of Africa.

Sub-point #2:

A variety of national laws and species-protection programs have been created to protect the Mediterranean monk seal.

Supporting Detail:

Protected areas have been established by Greece, Madeira, and Mauritania.

Concluding Sentence:

If nations do not take care to preserve the Mediterranean monk seal, a unique natural treasure will be lost forever.

Practice 1

Read and identify the parts of the paragraph. Write the number of the sentence next to the best description of it.

Qualities of a Good Marriage

(1) A long-lasting marriage is made up of three important qualities: good communication, unconditional acceptance, and humor. (2) First, communication is vital to a healthy relationship.

(3) Couples need to be honest about their needs, desires, and feelings. (4) If they are not honest, they will not be able to make decisions together about work, family, housing, and money. (5) Next, people in strong relationships love their partners, so they are more accepting of faults and offensive behavior. (6) Studies have shown that feelings of disdain and contempt in a marriage increase the likelihood of divorce. (7) Feelings of contempt are often directed toward the person, not the offensive behavior. (8) Since there can be so much conflict in relationships, humor is an important quality for a happy, long-lasting relationship. (9) Couples who laugh together and share good times feel more positive about their marriage. (10) In addition, couples who can see the funny side to life don't argue as much as couples who are more serious. (11) To conclude, couples who want their marriages to last a lifetime should work on communication, acceptance, and humor.

Topic Sentence: _____

Concluding Sentence: _____

1st sub-point: _____

2nd sub-point: _____

3rd sub-point: _____

Supporting Details for the 1st sub-point: _____ , _____ and _____ , _____

Supporting Details for the 2nd sub-point: _____ , _____ and _____ , _____

Supporting Details for the 3rd sub-point: _____ , _____ and _____ , _____

Practice 2

Order the sentences to make a complete paragraph.

Example:

_1_ *There are a number of reasons to go back to college as an adult.*

____ College can be an important place to network and talk to people about the kind of job you might want to do when you are finished with school.

____ Children of college-educated parents are more likely to see the value of a college education.

____ An additional reason to go back to college is to meet people in the field you are interested in.

____ The number-one reason to return to college is that people with a college education make more money.

____ In addition, it is almost impossible to take care of a family with a very low wage.

____ The final reason for attending college is to set an important example for your children.

____ Jobs that only require a high school education often pay the lowest wage.

____ Also, teachers and other students will become valuable resources.

____ As you can see, going back to school will contribute to your success in a number of ways.

Topic Sentence and Controlling Idea

Copyright © 2017 by Pearson Education, Inc. Duplication is not permitted.

Presentation

Topic Sentence and Controlling Idea

A **topic sentence** states the topic and the reason for writing. It is usually the first sentence in a paragraph.

A topic sentence has two parts:

Topic = who or what the paragraph is about
Controlling Idea = what the author's perspective on the topic is

Mistakes with Topic Sentences

A factual statement cannot be a topic sentence, because there is nothing to support. A fact is a fact and does not need to be supported.

A topic sentence that lacks a focused controlling idea introduces a subject that is too general or broad. It cannot be adequately supported. Make sure you have a controlling idea that is narrow enough that you can support it with detail.

A topic sentence with too much detail and explanation introduces a very limited subject that is too specific or narrow. There is not enough to say in one paragraph.

Sample Topic Sentences

Topic: Noise Pollution

There are three main sources of noise pollution in modern society.

The writer plans to classify three sources of noise pollution. This topic sentence is appropriate.

Noise pollution can have a number of serious effects on human health.

The writer plans to explain the health effects of noise pollution. This topic sentence is appropriate.

Noise pollution has a number of detrimental effects on people and animals.

The writer plans to discuss the negative effects of noise pollution. This topic sentence is appropriate.

Noise pollution is nothing new; it has been bothering people since the dawn of humankind.

The writer plans to discuss the history of noise pollution. The topic sentence is too general for one paragraph.

The main source of noise pollution is traffic because of the sound made near highways.

The writer introduces a topic that is too narrow.

Too much noise can be a problem.

This is an obvious factual statement that is not in need of support.

Practice 1

Read each topic sentence. Decide whether the topic sentence is appropriate, too factual, too broad, or too narrow for a paragraph. Circle the letter next to the correct answer.

Example:

1 *I believe that cats like to sleep all day because they are lazy.*

   a *appropriate*

   b *too factual*

   c *too broad*

   (d) *too narrow*

2 Stereotyping people based on race, gender, or religion is an ongoing problem that can be solved in several ways.

   a appropriate

   b too factual

   c too broad

   d too narrow

3 The Internet is an excellent tool for finding information.

   a appropriate

   b too factual

   c too broad

   d too narrow

4 Coffee is mainly grown in Africa, Central America, and South America.

   a appropriate

   b too factual

   c too broad

   d too narrow

5 Baseball and cricket are both played with a bat and a ball, but cricket only has two bases.

   a appropriate

   b too factual

   c too broad

   d too narrow

6 Scientists agree that there are seven traits that all living things share.

   a appropriate

   b too factual

   c too broad

   d too narrow

7 Democrats compete with Republicans for seats in the U.S. House of Representatives.

   a appropriate

   b too factual

   c too broad

   d too narrow

8 *The Diary of Anne Frank* was published in 1947.

   a appropriate

   b too factual

   c too broad

   d too narrow

Practice 2

Circle the letter next to the best topic sentence for each paragraph.

1 Topic Sentence: _____

First, cigarettes are more damaging to your health. Researchers have found that smoking causes lung cancer and heart disease. Drinking coffee has not actually been associated with causing any illnesses. The second reason is financial. Cigarettes cost a lot more money than coffee does. Finally, drinking coffee is a more socially acceptable activity. Smoking around others can expose them to harmful secondhand smoke, whereas drinking coffee around others will not expose them to anything harmful.

   a Cigarettes are different from coffee in a number of ways.

   b Cigarettes and coffee have a number of bad effects.

   c Cigarettes are a much worse habit than coffee for several reasons.

   d Two harmful habits are smoking and drinking coffee.

2 Topic Sentence: _____

Most automatic programmable slow cookers can be programmed to cook food for a certain amount of time, on a certain heat setting, or at a certain temperature. Before you start cooking with this kind of cooker, you will need to decide which method works best for your recipe. Once you have decided which method to use, you can start cooking. The first step is to turn the machine on. To cook using time, select the time button, and put in the amount of time. To cook on a particular setting, select the manual button, and choose the high or low setting. To cook to a certain temperature, you will need to plug the cord from the cooker's thermometer into the bottom of the machine and insert it through the top of the lid. The probe should be inserted into the food you are cooking. After you have set up the thermometer, select the probe button, and choose the right temperature.

   a An automatic programmable slow cooker is great for cooking.

   b There are a number of steps to follow when cooking with an automatic programmable slow cooker.

   c Slow cookers save time when you are cooking.

   d Cooking chicken in a slow cooker makes it tender and succulent.

3 Topic Sentence: _____

The first way is to keep your money in a savings account. Saving accounts generally have a very low interest rate, so there isn't a high return. However, with this method, your money is easily available if you need it. Another way is to buy a certificate of deposit (CD). CDs are purchased and accrue interest for a set period of time. The interest rate is higher than a savings account, but your money is not available during the set period of time. Next, if you are planning for the long term, you can put your money in an individual retirement account (IRA). These accounts are designed to help people save money for retirement. Money that you put in an IRA is tax deductible, and the interest rate is quite high compared to savings accounts and CDs. It's important to know that you will have to pay a penalty if you try to withdraw money from your IRA before you are 59 years old. The final way to save money is to buy some stock in a company. A company's value is divided in pieces, or shares, that anyone can purchase. If the value of the company's stock goes up, you can make a lot of money, but if the value goes down, you can lose a lot of money. There can be a lot of risk associated with buying stock.

a There are four ways to save your money for the future.
b Saving money is important.
c An important way to save money is to pay yourself first by saving before you pay your bills.
d People say you should save at least 20% of your income.

Concluding Sentences

Copyright © 2017 by Pearson Education, Inc. Duplication is not permitted.

Presentation

Concluding Sentences

Concluding sentences summarize the important ideas in the paragraph and sometimes provide a final thought. They are usually the final sentence in a paragraph.

Concluding sentences have three parts:

Conclusion Signals = *To sum up, In conclusion, Finally, To conclude, Thus*

Review of Ideas = a summary or re-statement of the topic sentences and the main reasons or ideas

Final Thought = why the information in the paragraph is important. The final thought is often an opinion, suggestion, or prediction.

Sample Paragraph

Green and black teas share similarities and differences. Both teas are harvested from the same plant, the *camille sinensis* bush. Also, the quality, taste, and price of both types of tea depend largely on the sub-species of *camille sinensis* that is used, the region it comes from, and the time the leaf is harvested.

The main difference between the two teas is in the way they are processed. For green tea, the process is relatively quick: The leaves are harvested, withered (dried in the sun until they become soft and pliable), and immediately heated at a high temperature to prevent fermentation. For black tea, the process is longer: The leaves are harvested, withered, and allowed to ferment until they turn a dark brown or black. At that point, they are heated to stop further fermentation.

Possible Concluding Sentences

1. *In conclusion, the differences in taste and color are mainly the result of the way green and black teas are processed.*

   The writer only provides a review. There is no final thought.

2. *To sum up, it's helpful to know how green and black teas are produced and processed.*

   The writer's opinion is that the information is helpful.

3. *To conclude, the variety of teas created by processing* camille sinensis *leaves are delightful and should be enjoyed.*

   The writer suggests that people should enjoy the tea.

Practice 1

Circle the letter next to the best concluding sentence to complete each paragraph.

1 Language and cultural barriers often force new immigrants to the United States to isolate themselves in their own communities. While these communities provide a sense of comfort and security for the immigrants, they also prevent them from integrating into American society. There are many ways we can help immigrants make the adjustment to their new environment. For example, our educational institutions could offer free or low-cost English classes. Also, schools and libraries could set up language-practice programs that pair English speakers with immigrants. Finally, community-based organizations could offer services that help immigrants with daily life, such as work, health care, and housing.

Concluding Sentence:

a In short, several programs can help new immigrants speak English, get jobs, and become citizens.

b To conclude, helping immigrants integrate into our culture makes the United States a better place to live for everyone.

c In conclusion, immigrants should learn to speak English so that they can participate in society.

2 Recycling is easy if you follow these three suggestions. First, learn the rules for your area—what is recyclable and how it is collected. In most cities, glass, paper, aluminum, and certain types of plastic are recyclable. Buy items that you know can be recycled. For example, if a certain type of plastic is recyclable in your city, buy plastic products that are made only from that type. Second, organize your home so that recycling is easy. For this, you will need different containers to separate the different kinds of recyclables. Third, instead of throwing everything in the trash, find ways to recycle it. For example, look for organizations that will take large appliances to recycle. Also, make a compost of your dead plants and leaves, food waste, and untreated paper to use as a nutrient-rich soil for your garden.

Concluding Sentence:

a You should follow these suggestions to recycle.

b To recycle, gather information about your neighborhood and organize so that recycling is easy.

c In short, following these three simple suggestions will help make it easy to recycle.

3 Asperger's syndrome is a disorder that affects a child's ability to socialize and communicate effectively with others. Many experts believe that the disorder is a mild form of autism. However, unlike with autism, a child with Asperger's syndrome frequently has normal intelligence and language development. He or she may, however, show signs of motor-skill delay and, at times, appear unusually awkward or clumsy. A major problem facing a child with Asperger's syndrome is his or her desire to fit in but inability to do so. There is no cure for Asperger's syndrome, but, if the disorder is diagnosed early, treatment can teach a child how to act appropriately in social situations and give him or her a better chance at having a successful life.

Concluding Sentence:

a In sum, Asperger's syndrome presents challenges to a child, but early detection and treatment can help him or her overcome these difficulties.

b Asperger's disorder, to conclude, is a milder form of autism.

c In conclusion, a child with Asperger's syndrome often has trouble communicating and fitting in with others.

Practice 2

Circle the letter next to the best concluding sentence to complete each paragraph.

1 In the painting *A Sunday Afternoon on the Island of Grand Jatte* Georges Seurat's unique style gives the languid scene a dreamlike quality. The painting depicts people enjoying a park on the Seine River in the late 19th century. The lazy river appears in the distance at the top of the

painting and gently curves around to the bottom left of the painting. In the distance, beyond the sailboats and through the trees, the viewer can just begin to see the other bank. In the center of the painting, sunbathers and idlers from all walks of life stand, sit, and lie around. Some of them are reading or taking pictures, and others are fishing or strolling. On the right side of the painting, the trees from the forest cast a darker shadow across the foreground of the painting. Seurat used tiny dots of color to paint this scene, causing colors to swim together like a picture under water. Seurat's images are indistinct and somewhat cloudy.

Concluding Sentence:

a Seurat's method of painting, which uses tiny dots of color, was called Impressionism.
b In brief, this timeless painting conveys the unhurried, leisurely feeling of a particular Sunday afternoon.
c The painting, to sum up, is quite beautiful.

2 Social media on the Internet has had a few important effects on modern politics. First of all, free public access to Twitter, blogs, Facebook, and other social media have given people the ability to comment on political decisions and breaking news in real time. Virtually anyone can make his or her voice heard immediately and publicly on issues that affect him or her. Second, politicians and others holding power are likely to read what people are saying online and act or react accordingly. Finally, people communicate with each other through social media in order to organize and protest. Social media sites allow them to sign petitions, engage in civil action, and coordinate protests.

Concluding Sentence:

a In conclusion, social media allows everyone to express his or her views on contemporary issues, thus creating a more democratic and global society.
b Therefore, people use social media to communicate on important political issues.
c Anyone can speak his or her mind about the issues of the day using social media.

3 The question of whether online classes or traditional classes are better and more effective is not an easy one to answer. Both have advantages and disadvantages. For example, traditional classes require students to be in class on a specific day and at a specific time, whereas online classes allow students to "attend" whenever it is convenient for them to do so. In traditional classes, the teacher interacts directly with students, and students can ask questions and get immediate answers. In online classes, however, there is no interaction with the teacher. Students typically have to send an email or post a question to a class blog or discussion board. Then they have to wait for a response.

Concluding Sentence:

a Both types of learning are important and have many similarities.
b Obviously, the traditional classroom is still relevant even though more students are studying online.
c To sum up, taking a course online or in a traditional classroom depends on the needs and preference of the individual students.

Supporting Sentences
COMPARISON SIGNALS

Presentation

Supporting Sentences: Comparison Signals

Use comparison signals in supporting sentences to compare the similarities between people, places, things, and concepts. The different types of comparison signals include adjectives, adverbs, prepositions, sentence connectors, and conjunctions.

Types of Signals	Examples
Nouns: *similarities, comparison*	Many cities share **similarities**.
Adjectives: *similar, equal, the same, common*	New Orleans and Paris are **similar** cities.
Comparatives: *as . . . as*	The nightlife in New Orleans is **as** exciting **as** the nightlife in Paris.
Prepositions: *similar to, equal to, like, the same as, just as, in common, as*	The architecture in New Orleans is **similar to** French architecture.
Sentence connectors: *similarly, likewise, also, too, in addition, additionally*	**Likewise**, New Orleans and Paris share the same French dishes.
Coordinating conjunctions: *and, nor*	People in New Orleans **and** Paris speak French.
Paired conjunctions: *both . . . and, neither . . . nor, not only . . . but also*	**Both** New Orleans **and** Paris are located on the banks of a river.

Practice 1

Write the appropriate comparison signals from the word box into the paragraph to complete the sentences.

similar	and	common
Both	neither Harry Potter nor	Similarly
not only Harry Potter but also	comparison	

Example:

A <u>*comparison*</u> of the Harry Potter stories and the King Arthur legend reveals a number of

_____ events and characters. First, _____ young

King Arthur are hidden after their parents die to protect them. _____ ,

_____ Arthur is aware of his special heritage, because both are adopted

by new families. _____ boys, in addition, are rescued from these families by

events that mark them as special. Harry Potter discovers he is a wizard when he talks to a snake,

_____ King Arthur discovers he is meant to be king when he pulls a sword

out of a stone. Once Arthur is marked as king, he goes to study with a teacher named Merlin, an

old white-haired man with a beard. Harry Potter has a _____ teacher

named Dumbledore. Both popular stories explore heroic themes that have been popular in

literature throughout centuries.

Practice 2

Write the appropriate comparison signals from the word box into the paragraph to complete the sentences.

the same material as	Both	not similar	Not only
many similar features	similar to	but also	and
Likewise	the same	similarities	

Example:

Baseball and cricket have several <u>*similarities*</u>. _____ cricket _____

baseball began in England _____ later came to the United States.

_____ sports are bat and ball games. The games mostly use _____

equipment, but the bats are _____ in shape. Cricket bats are flat, and baseball

bats are round. However, the balls in baseball are made of _____ the balls in

cricket. The objective in both sports is to win points called runs by batting the ball when the

opposing team throws it, _____ other bat and ball games. _____ ,
in both sports, the hitting team wins points by hitting the ball and running from one base to
another. The opposing team tries to strike out or stop the hitting team so that they can take a turn
at hitting. As you can see, the popular sports share _____ .

CONTRAST SIGNALS

Presentation

Supporting Sentences: Contrast Signals

Use contrast signals in supporting sentences to compare the differences in people, places,
things, and concepts. The different types of contrast signals include adjectives, adverbs,
prepositions, sentence connectors, and conjunctions.

Types of Signals	Examples
Nouns: *differences, contrast*	The two cities have many **differences**. The **contrast** between the two is marked.
Verbs: *differ in, differ from*	New Orleans **differs from** Paris in its history.
Adjectives: *different*	New Orleans and Paris are **different** in many ways.
Comparatives: *More / less … than, the most / least …*	New Orleans is **smaller than** Paris.
Prepositions: *different from, unlike, instead of*	**Unlike** New Orleans, Paris has a temperate climate.
Sentence connectors: *by contrast, on the other hand, however*	Paris is relatively safe; **by contrast**, New Orleans can be quite dangerous.
Coordinating conjunctions: *but, yet*	Paris has many beautiful parks and boulevards, **but** New Orleans only has a few.
Paired conjunctions: *not … but*	Paris is **not** cheap, **but** the cost of living in New Orleans is quite inexpensive.
Subordinating conjunctions: *while, whereas* (opposites) *although, though, even though* (surprising contrast)	**While** Paris is known for love and romance, New Orleans is known for voodoo and mystery.

Practice 1

Write the correct contrast signals from the word box into the paragraph to complete the sentences.

while	on the other hand	However	differ
different	more social than	whereas	In contrast
yet	contrast	difference	

Example:

The _contrast_ between dogs and cats is not always obvious, _____ the two animals

are _____ in many ways. One way they _____ is in their behavior.

Dogs are far _____ cats. For example, because dogs are eager to please their

owners, they can be trained to do tricks and to obey simple commands like come, sit, and fetch.

Cats, _____ , have no interest in pleasing their owners and cannot be trained

in this way. Also, dogs are pack animals, _____ cats are solitary creatures. This

means that dogs like (and sometimes need) to travel and be in the company of other

dogs. _____ , cats are loners whose main concern is protecting their territory, not

spending time with other cats. Another _____ is that cats are good jumpers

and climbers, dogs are not. Cats in the wild climb and jump to hunt and escape from

danger. _____ , dogs do not climb and jump well, so they need to travel in packs

to hunt effectively, and they fight rather than flee when they feel threatened.

Practice 2

Write the correct contrast signals from the word box into the paragraph to complete the sentences.

instead of	In contrast	difference
whereas	better for the environment than	however
but	unlike	differs from
final contrast	while	

Conventional farming _____ organic farming in several ways.

First, _____ organic farmers, conventional farmers use many

non-natural substances. For example, they use chemical fertilizers to promote plant growth,

_____ organic farmers use compost or manure to fertilize

the soil. Conventional farmers use insecticides to eliminate pests and disease,

_____ their organic counterparts use insects and birds,

traps, and other methods. Conventional farmers use herbicides to control weeds;

_____ , organic farmers control them by rotating crops or

removing the weeds by hand. Another key _____ is in the

food that the animals eat and the conditions in which they live. Conventional animals eat a variety

of food , _____ they are also given antibiotics and growth hormones

to prevent disease and make them grow faster. The animals are also housed in small,

crowded spaces indoors. _____, organic animals eat a strict

diet of grass and organic feed, and, living in confined spaces, they are allowed to roam freely

outdoors. A _____ is the impact that farming has on the land.

Because organic farming helps to reduce pollution and conserves water and soil, it is

_____ conventional farming.

DESCRIPTIVE DETAILS

Presentation

Supporting Sentences: Descriptive Details

Use descriptive details in supporting sentences to say what a person, place, thing, or concept looks, sounds, smells, feels, and tastes like. Descriptive details also answer questions about *who, what, where, when, why,* and *how.*

There are several ways to include descriptive details in your writing.

- Use adjectives to depict the five senses:

  Sight – bright, dark, colorful, bent, round, tall, short

  Sound – noisy, quiet, melodic, dissonant, booming, silent

  Smell – scented, pungent, aromatic, stinky, smelly

  Touch – rough, smooth, silky, soft, hard, bumpy

  Taste – sweet, sour, bitter, salty, bland, spicy

- Use appropriate adjective order when listing descriptive words:

  Opinion: ugly, beautiful, expensive

  Size: small, round, torn

  Age: old, young, new

  Shape: round, flat, square

  Color: green, yellow, blue

  Origin/Religion: – Chinese, Christian, Martian

  Material: wooden, cotton

  Purpose: wedding, baseball, as in "wedding cake" or "baseball glove." The noun-adjective tells us the purpose of the object. Main noun: The main noun comes last: *cake, glove*

Example:

  The beautiful, tall, young woman wore a long, yellow, mohair sweater.

- Use feeling words and participial adjectives (adjectives that end in *–ed* or *–ing*, such as *talented* or *annoying*) to give emotional detail.

Examples:

   The girl was excited when she saw her brother.

   Roman became frightened when he saw a big brown bear approaching his tent.

- Use *like*, *as*, and *as…as* to compare items.

Examples:

   That movie was awful. It was as bad as a visit to the dentist for a root canal.

   She runs like a well-trained athlete.

- Use prepositional phrases to give background information about time and place.

Example:

   Yesterday morning, she dressed in her room and then went to the kitchen for breakfast.

- Use adverbs to say *how, why, when,* and *to what degree*.

Example:

   Yesterday morning, she dressed hurriedly in her room and then dashed quickly to the kitchen for breakfast.

Practice 1

Sort the sentences into the groups based on the type of descriptive detail by writing whether the sentence describes *physical appearance, background information,* or *personality*.

Topic Sentence: My grandfather was a handsome man with a quiet strength.

He was not a man given to flowery speeches and long explanations. _____

He never wasted anything, including words. _____

Every Sunday, he would sit and cut coupons carefully from the paper to save money. _____

When he stood still, he was like a tree rooted to the earth. _____

When he talked, he had a quiet stern voice that rumbled like distant thunder. _____

At 6 feet 4 inches, he was a tall man with large bones and a heavy frame. _____

He had an angular face with high cheekbones, and his skin was the color of reddish-brown clay. _____

He was all economy and efficiency because of his poor rural upbringing in Oklahoma. _____

When he spoke, it was always carefully measured and brief. _____

Practice 2

Read the topic sentence and the supporting sentences. Circle the letter next to the correct type of descriptive detail in each supporting sentence.

Topic Sentence: The Paintpots in Yellowstone Park are one of the most unusual natural features in the world.

1 As you look out onto the landscape, you might get an uneasy feeling of wonder at the strangeness of it all.
   a How it smells
   b What it looks like
   c How you feel
   d What it sounds like

2 The hot, dry air gives off the scent of rotting eggs from the sulfur.
   a How it smells
   b What it looks like
   c How you feel
   d What it sounds like

3 The sun burns down on the parched and cracked earth that surrounds the pools of bubbling mud and scalding blue water.
   a How it smells
   b What it looks like
   c How you feel
   d What it sounds like

4 Mud sinkholes are stained deep red, orange, blue, and green from mineral deposits as the acid from the steamy pools eats away at the rock around it.
   a How it smells
   b What it looks like
   c How you feel
   d What it sounds like

5 If you listen, you can hear soft gurgling and popping sounds from the craters below.
   a How it smells
   b What it looks like
   c How you feel
   d What it sounds like

6 The pots of mud and water are like an artist's palette of oil colors, ready to be smeared across a canvas.
   a How it smells
   b What it looks like
   c How you feel
   d What it sounds like

EXAMPLES AND REASONS

Presentation

Supporting Sentences: Examples and Reasons

Use supporting details, such as examples and reasons, to provide more information about sub-points in a paragraph. A supporting detail can be an explanation, an example, a fact, an expert opinion, or a statistic. It is common to provide at least one example, fact, statistic, or expert opinion to support a sub-point in a paragraph and then explain and connect it to your sub-point. Review the different sentence structures for each type of supporting detail.

Types of Support	Examples
Examples: *for example, for instance, such as, specifically, in particular*	A superstition is a belief in the power of an object or action. **For example**, one superstition is that if you break a mirror, this can cause you seven years of bad luck.
Facts, expert opinions, and statistics: *statistics show that, according to, data show that*	Superstitions are explanations of observable phenomena. **According to** the *Oxford Dictionary of Superstitions*, most superstitions began as a misunderstanding of an observable phenomenon.
Reasons: *the reason is (that), the cause of, that is why, as a result, consequently, so, for, because, due to, provided that, thus, therefore*	**The main reason** that superstitions are so common is **because** people want to be able to control what happens to them. **Therefore**, they try to explain events as best they can.

Practice 1

Write in numbers from 1 to 10 to put the sentences in the best order by topic sentence, sub-points, and supporting details.

_____ According to a report from the U.S. Census Bureau, a high school graduate makes about $20,000 less than a college graduate annually.

_____ Second, college tuition is rising, and many students need to take out student loans to pay for their education.

_____ Finally, because high school graduates are no longer able to get good jobs, and many are unable to afford college tuition, the government should prepare citizens for the workforce by offering free college education.

_____ More and more students are leaving college with too much debt.

_____ In my opinion, there are two important reasons to make college education free for anyone who wants to attend.

_____ For example, it is common for a university graduate with a bachelor's degree to leave school with $100,000 or more in student loans.

_____ First, it is no longer possible for a person to make a decent salary with only a high school education.

_____ Thus, it is clear that a college education can prevent the likelihood that someone will be poor.

_____ Therefore, college graduates may struggle financially even with their earning potential because of debt.

_____ For instance, many high school graduates end up in minimum-wage jobs that pay less than $9 an hour.

Practice 2

Underline the best two details to support each sub-point in each paragraph

Topic:

Obesity is on the rise in many Western societies for a number of reasons.

1 The first reason is the way people eat.

More and more people are eating larger amounts of fatty and sugary food.

People mostly eat meat and potatoes, because they do not like vegetables.

Since more and more people can afford food, they are choosing to buy leaner, healthier options.

For instance, a McDonald's value meal in the United States 20 years ago consisted of a 12-ounce soda, a small side of French fries, and a 3-ounce hamburger; however, the current "super-sized" value meal consists of a 20-ounce soda, a large side of French fries, and an 8-ounce hamburger.

For example, in the past, people put a lot of cream and sugar in their coffee, but now they prefer to buy espresso drinks from Starbucks.

2 Furthermore, many people do not get as much exercise.

There are many types of exercise that promote a healthy weight, including yoga, walking, and dancing.

According to the Food Research and Action Center, many people spend too much time on sedentary activities.

Researchers have found that in the United States alone, people spend more than $30 billion a year on diets and weight-loss programs.

In addition, exercise can promote cardiovascular health.

The average person spends at least half of the day sitting at a desk, playing video games, surfing the Internet, and driving from one place to another.

3 Third, studies have shown a direct link between poverty and obesity due to unhealthy eating habits.

People in poor neighborhoods are often too tired to cook.

People with low incomes have more obesity-related health problems.

Grocery stores in low-income neighborhoods do not stock healthy foods like fruit, vegetables, and whole grains, because most people cannot afford to buy them.

It is unacceptable that in many countries an apple costs more than a candy bar.

In fact, some politicians have suggested that we should make overweight people pay more for health insurance, because they cost us more money.

4 The final reason is that higher levels of chronic stress may cause people to overeat.

The top causes of chronic stress include worry about relationships, money, and work.

The average person's lifestyle is more stressful than ever because of increasing work hours, lack of health care, lack of community connection, and rising cost of living.

People tend to eat when they are depressed and unhappy about their lives for a number of reasons.

People with a stressful lifestyle may overeat because they do not have time to prepare healthy food, or because they use food as a way to relax.

Some scientists believe that people under extreme stress release high levels of cortisol, a hormone that leads to weight gain.

SPATIAL ORDER

Presentation

Types of Spatial Order	Examples
From top to bottom: *at the top of, above, between, below, beneath*	The bookcase has three shelves. **On the top** shelf, there is a pink shell, a photo album, and a yellow piggy bank. **Beneath** the first shelf, a number of small books line the second shelf. Finally, there are larger books **on the bottom** shelf.
From right to left: *on the right / left, in the center, next to*	The old cabin had one room. **From** the door, you could see a single window **to the right**, the only source of light. A rocking chair sat **in the middle** of the room with a rug underneath it. If you looked **to the left**, you would see a rusty cast iron stove with a chimney pipe.
From front to back: *in front of, behind, in the back of, across from*	The blouse I bought for the party had a lace collar with small pearl buttons **down the front**. The sleeves were cut off at the elbow with lace frills hanging **on either side**. **On the back of** the blouse, near the shoulders, there were small lines of delicate embroidery.
From near to far: *here, (over) there, near to, far from*	**At the entrance** of the park, there are a number of picnic tables. As you walk **past** the picnic tables, you will see a wading pool **between** the trees. **Farther on**, you will reach the lakeshore and the beach.

Practice 1

Write in numbers from 1 to 8 to organize the sentences in the paragraph so that the spatial order is from left to right. Some of them have been done for you.

Topic Sentence: This is my favorite family photo because it has such a warm, antique feeling.

_____ To my right are our parents.

_____ At the far left is my sister, Yolanda, who's holding her oldest child.

__7__ We all dressed in black and white outfits for the photo.

__1__ The photo was taken by a professional photographer who used sepia tones to get the warm, antique effect.

_____ That's my sister Cerise and me next to Yolanda's husband.

_____ Then at the far right is my eight-year-old nephew, who, as you can see, loves having his picture taken!

__8__ The sepia tones and our simple black and white outfits give the photo its old-time look.

_____ Next to Yolanda is her husband, Raul, who's holding their six-month-old baby.

Practice 2

Write in numbers from 1 to 9 to organize the sentences in the paragraph using left to right spatial order. Some of them have been done for you.

Topic Sentence: My favorite family photograph is special because of its aged, vintage appearance.

_____ Yolanda's husband is standing behind her holding their six-month-old baby.

_____ My mother and father are to the right of Cerise and me.

__5__ I am sitting on a stool at the center of the photograph with Cerise behind me.

_____ To the left, my sister, Yolanda, is sitting in a high-backed chair and holding her oldest child in her lap.

__1__ The photograph was professionally done using sepia tones that give the picture a warmer appearance than a stark black and white photograph would have.

__9__ My father and my sister's husband are dressed simply in plain black suits and white shirts, and my mom, my sisters, and I are all in simple black dresses.

_____ My other sister, Cerise, and I are next to Yolanda and her husband.

_____ My father is sitting next to me, and my mother is on his right side.

_____ Cerise is standing next to Yolanda's husband with her hands on my shoulders.

TIME ORDER SIGNALS

Presentation

Supporting Sentences: Time Order

Use time order in supporting sentences to tell what happened from past to present. Use time order to describe an event, tell a story, or explain a procedure chronologically.

Types of Signals	Examples
Adverbs: *yesterday, today, last night*	**Last night**, I went on the worst date of my life. **Earlier that day**, I met a man while choosing apples to buy in the grocery store.
Prepositions: *in the morning, at noon*	We talked **for a while**, and he asked me out to dinner that night. He came to my house **at 8 o'clock**, but he didn't have a car. We had to take the bus.
Sentence connectors: *first, later, next, finally*	**Later**, at the restaurant, he told me he forgot his wallet and asked me to pay.
Subordinating conjunctions: *after, as, meanwhile, when, as soon as, until, since, as long as, before, after*	**After** I paid for dinner, he wanted to know if I wanted to go to the movies. **Since** I wasn't having a good time, I told him no and went home.

Practice 1

Circle the correct time order signals to complete the sentences.

Making low-fat yogurt at home is not difficult to do. [Before you start / As long as / Next], have the following items ready: a quart of 2% milk, a one-quart ceramic or glass container with a lid, a cooking thermometer, and a half cup of store-bought plain yogurt. [First / After / Next], warm the milk in a medium-sized saucepan until it reaches a temperature of 175–180°F. [As soon / As long / Until] as the milk reaches that temperature, remove it from the heat. [Once / First / Until] you have removed it from the heat, let it cool to a temperature of 100–115°F. [After / Finally / Next] the milk has cooled to that temperature, mix in the half cup of plain yogurt a little at a time. [Next / As soon as / Before you start], pour the milk and the yogurt mixture into the container, cover it with the lid, and leave it in a warm place for 8 to 12 hours. The milk will turn to yogurt [as long as / after / until] the temperature remains constant at about 100–110°F. Wait for the yogurt to set. [Finally / As long as / Next], put it in the refrigerator to completely cool. Keep the yogurt refrigerated [until / after / once] you are ready to serve it.

Practice 2

Write the numbers next to the sentences in order, using the time order signals as a guide. Some of them have been done for you.

Topic Sentence: My parents met by chance because of their mutual interest in basketball.

_____ Meanwhile, my father had decided to coach a women's basketball team to meet girls.

_____ My father, on the other hand, is American.

__10__ If it hadn't been for basketball, my parents might never have met 40 years ago.

__6__ Both teams played against each other in the spring of 1973.

__3__ He moved to Seattle, Washington, when he returned from the Vietnam War in 1969.

_____ At the party, my parents were introduced to one another by a mutual friend.

__1__ My mother is from San Juan, Puerto Rico, but she left when she was 18 years old to move to Vancouver, B.C., in Canada.

_____ My father's team lost, but the Canadian team hosted a party for them anyway.

_____ After my mother moved to Vancouver, she began to play on a women's basketball team to make friends.

_____ It was love at first sight.

Coherence

LOGICAL DIVISION OF IDEAS

Presentation

Coherence: Logical Division of Ideas

In coherent writing, the ideas should be organized logically. Ideas may talk about steps, reasons, advantages, disadvantages, similarities, differences, causes, effects, solutions, qualities, types, or kinds. To order them logically, choose one of the methods described below:

most to least important

the most important reason -> an important reason -> yet another reason

general to specific

a general quality -> a more specific quality -> a unique quality

familiar to unknown

the well-known effect -> another effect -> a surprising effect

oldest to newest

the oldest type -> another type -> most recent type

simple to complex

the easy solution -> a more challenging solution -> the most complex solution

Topic: Swing Dancing

Examples:

Swing is an American dance form that has developed into three popular types.

The oldest type of swing is Lindy Hop.

Another type is East Coast Swing.

The most recent type of swing started on the West Coast and is called …

Order: oldest to newest

Swing is a type of American dance with a number of characteristics.

First, swing developed from jazz music.

Next, swing has syncopated steps.

Finally, swing is danced with a partner.

Order: most to least important

Use **sentence connectors** to indicate the logical order of arguments and to signal transition from one to the other. This will make your writing more coherent.

Examples:

First (of all), …   Second, …

The first step/ reason/ effect/ solution/ type etc. is …

Another step/reason/effect/ solution/ type etc. is …

Furthermore, also, moreover, in addition

Finally, …

The final step/reason/effect/ solution/ type etc. is …

Practice 1

Underline the best answer.

1 **Topic sentence:** There are a number of methods parents can try when dealing with their teenager's difficult behavior.

   Which of the following sub-points is the most logical division for the topic?

   Emotional mood swings, talking back, not doing what you say.

   Teens make more of their own decisions, they spend more time away from home, they want to be an adult.

   Tell them the rules, be consistent about punishment, don't get angry and criticize.

   How is the topic divided into sub-points?

   Solutions to a problem

   Examples

   Reasons for something

   What is the most logical order for the sub-points?

   General to specific

   Easy to difficult

   Familiar to unknown

2 **Topic sentence:** Anyone can stop biting his or her nails by following a few easy steps.

   Which of the following sub-points is the most logical division for the topic?

   Some people do it when stressed, some when bored, some to relax.

   Your fingers bleed, you can get infections, it can cause dental problems.

   Use an unpleasant solution on your nails, find new ways to release your anxiety, and do things that help you relax.

   How is the topic divided into sub-points?

   Qualities

   Steps

   Effects

   What is the most logical order for the sub-points?

   Most to least important

   First to last

   General to specific

3 **Topic sentence:** It is important to be aware of how a particular college defines plagiarism.

   Which of the following sub-points is the most logical division for the topic?

   Copying someone's assignment, not citing a source, using your own work from a different class

   Dishonest, unprofessional, wrong

   Receive a zero on an assignment, fail the class, suspended from the school

How is the topic divided into sub-points?

Similarities

Causes

Types

What is the most logical order for the sub-points?

General to specific

Most obvious to least obvious

Simple to complex

Practice 2

Circle the best transition signals to complete the sentences.

Topic: A classical Greek tragedy has a number of elements.

[First of all, / Most interestingly, / The most important one is] a classical Greek tragedy usually has a protagonist or hero who is unaware of his destiny. [Furthermore / Finally / To begin], the events lead to a catastrophe for the hero of the story. [In addition / Finally / Next], the tragic events are not usually the hero's fault but rather his or her destiny. [Finally / First / At last], most tragedies contain a moment when the hero gains a new insight about life because of the tragedy he or she has endured.

NOUNS AND PRONOUNS

Presentation

Coherence: Nouns and Pronouns

In coherent writing, ideas are connected from the beginning to the end of the paragraph. Consistent use of key words and pronouns provides coherence in writing.

- Use the same words and phrases to talk about key people, places, things, and concepts.
- Use the same pronouns to rename nouns. Review the section on pronoun agreement for more information.
- Use pronouns that avoid gender bias.

Examples:

We want **someone** who can type. We need to hire **him or her.** (Note that the use of both genders to avoid bias can be awkward.)

We want **people** who can type. We need to hire **them**. (Use plural to avoid using both genders.)

We want **someone** who can type. We need to hire **you**. (Use 2nd person, informal pronoun.)

We want **someone** who can type. We need to hire a **person**. (no pronoun used)

- Only use pronouns when they clearly refer to a previously named person, place, thing, or concept in the paragraph.

Practice 1

Circle the correct noun or pronoun to complete the sentences correctly.

Coulrophobia is the irrational fear of clowns. While the phobia affects mostly children, [it / its / they] can also be found in teenagers and adults. People who suffer from [coulrophobia / its / phobia] experience a range of symptoms—from mild discomfort to severe panic attacks—depending on the intensity of [their / his or her / its] fear. According to experts, most people develop [coulrophobia / intensity / them] in early childhood after one or more traumatic experiences with clowns. [Their / His or her / Its] exaggerated makeup, colorful costumes, and distorted features make clowns quite frightening to children, and [they / he / it] carry this fear with [them / her / they] into adulthood. Other people are known to develop [the phobia / adulthood / them] later in life after reading a book or watching a movie about an evil clown, such as the one portrayed in Stephen King's novel *It*.

Practice 2

Underline the five mistakes in pronouns in the paragraphs.

Academic cheating is a problem on college campuses. My college recently announced strict new rules for dealing with them. Based on it, any student caught cheating will fail the course in which the cheating occurred. If they happens again, the student will be expelled from the university. Many students were upset about the policy. They said that she wasn't fair because, under the new rules, a student's entire career could be destroyed by one "mistake."

My roommate Bob was one of the first people punished under the new regulations. His physics professor caught him cheating during a test. He saw Bob looking at notes he had hidden in his sleeve. Since it was his first offense, he got an F, and he will have to repeat him in summer school. When I asked Bob why he had cheated instead of studying a little harder, his excuse was "Everyone does it."

Unity

Unity

A paragraph is unified if every supporting sentence is clearly connected to the topic sentence. To achieve unity in writing, check that each sentence is relevant and is placed appropriately. Delete any sentences that are off or irrelevant to the main idea of the paragraph. Move sentences to a more appropriate place if necessary.

Example Paragraph:

There are three main reasons people develop eating disorders. The first is the failure to cope with traumatic events. People who develop eating disorders have often suffered severely traumatic events in their lives, and they have often not coped with them. In particular, verbal, physical, and sexual abuse can trigger an eating disorder if the person does not get help.

There are three types of disordered eating; anorexia, bulimia, and binge eating. (Relevant but not appropriate here. It should be moved to the first sentence.)

The second reason is low self-esteem. Researchers have found that people with low self-esteem are overly concerned with what others think about them due to their poor self-image. ***People with a poor self-image also have trouble in school.*** **(Irrelevant to the topic)** Since people with low self-esteem don't feel good about themselves, they might become depressed and eat or purge to feel better. ***They might spend a lot of money on clothes and fashion to impress others.*** (Off-topic)

The final reason someone might develop an eating disorder is an excessive focus on weight loss and dieting. For example, a person who spends a lot of time dieting and exercising might become obsessed with body weight. This obsession might cause him or her to refuse to eat (anorexia) or vomit (bulimia). In conclusion, trauma, poor self-image, and an obsession with body size can all lead to an eating disorder.

Practice 1

Circle the letter next to the best description for each sentence in the paragraph.

Topic Sentence: Cellist Yo-Yo Ma is not only one of the most brilliant but also one of the most beloved musicians in the world today.

Example:

1 *The cello is a very difficult instrument to master.*
   a *Off-topic*
   b *Relevant*
   c *Wrong place*

2 Yo-Yo Ma is an amazingly diverse artist, famous not only for his performances of classical music but also for his participation in projects involving other musical styles, such as jazz, country, and traditional Chinese folk music.
   a Off-topic
   b Relevant
   c Wrong place

3 Once, Ma accidentally left his cello in the trunk of the taxi he was riding in.

   a Off-topic

   b Relevant

   c Wrong place

4 For example, Ma has recorded more than 45 albums and won 14 Grammy Awards.

   a Off-topic

   b Relevant

   c Wrong place

5 Yo-Yo Ma is married and has two children.

   a Off-topic

   b Relevant

   c Wrong place

6 In addition, he has played the cello in such hit films as *Crouching Tiger, Hidden Dragon* and *Seven Years in Tibet.*

   a Off-topic

   b Relevant

   c Wrong place

7 Born October 7, 1955, to Chinese parents living in Paris, he began playing the cello at the age of four.

   a Off-topic

   b Relevant

   c Wrong place

8 The *Los Angeles Times* described Yo-Yo Ma as "an artist possessing tremendous technical brilliance and musicality."

   a Off-topic

   b Relevant

   c Wrong place

9 He has performed as a soloist with symphony orchestras around the world, including those of Boston, Toronto, New York, Israel, and the Los Angeles Philharmonic.

   a Off-topic

   b Relevant

   c Wrong place

10 In his free time, Ma also likes to write poetry.

   a Off-topic

   b Relevant

   c Wrong place

Practice 2

Circle the letter next to the best description for each sentence in the paragraph.

Topic Sentence: San Francisco is an outstanding city to visit on vacation for three reasons.

Example:

1 *First, it has many great tourist attractions, such as its cable cars, Chinatown, Alcatraz Island, and Union Square.*
   a *Off-topic*
   (b) *Relevant*
   c *Wrong place*

2 Restaurants in San Francisco feature every imaginable type of ethnic food as well as outstanding fish dishes.
   a Off-topic
   b Relevant
   c Wrong place

3 More than 10 million tourists visit San Francisco each year, and some of these attractions, such as Alcatraz, are so popular that it's necessary to make reservations ahead of time.
   a Off-topic
   b Relevant
   c Wrong place

4 A second reason for San Francisco's popularity with tourists is the quality of its world-famous restaurants.
   a Off-topic
   b Relevant
   c Wrong place

5 Tourists can find a unique type of bread called "sourdough."
   a Off-topic
   b Relevant
   c Wrong place

6 Though many people think it tastes strange at first, they soon develop a taste for it.
   a Off-topic
   b Relevant
   c Wrong place

7 That's why many tourists leaving from San Francisco International Airport can be seen boarding their planes with a loaf of bread under their arms.
   a Off-topic
   b Relevant
   c Wrong place

8 However, I ate at one restaurant in Chinatown where the service was terrible.
   a Off-topic
   b Relevant
   c Wrong place

9 The third thing that makes San Francisco a great vacation city is its geographical location.

   a Off-topic

   b Relevant

   c Wrong place

10 This city is small—only 49 square miles.

   a Off-topic

   b Relevant

   c Wrong place

11 The ocean surrounds it on three sides, and there are many hills.

   a Off-topic

   b Relevant

   c Wrong place

12 For this reason, beautiful views of the water can be seen from the downtown skyscrapers.

   a Off-topic

   b Relevant

   c Wrong place

13 These are just three of many reasons why San Francisco is a popular vacation destination for people from all over the world.

   a Off-topic

   b Relevant

   c Wrong place

Essay Structure

Presentation
Essay Structure

Essays, like paragraphs, have three main parts: an introductory paragraph, a number of body paragraphs, and a conclusion paragraph.

An introductory paragraph has an opening hook to get the reader interested in the topic and states the overall main point in a thesis statement.

The essay opening can:

- give background information about the topic.
- tell a story related to the topic.
- make a surprising statement (quote, fact, statistic, or question) related to the topic.

A thesis statement can:

- tell what the topic is.
- state the writer's idea about the topic.
- say why the writer is writing.

Body paragraphs divide the overall main point into a number of sub-topics that further support and provide evidence for the claim in the thesis statement. Each body paragraph has a topic sentence and supporting sentences. The topic sentence states the sub-topic related to the thesis statement.

Supporting sentences provide facts, examples, details, and explanations related to the topic sentence.

A conclusion paragraph summarizes the main point and sub-points and finishes up the essay with a final thought, suggestion, or prediction related to the essay.

Practice 1

Read and identify the parts of the essay. Circle the letter next to the correct answer in each of the questions that follow.

(1) Are you a shy person? If so, you are not alone. According to research by Dr. Philip Zimbardo of Stanford University, more than 40% of Americans say they are shy in most situations; in addition, another 15% say they are shy in certain situations. In contrast, only 5% say they have never experienced shyness.

(2) Doctor Zimbardo distinguishes between two kinds of shyness.

(3) The first kind is called "situational" shyness. As the name suggests, this is a temporary kind of shyness that most people feel if, for example, they meet an attractive person for the first time, or if they have to speak in public. In other words, this kind of shyness is caused by external circumstances.

(4) On the other hand, some people are born shy and feel shy all the time in nearly every situation. For such people, shyness can lead to a variety of negative consequences. For instance, shy people have fewer friends and are more likely to be depressed than outgoing people.

(5) If shyness is a problem for you, what can you do about it? Doctor Zimbardo has a number of recommendations. First, it may help to remember that nearly half of all people are shy like you. If you are in a social situation, such as a party, try to find other shy people and talk to them. Start the conversation by admitting that you are shy. This will help put them at ease and may even get a conversation going. Since shyness can be a crippling problem for so many people, Doctor Zimbardo and his colleagues at Stanford started the Shyness Institute devoted to researching the causes of and treatments for this widespread condition.

1 Which sentence is the introductory hook?
  a 1
  b 2
  c 4
  d 5

2 What type of opening does the essay have?
  a Background information
  b Story or anecdote
  c Surprising statement
  d Question

3 Which sentence is the thesis statement of the essay?
  a 1
  b 2
  c 4
  d 5

4 Which paragraph is not a sub-topic for this essay?
  a 3
  b 4
  c 1
  d 5

5 Which sentence reviews the essay?
  a 1
  b 2
  c 3
  d None

Practice 2

Read the thesis, body paragraphs, and sentences/phrases. Write the number that is next to each sentence/phrase into each outline.

Sentences

1 The most familiar note-taking system is the outline.

2 The final type of note-taking is the Cornell Method.

3 Another familiar system is a T-chart graphic organizer.

4 using an outline, T-chart, or Cornell Method for taking notes can improve your success in college.

Essay Outline

Introduction

Thesis: Three familiar types of note-taking systems are effective for use in college lectures.

Body Paragraphs

a _____

- It uses lists with bullets or numbering.
- It is organized by topic and details.

b _____

- This uses a visual map or chart to organize.
- It can organize in multiple ways.

c _____

- This uses a combination of lists and charts.
- It provides a summary at the end.

Conclusion

In conclusion, _____

Sentences

1 Second, Spanish and Italian people have similar attitudes about work and daily life.

2 First, both languages derive from Latin and have similar features.

3 the Spanish and Italian people have similar languages, attitudes, and cultures.

4 A comparison between Spanish and Italian cultures demonstrates some remarkable similarities.

5 Finally, the Spanish and Italian people have similar cultures.

Essay Outline

Introduction

Thesis: _____

Body Paragraphs

a _____

- vocabulary
- grammar

b _____

- work and schedule
- family and home life

c _____

- religion
- Mediterranean diet

Conclusion

To sum up, _____

INTRODUCTORY PARAGRAPHS AND THESIS STATEMENTS

Copyright © 2017 by Pearson Education, Inc. Duplication is not permitted.

Presentation

Introductory Paragraphs and Thesis Statements

An introductory paragraph has an opening hook to get the reader interested in the topic and states the overall main point or perspective of the essay in a thesis statement. In general, all introductions start with a general statement about the topic. Each sentence becomes more and more specific until the writer has introduced the thesis.

There are various kinds of essay openings. An essay opening can:

- give background information about the topic.
- tell a story related to the topic.
- make a surprising statement (quote, fact, statistic, or question) related to the topic.

Thesis statements:

- state the topic.
- state the writer's purpose for writing about the topic.
- indicate how the essay is structured (cause/effect, classification, comparison/contrast, definition, description, narrative, opinion, problem/solution, process).

Sample Introductory Paragraph

In the United States, students at private, independent, and religious schools have always worn uniforms, while students in public schools have not been required to do so. This trend is changing, however. More and more public schools across the nation, including the influential New York City school system with its 550,000 elementary school children, are requiring students to wear uniforms for a number of reasons.

Practice 1

Number the sentences in the paragraph in order from general to specific by writing them in the blanks. Start with a hook, and put the thesis statement last.

____ These couples think that divorce will solve their problems and make life easier.

____ The latest figures say that more than 50% of marriages end in divorce.

____ However, there is evidence that divorce might actually have a number of harmful effects as well.

____ A surprising number of marriages fail in the United States.

____ Most couples get divorced because of money problems or because of lack of commitment.

Practice 2

Write the letters into the blanks that place the sentences in the best order.

Sentences

a After ten years of working as a teller, I received a notice one day that the bank was letting me go.

b Like me, many adults face challenges when they return to college.

c So, I decided to go back to school and get a degree.

d I started the job right after high school and had no training to do any other kind of work.

e Although I'm happy I finished, I must say that returning to college was one of the most challenging experiences of my life.

Paragraph

_____

I was out of a job.

I didn't know what to do.

_____

_____

_____

_____

BODY PARAGRAPHS

Body Paragraphs

Body paragraphs divide the overall main point into a number of sub-topics that further support and provide evidence for the claim or claims of the thesis statement. Each body paragraph has a topic sentence, supporting sentences, and a concluding/transitional sentence.

The topic sentence states the sub-topic as it relates to the thesis statement. Each topic sentence should have a controlling idea that states what the writer will say about the sub-topic. Use transition signals to indicate the paragraph pattern.

Supporting sentences provide facts, statistics, expert opinions, examples, details, and explanations related to the topic sentence. These sentences are organized in the following ways: logical, spatial, or time order. It's common to relate a sub-point to the topic sentence or provide a supporting detail and explain it.

The concluding sentence in a body paragraph provides a brief review of the points in the paragraph. It then transitions to the next body paragraph.

Example:

Introductory Paragraph:

Seoul, Korea, has one of the worst traffic problems in the world. Since there are so many cars on the road, traffic accidents are frequent. These accidents cause injuries and deaths. One reason this problem persists is that there are few penalties for traffic violations. Also, automobile insurance rates are very low. Nonetheless, the traffic problem in Seoul can easily be solved in several ways.

Body Paragraph Structure:

- Topic Sentence — If the government increased traffic fines, there would be fewer traffic problems.
- Sub-point #1 — People would drive more carefully to avoid a traffic ticket.

Practice 1

Circle the letters next to the three best sub-points for each thesis statement.

1 Thesis: Divorce can have a number of harmful effects on adults.
  a Divorce has increased in the last couple of decades.
  b The most important effect on people who experience divorce is a financial one.
  c Divorce can have a devastating immediate emotional effect on people.
  d Furthermore, children of divorced parents often need therapy for behavior problems.
  e Divorce can affect future psychological health.
  f In addition, property must be divided when people divorce.

2 Thesis: Adults returning to college face many challenges.
  a Paying for college can be a huge burden for an adult returning to college.
  b Adults may need to return to college to update their skills.
  c Adults might also find balancing their work and home responsibilities with their studies difficult.
  d Adults who have not studied for a long time might lack confidence and feel lost or out of practice.
  e After losing a job, many unemployed workers return to college to train for another career.
  f Often, people return to college to win promotions at work.

3 Thesis: There are a number of ways to reduce your impact and live a more environmentally sustainable life.
  a There are daily practices that impact the environment negatively.
  b Many people choose to use fewer products and services that have a negative impact on the environment.
  c If we don't limit our influence on the environment soon, we will face a global crisis.
  d It is important to recycle old products to reduce the amount of trash that goes into landfills.
  e Sustainable practices often help us reduce waste and save money.
  f It is a good idea to research items that have the least impact on the environment.

Practice 2

Underline the sub-points and supporting details in the correct body paragraph to complete the essay.

Hurricane Katrina was one of the worst storms in American history. The hurricane hit the southern United States on August 29, 2005. Although people had warning days before the storm, they were not prepared to evacuate, and the government was not prepared to help. The state of Louisiana and surrounding areas are still trying to recover after the disaster. Many people believe that the hurricane has had three major lasting effects on that region.

First, Hurricane Katrina destroyed the social systems in New Orleans and surrounding areas. More than 1,800 people died in the initial days after the storm, and more than one million people were moved to other areas of the United States. Many of these people were never able to return to their original homes. They left the city for good, and the rich cultural roots of New Orleans were weakened. The huge migration of all people devastated by Katrina represents the largest U.S. migration since the Great Depression.

Next, the storm severely damaged the environment in the southern coastal areas. The massive flooding covered more than 215 square miles of beaches, swamps, marshes, and islands in water. Acres of land have been lost forever. A number of oil refineries malfunctioned as well because of the storm. All in all, there were more than 40 oil spills, and a total of seven million gallons of oil leaked into the water.

Economically, the hurricane cost local, state, and federal governments a lot of money. Since the canal levees broke in New Orleans, there was a huge amount of damage to historical buildings. Restoring these buildings is still costing a lot of money. So far, the government has spent more than $100 billion. However, the economic stability completely vanished from the region. People were unable to resume normal economic activities for months after the storm. For instance, the two biggest industries in the area are tourism and oil production. With the city in ruins and oil refineries shut down, it became impossible for many people to resume working.

To conclude, Katrina has affected the social, environmental, and economic systems in a number of southern states in the United States. The damage has been quite extensive and long lasting, but the people of that region have not given up. Efforts continue to restore the cities and rural areas. It's possible that there will be little evidence of the storm in another decade or so.

CONCLUDING PARAGRAPHS

Concluding Paragraphs

A concluding paragraph is the essay's final paragraph. It summarizes the main point and sub-points and finishes up the essay with a final thought related to the essay as a whole.

Concluding Paragraphs have three parts:

Conclusion Signals = *To sum up, In conclusion, Finally, To conclude, Thus.*

Review of Ideas = a summary or re-statement of the topic sentences and the essay's main ideas.

Final Thought = why the information in the essay is important. This might be an opinion, a suggestion, or a prediction.

Essay Outline

Thesis: Shopping online can be a rewarding experience when you follow some simple steps.

1. Before you begin shopping, it is important to familiarize yourself with issues around Internet safety to avoid identity theft.

2. Once you are prepared to protect your information, you are ready to use consumer reviews to find the best product.

3. The next step is to find the most reputable website with the cheapest price.

4. The final step is to purchase the item and make decisions about shipping.

Sample Concluding Paragraphs

In conclusion, it is important to research carefully and protect your financial information when you buy online. As online sales increase and in-store sales decrease, it is probable that more and more of our shopping will take place in the comfort of our living rooms. However, shopping online might only work for some types of products. It is clear that certain types of in-store shopping, such as shopping for groceries, will continue. (Prediction)

To sum up, the steps to a successful online shopping experience involve taking time to research what's available and protecting your financial information. Many people find shopping online very convenient and cost effective, because it can offer a consumer many choices. The number of choices ensures that the consumer gets the best type, quality, and price available. (Opinion)

Practice 1

Number the sentences in the concluding paragraph in the best order. Start with a review and conclude with a final thought.

Thesis: Adults returning to college face many challenges.

Essay Outline:

1 Paying tuition can be a huge burden for an adult returning to college.

2 Adults might also find it difficult to balance their studies with work and home responsibilities.

3 Adults who have not studied in a long time might lack confidence and feel lost or out of practice.

Concluding Paragraph:

_____ In addition, adults may find school work and the classroom overwhelming if they been out of school for a while.

_____ Since more and more adults are going back to school, colleges need to be more prepared to help these students transition.

_____ They have to balance their responsibilities to family and work with their responsibilities at school.

_____ To conclude, adult students may find college difficult.

Practice 2

Write the number next to the sentences in the concluding paragraph that places them in the best order. Start with a review and conclude with a final thought.

Thesis: Divorce can have a number of effects on an adult.

Essay Outline:

1 The most immediate effect is a financial one.

2 Secondly, divorce can have a negative or positive emotional effect.

3 The final effect divorce can have is on health.

Concluding Paragraph:

_____ In order to determine this, people should always seriously consider if a divorce is right for them.

_____ Ultimately, only the individual can really determine the best decision for himself or herself.

_____ Divorce can be emotionally painful but in some cases may lead to a better situation.

_____ To sum up, people who get divorced often experience financial, emotional, and/or health effects.

Body Paragraph Organization
BLOCK VS. POINT-BY-POINT

Paragraph Organization: Block vs. Point-by-Point

We often **compare and contrast** two or more options to come to a decision or explain a preference. When comparing and contrasting two or more options in writing, discuss similarities and differences between the two subjects using one of two organizational patterns. Use signal words to indicate comparison and contrast.

Comparison Signals: *similarly, likewise, as … as, just like, both … and, not only … but also*

Contrast Signals: *on the other hand, in contrast, however, but, while, although, unlike*

In a **Block Pattern**, compare all the similarities between two or more things. Then contrast the things.

In a **Point-by-Point Pattern**, organize your comparisons and contrasts so that you alternate between them as you go along.

Practice 1

Read the nine sentences about the Android phone and the iPhone. Then write the letter of each sentence in the correct group.

1   Both types of smartphones allow the user to control the device by touching the screen.
2   There is a wide variety of phone companies that use the Google Android system, so consumers have more options.
3   Tests have determined that the iPhone is less prone to problems.
4   The Android may have more problems with overheating and freezing.
5   The Apple iPhone system is exclusively used with one type of phone; therefore, there is less variety.
6   Smartphones like the Android and the iPhone offer services, such as Internet access, GPS navigation, and text messaging.
7   Google is slower to release updates to the Android system.
8   The Android and the iPhone offer hundreds of programs called apps that perform different tasks.
9   Apple is much faster at updating than Google is.

Similarities	Android	iPhone
1 [Both types of smartphones allow the user to control the device by touching the screen.]		

Which of the outlines uses point-by-point organization? Circle the letter next to the correct answer.

2 a Thesis: The Android phone and the iPhone have a number of important similarities and differences.

Paragraph 1
- Touchscreen technology
- Apps
- Services

Paragraph 2
- Varieties
- Problems
- Updates

b Thesis: Though smartphones share many similarities, the Android phone and the iPhone have a number of important differences.
Paragraph 1 • Types of Android and iPhones
Paragraph 2 • Problems with Android and iPhones
Paragraph 3 • How often are Android and iPhones updated

c Thesis: A comparison between the Android and the iPhone smartphones reveals important similarities and differences.
Paragraph 1 (Androids)
- Types and variety
- Problems
- Updates

Paragraph 2 (iPhones)
- Types and variety
- Problems
- Updates

Practice 2

Read the nine sentences about the education systems in the United States and China. Then write the number of each sentence in the correct group.

1 Americans believe that some people have more talent than others; therefore, individual students are expected to keep up with the class as best they can.

2 Like the United States, China has compulsory and free public education for all its citizens.

3 The Chinese believe that students should study and practice until they learn the subject.

4 Parents in U.S. schools are not expected to contribute to their children's education, so parental participation in school varies.

5 Children in the United States and China study the same subjects.

6 Schools in the United States and China have schedules that are very similar.

7 At the end of every year, students in China take standardized tests in order to move on to the next grade.

8 Standardized tests are used in the United States mainly to separate high-performing students from low-performing students.

9 There is an expectation for Chinese parents to be highly involved in their children's education.

Similarities	U.S. education system	Chinese education system

Which of the outlines uses point-by-point organization? Circle the letter next to the correct answer.

2 **a** Thesis: The education systems in China and the United States have a number of important similarities and differences.

Paragraph 1
- Free education
- Weekly schedule
- Curriculum

Paragraph 2
- Philosophy
- Purpose of testing
- Role of parents

b Thesis: Though the educational systems in the United States and China share many similarities, they have a number of important differences, too.

Paragraph 1
- Philosophy of education

Paragraph 2
- Purpose of testing

Paragraph 3
- Role of parents

c Thesis: There are a number of similarities and differences in the educational systems in the United States and China.

Paragraph 1 (U.S. education)
- Philosophy
- Purpose of testing
- Role of parents

Paragraph 2 (Chinese education)
- Philosophy
- Purpose of testing
- Role of parents

WRITING ASSIGNMENTS

Paragraph

Writing a Narrative

Model Paragraph

Overcoming Stage Fright

Though I have always loved to sing, I have also always had stage fright—that is, until the day I performed a solo. Hooked on music by the time I was five years old, I would dance around the house, singing along, as best I could, with the old records my parents used to listen to. I wasn't shy at home and often sang in front of my family and friends. My parents encouraged my interest in music by sending me for piano lessons and enrolling me in a girls' choir. They thought I had the makings of a great performer, but, in reality, I was painfully shy at school and in public. For instance, I dreaded when teachers called on me in class, and, when they did, I'd get flustered, and my face would turn bright red. I also hated being in front of the class alone. My heart would pound, and I'd feel sick to my stomach. Things were different when I sang with the choir, though. I didn't have any of those bad feelings, because I wasn't alone—I was a part of a group, and no one was looking at me. Then one day, my choir director asked me to perform a solo at our next recital. I didn't want to, but my father encouraged me to do it. He told me that I shouldn't let fear stop me from doing what I loved most to do—sing! The night of the performance, I was so nervous that I couldn't eat. When it was time for me to step up to the microphone alone, I was terrified. My knees were trembling so much that I didn't think I'd make it to the front of the stage, but I did. The music started, and my mind started racing. Would I remember the words? What was the first note again? Then I saw my father looking up at me from the audience. His smile was reassuring. I took a deep breath, opened my mouth, and began to sing. The more I sang, the calmer I became. Then it happened—the stage fright was gone, and I was actually enjoying the spotlight! It was a great moment and one that I would not have had if I had not let go of my fear. That evening, I learned an important lesson: Don't let fear stand in the way of life dreams and ambitions!

Write a paragraph about one of the topics listed below (or the topic your teacher assigns). You will have 40 minutes.

1 Choose a current news event. Tell the story about what happened.

2 Choose an important moment in your life. Tell the story about what happened.

3 Choose a historical event. Tell what happened.

Editing Checklist

Are the grammar, sentence structure, mechanics, and punctuation correct?

Is the vocabulary appropriate? Are the words spelled correctly?

Is the paragraph well organized, well developed, and clear?

_____

_____

_____

_____

_____

_____

_____

_____

_____

_____

_____

_____

_____

_____

_____

_____

_____

_____

_____

Writing a Descriptive Piece

Model Paragraph

The Kukulkan Pyramid in Chichén Itzá

The Kukulkan Pyramid is a combination of imagination and scientific ability. This pyramid is located in Chichén Itzá on the Yucatán Peninsula. It was built around the 11th century BCE by the Mayan people. The pyramid is about 181 feet wide and 75 feet tall with nine terraces rising to a platform, on top of which is a temple. The pyramid has four sides, with a central staircase of 91 steps on each side. There is a giant snake head at the bottom of the staircase on the northern side. The top platform of all four staircases leads to the temple. These numbers are not accidental. The steps of the four staircases add up to 365, the number of days in a solar year. Moreover, the central staircases divide the nine terraces into two, resulting in 18, which corresponds to the 18 months of the Mayan calendar. The mathematical nature of this structure demonstrates an incredible understanding of astronomy and geometry. The pyramid is, in essence, a giant calendar. The Maya used it to indicate the end of winter and summer. Twice a year, around March 21 and September 23, a shadow in the shape of a snake crosses the northern side of the pyramid. This image is meant to represent the Mayan god Kukulkan. The Maya used the pyramid to tell them when to plant and when to harvest. It's no wonder that this pyramid was recently listed as one of the New Seven Wonders of the World. The pyramid is truly an amazing example of the genius of this civilization.

Write a paragraph about one of the topics listed below (or the topic your teacher assigns). You will have 40 minutes.

1 Describe a product you are familiar with. What is it like, and how does it work?

2 Choose a well-known company. Describe what it does and how it operates.

3 Describe a favorite piece of furniture you own. Describe its appearance and why you like it.

Editing Checklist

Are the grammar, sentence structure, mechanics, and punctuation correct?

Is the vocabulary appropriate? Are the words spelled correctly?

Is the paragraph well organized, well developed, and clear?

_____

_____

_____

_____

_____

_____

_____

Defining an Idea

Model Paragraph

April Fools' Day

April Fools' Day is celebrated in the United States and other Western countries. It occurs annually on April 1st. While it is not a national or international holiday, it is beloved by people around the world. On this day, people come up with elaborate pranks and jokes to trick their families, friends, and coworkers. A common feature of April Fools' Day jokes is convincing someone of something illogical or impossible. One example of such a prank is to glue a one hundred dollar bill to the ground so that passersby try to pick it up. No one knows exactly when April Fools' Day began, but some say the tradition began in the 1500s, when France and other European countries adopted the Roman calendar. Romans celebrated the New Year on January 1st, while Renaissance Europeans celebrated the beginning of the year at the end of March. Legend says that people who forgot this and celebrated the New Year in the spring were teased as "April fools." Though entertaining, this story is implausible. What's more likely is that the celebration was a part of springtime festivities. One thing is clear, however: April Fools' Day is a much-needed rite of spring that lightens people's moods after the cold days and long nights of winter.

Write a paragraph about one of the topics listed below (or the topic your teacher assigns). You will have 40 minutes.

1 Choose a custom from your country. Explain its purpose and what people do.

2 Choose a type of alternative medical treatment. Define it and explain how it works.

3 Choose a sport or artistic or scientific practice. Define what it is and describe how it is practiced.

Editing Checklist

Are the grammar, sentence structure, mechanics, and punctuation correct?

Is the vocabulary appropriate? Are the words spelled correctly?

Is the paragraph well organized, well developed, and clear?

_____

_____

_____

_____

_____

_____

_____

Comparing and Contrasting

Model Paragraph (block pattern)

Yoga Practices in India and the U.S.

There are some similarities and differences in the yoga practices of India and the United States. Yoga in both places includes two types of activities. First, there is a series of poses called *asanas*. These are positions people hold for one to three minutes at a time. The second type of exercise involves a special kind of breathing called *pranayama*. These breathing exercises help people focus and calm down. In both countries, teachers lead students through a series of asanas during class. A yoga session in both countries will usually begin or conclude with pranayama. People in India and the United States practice yoga for different reasons. Yoga began in India thousands of years ago as a spiritual practice. In the United States, it has only recently become popular as a type of exercise. In India, yoga is a part of the Hindu spiritual tradition. People there believe that yoga prepares the body and the mind for spiritual practice. The practice helps people calm down so that they can sit for long periods of time during meditation. In contrast, people in the United States see yoga as exercise. Many Americans feel that yoga is a good defense against health problems, such as depression and heart disease. Unlike in India, yoga is often faster and more athletic in the United States. This kind of practice raises heart rate and tones muscles. In conclusion, it's clear that yoga is popular in both countries for different reasons. Moreover, the practice is beneficial to one's spiritual and physical health.

Model Paragraph (point-by-point)

The Difference between Books and Movies

Books and movies share many similarities, but they also differ in important ways. One of the main differences between reading a book and watching a movie is sensory. When you watch a movie, you can see actors and hear what they say. Many people prefer movies, because they are more vivid and life-like. However, when you read a book, you rely on a written description to imagine the story. People who like reading books prefer to use their own imaginations to re-create what they read. Another difference between a book and a movie is the amount of detail each has. Movies tend to have less plot detail, because they have to tell the story in two or three hours. Oftentimes, movies leave out important information about characters and previous events. This can make the story inconsistent and leave viewers with questions. Books, on the other hand, are designed to be read over a long period of time, and they therefore contain a lot of information about the characters and the events that preceded the plot. A final difference between books and movies is the use of language. In movies, there does not have to be a narrator or person to tell the story. Communication generally happens through dialogue and interaction between characters. By contrast, books have greater access to different narrative modes. There is often a third-person narrator who describes the scene or explains what people are thinking and feeling. Depending on the person, reading a book can be more or less exciting than watching a movie. Differences in the experience, the amount of detail, and the use of language can affect people's preferences for reading books or watching movies.

Write a paragraph about one of the topics listed below (or the topic your teacher assigns). You will have 40 minutes.

1 Compare and contract two cities.

2 Compare and contrast two people you know well.

3 Compare and contrast two types of animals from the same family (e.g., lions and tigers).

Editing Checklist

Are the grammar, sentence structure, mechanics, and punctuation correct?

Is the vocabulary appropriate? Are the words spelled correctly?

Is the paragraph well organized, well developed, and clear?

_____

_____

_____

_____

_____

_____

_____

_____

_____

_____

_____

_____

_____

_____

_____

_____

_____

_____

Describing Causes and Effects

Model Paragraph (causes)

Why People Don't Vote

One of the features of democratic life is the average citizen's right to vote for officials and laws. However, even in the United States, a country known for its democratic practices, only 50–60 percent of people who can vote exercise this right. Research has shown that socioeconomic status and convenience are factors that influence whether people decide to vote or not. Socioeconomic status influences voter turnout in a few ways. Studies show that more educated people vote more often than less educated people. There could be several reasons for this. Education is linked to social status and class in the United States. People with more education tend to have better paying jobs and more satisfying lives. Perhaps due to their success, people with more education have more positive attitudes about the role of government in their lives. Highly educated citizens are also more likely to follow the news. They are probably better informed than less educated citizens. Therefore, they are probably more aware of the issues and more interested in doing their part.

Another reason people don't vote has to do with convenience. People who live in rural areas vote less often than people who live in more urban areas. There are probably fewer voting stations in rural areas. Thus, it would take more time and effort to vote. States that give citizens the choice to mail in ballots have higher voter turnout than states that don't. This suggests that people would be more likely to vote if the process were more convenient and took less time. It is clear that education and convenience play major roles in voter turnout. An understanding of why people make time to vote can have clear implications for countries that are interested in increasing how many citizens choose to vote.

Model Paragraph (effects)

The Effects of Facebook on Modern Society

Facebook has had several effects on people's social behavior. With millions of users, Facebook has made it possible for people to maintain relationships in unprecedented ways. Psychologists agree that people are more likely to socialize frequently in their late teens and early 20s than in later years. Maintaining a large network requires a lot of effort. Therefore, there is less time to build close relationships. As people start families and begin to age, they maintain fewer intimate relationships. The advent of social networking has allowed people to connect with people from different times in their lives. A potential community is now much larger than ever. However, it may not be as satisfying as a non-digital one. People have to spend a lot of time on the computer to maintain these relationships. Thus, they spend less time with people in person. In addition, Facebook has changed the way people communicate. When people post messages to Facebook, they would rather entertain than convey information. They also share details about themselves or others that would be considered antisocial and awkward in a face-to-face conversation. Since posts are available to everyone in a network, there is no privacy. Facebook invites people into our homes, on our vacations, and into our thoughts. Even if we choose to opt out, our friends, family, and acquaintances can post information about us. Social networking has definitely made our lives more open to scrutiny. For example, I was recently at a dinner where a friend took a photograph of us. When I asked why, she said she wanted to post it to Facebook. What might have been an intimate dinner with friends became a performance broadcast to millions. To conclude, social networking has unexpectedly changed attitudes about community and privacy in some beneficial and in some harmful ways.

Write a paragraph about one of the topics listed below (or the topic your teacher assigns). You will have 40 minutes.

1 Describe the causes of pollution and the effects it has on the environment.

2 Describe the causes of a particular disease and the effects it has on people's lives.

3 Describe the causes of marital problems and the effects they have on families.

Editing Checklist

Are the grammar, sentence structure, mechanics, and punctuation correct?

Is the vocabulary appropriate? Are the words spelled correctly?

Is the paragraph well organized, well developed, and clear?

_____

_____

_____

_____

_____

_____

_____

_____

_____

_____

_____

_____

_____

_____

_____

Expressing an Opinion

Model Paragraph

Mandatory Parenting Classes?

Raising children is a huge responsibility. Parents have a big impact on who their children become as adults. Poor parenting practices can leave children with a number of social problems. Since parenting is so important, I believe all parents should be required to attend a parenting class once a year. First, parents often make mistakes, because they are not well informed. Classes can give parents important information about the latest theories in child and adolescent psychology. Every stage in a child's life is different, which means parents will need new information every year. A second reason for requiring these classes is to help parents discuss their values with an expert and develop a parenting plan. Often, couples decide to have children without ever discussing such important issues as education, punishment, and appropriate pastimes for their children. Parents need to make decisions about these issues using expert advice. The final reason parents should be required to attend classes is to provide them with resources and community. Families manage better when they have strong ties to a supportive community. Parents need to talk with other parents to discuss their challenges. They also need to have access to resources when having a hard time. Potential parenting problems could then be addressed before they get out of control. All in all, mandatory ongoing parenting classes would have positive effects on families and the community at large. If the government wants to reduce crime, drug addiction, and other social problems, it can start by helping parents raise their children.

Write a paragraph about one of the topics listed below (or the topic your teacher assigns). You will have 40 minutes.

1 Should young people have tattoos and other body art? Support your opinion with reasons and examples.

2 Is violence in movies dangerous for young people? Support your opinion with reasons and examples.

3 Are people too cruel to animals? Support your opinion with reasons and examples.

Editing Checklist

Are the grammar, sentence structure, mechanics, and punctuation correct?

Is the vocabulary appropriate? Are the words spelled correctly?

Is the paragraph well organized, well developed, and clear?

_____

_____

_____

_____

_____

Describing a Process

Model Paragraph

How to Become a U.S. Citizen

There are many reasons immigrants from around the world want to settle in the United States, but the process to citizenship can be long and confusing. There are a number of procedures you should follow if you are interested in becoming an American citizen. At the beginning of the process, it is important to understand what makes you eligible. For example, you cannot apply for citizenship unless you are at least 18 years old. You also must either have a green card or be married to a U.S. citizen in order to begin the process. In addition, at the time you apply, you will have to prove that the United States has been your primary residence for a certain number of years. Next, you will have to take an English language test and a U.S. civics test. If you are from a country that is not English speaking, you may need to improve your English. If that's the case, you may want to enroll in a low-cost or free ESL class. The civics test examines your knowledge about U.S. history, the government, and citizen rights and responsibilities. There are many books, websites, and free civics classes available to help you prepare for this test. Finally, the government will not give citizenship to people who don't obey the law. You must be of "good moral character" to become a citizen. That is, you cannot have committed serious crimes, you must have paid taxes if you are working, and, above all, you must not lie in any part of your application. In addition, if you are a man between the ages of 18 and 25, you may be required to register with the Selective Service System. To sum up, the process of becoming a U.S. citizen can take many years. If you are aware of the requirements beforehand, you will be prepared to complete your application when the time comes.

Write a paragraph about one of the topics listed below (or the topic your teacher assigns). You will have 40 minutes.

1 Describe how to play a game that you are familiar with.

2 Describe how to make a special food or drink from your country.

3 Describe how to drive a car or ride a bicycle.

Editing Checklist

Are the grammar, sentence structure, mechanics, and punctuation correct?

Is the vocabulary appropriate? Are the words spelled correctly?

Is the paragraph well organized, well developed, and clear?

_____

_____

_____

_____

_____

Division and Classification

Model Paragraph

Types of Intelligence

In the 1980s, Howard Gardner developed a theory to classify different types of intelligence. In Gardner's model, intelligence can be classified into seven categories. First, Gardner identified interpersonal intelligence. People who have this intelligence are great with others. They tend to learn better in groups and understand the world through their relationships. Another type is intrapersonal. People who have this intelligence are highly self-aware. They are primarily interested in their own reasons for doing things. They tend to learn better when the material is personally meaningful. Next, some people have visual intelligence. They have a strong sense of physical space and the environment, so they learn better with visual aids and drawings. Others have physical intelligence. That is, they learn through hands-on activities and movement. An additional type of intelligence is verbal intelligence. People who are verbally intelligent are great with language and words. They are good readers but can learn through listening as well. People who have musical intelligence remember and work better with music. Musical learners can use rhymes to memorize information or play music when they are studying. The final category of intelligence is logical or mathematical intelligence. People with this type find it easy to think critically about concepts and abstract ideas. They learn better when they can see the big picture. Gardner theorized that every person has an orientation to one of these seven types of intelligence. He wanted to debunk the idea that some ways of thinking or grappling with the world were not as important as others. He also wanted to help learners become more aware of their thinking to help them succeed.

Write a paragraph about one of the topics listed below (or the topic your teacher assigns). You will have 40 minutes.

1 Describe the different types of personalities required for a successful family life.
2 Describe the different types of foods and flavors that are important to planning a good meal.
3 Describe the different types of vacations that appeal to people of different interests and income levels.

Editing Checklist

Are the grammar, sentence structure, mechanics, and punctuation correct?

Is the vocabulary appropriate? Are the words spelled correctly?

Is the paragraph well organized, well developed, and clear?

_____

_____

_____

_____

_____

Writing a Character Analysis

Model Paragraph

Pride in "A Sound of Thunder"

They say that "pride comes before the fall." This is very true in the well-known American story "A Sound of Thunder" by Ray Bradbury. This story, set in 2055 BCE, follows a hunter named Eckels as he travels back in time to hunt a Tyrannosaurus Rex. In the story, Eckels is frightened when he sees the animal, and he makes a deadly error. When he and his companions return to the year 2055, they discover that the future has been altered because of Eckels's mistake. Eckels's pride in his skill as a hunter causes him to misjudge the Tyrannosaurus Rex, and his fear leads to a fatal mistake. While we learn that Eckels is indeed a skilled and experienced hunter, his pride in this skill causes him to become excessively confident and to believe that hunting shows how brave he is. When the guide, Travis, warns him to stay on a specific path to avoid altering the future, Eckels doesn't listen. He treats the hunt like a game. However, when Eckels first sees the dinosaur, he is afraid and loses his confidence. He remarks that "[they] were fools to come." He doesn't think he will live through the experience. In his fear, he steps off the path and kills a butterfly. This seemingly trivial act changes the future irrevocably and leads to his demise. "A Sound of Thunder" illustrates how important it is to be humble and not take unnecessary chances that might have terrible consequences.

Bradbury, Ray. "A Sound of Thunder." *R Is for Rocket*. New York: Doubleday, 1952.

Write a paragraph about one of the topics listed below (or the topic your teacher assigns). **You will have 40 minutes.**

1 Choose a character you are familiar with from a movie. Describe the character's personality and what motivates that character in the movie.

2 Choose a character you are familiar with from a TV show. Describe the character's personality and what motivates that character in the show.

3 Describe the personality of a friend, family member, or colleague. Explain what motivates this person in his or her everyday life.

Editing Checklist

Are the grammar, sentence structure, mechanics, and punctuation correct?

Is the vocabulary appropriate? Are the words spelled correctly?

Is the paragraph well organized, well developed, and clear?

_____

_____

_____

_____

_____

Writing a Review and Making a Recommendation

Model Paragraph

Accuracy with Some Eccentricities

I bought the Ozmerk Digital Kitchen Scale one month ago. For years, I used a manual scale for cooking, but I have recently been doing a lot more entertaining and have found I needed a faster, more precise way to measure ingredients. I decided to try the Ozmerk Digital Kitchen Scale, which comes in a stainless steel or white glass version. These scales are less than half an inch thick and about the size of an 8.5-x-11-inch piece of paper, so they are easy to store. Both types have different units of measurement, so it's easy to change to ounces, fluid ounces, grams, and milliliters using the Unit button. Since the scale has a capacity of 11 pounds, it handles large ingredients nicely. With a manual scale, I would have to weigh each ingredient separately and then put them into a bowl. With the Ozmerk, I can put the bowl on the scale and set the Tare button to "zero out" after adding each ingredient. Overall, the Ozmerk scale has been extremely useful, and I have been pleased with its accuracy. Before the Ozmerk, the same dish would taste a bit different each time. Now, this never happens. The stainless steel model is easy to clean. However, this scale does have some quirks. While it does have an automatic shut-off feature, it can take a long time. If you forget to turn it off, you will have to replace the batteries frequently. You must store the scale on a flat surface, because it's very sensitive. If you use it on an unstable surface, it will not work. Finally, it is better to turn the scale on before putting anything on it to avoid getting an "error" message. If you are interested in this scale, it's best to search for it online. But be careful: I found the scale offered at many different prices. I got mine for about $20, but I have seen it offered for much more.

Write a paragraph about one of the topics listed below (or the topic your teacher assigns). You will have 40 minutes.

1 Write a review of a movie you have seen. Who is in it? Where is it set? What's it about? Would you recommend this movie to others?

2 Write a review of a restaurant where you have eaten. What kind of restaurant is it? What does it serve? How is the service and the atmosphere? Would you recommend it to others?

3 Write a review of a class you have taken. What is the subject? Who teaches it? Would you recommend this class to other students?

Editing Checklist

Are the grammar, sentence structure, mechanics, and punctuation correct?

Is the vocabulary appropriate? Are the words spelled correctly?

Is the paragraph well organized, well developed, and clear?

_____

_____

_____

Writing a Summary

Model Paragraph

A Summary of "La Gringuita"

In her essay "La Gringuita," Julia Alvarez writes about her experience of falling in love with a boy during a visit to the Dominican Republic, her ancestral home. Through her story, she illuminates her feelings about growing up as an American with strong Hispanic roots. Alvarez was born in the Dominican Republic and spoke Spanish in her early years. Then she came to the United States at a young age and had to learn English and adapt to a new culture. She talks about her early encounters with American prejudice against non-native speakers. For example, her teachers discouraged her from studying Spanish so she would fully assimilate. On the other hand, she tells how the English language became a way to rebel against her parents and their more traditional ways of thinking. Embedded in the English language and in American culture, she explains, she found different expectations for women. One summer, she returns to the Dominican Republic and falls in love with a boy she nicknames Mangu. She has fun with him, but she has trouble understanding him, because her Spanish isn't good enough. At the summer's end, Mangu wants to discuss their future together, but she realizes that there is no future for her with him or in the Dominican Republic. She describes her sadness at being a "hybrid" and concludes that she doesn't fit in either in the United States or in the Dominican Republic.

Alvarez, Julia. "La Gringuita." *Something to Declare.* Penguin, 1999. 61–74. Print.

Write a paragraph about one of the topics listed below (or the topic your teacher assigns). You will have 40 minutes.

1 Write a short summary of a movie you have seen.
2 Write a short summary of a book or an article you have read.

Editing Checklist

Are the grammar, sentence structure, mechanics, and punctuation correct?

Is the vocabulary appropriate? Are the words spelled correctly?

Is the paragraph well organized, well developed, and clear?

_____

_____

_____

_____

_____

_____

_____

Essays

Writing an Expository Essay

Presentation

Model Essay

April Fools' Day

Many days marked for celebration in the United States and other Western countries have a long and strange history. Oftentimes, this is because they represent a blending of cultures. April Fools' Day is a popular and ancient Western celebration of foolishness that has an odd history and occupies an unusual place in modern society.

No one knows the exact origins of April Foods' Day, but there is a popular story that attempts to explain it. The tradition allegedly began in the 1500s, when France and other European nations adopted the Roman calendar. Romans celebrated the New Year on January 1st, while Renaissance Europeans were used to celebrating the beginning of the year at the end of March. Legend says that people who forgot and celebrated the New Year in the spring were teased as "April fools." Though entertaining, this story is implausible. What's more likely is that the holiday was part of spring festivities.

April Fools' Day occurs annually on April 1st. While it is not a national or international holiday, April Fools' Day is beloved by people around the world. People come up with elaborate pranks and jokes to trick their family, friends, and coworkers. A common feature of many April Fools' jokes is to try to convince someone that something illogical or impossible has occurred. One example of an April Fools' prank is to glue a one hundred dollar bill to the ground so that passersby try to pick it up.

Even with its murky history, it's clear that April Fools' Day still occupies an important place in our hearts. It is a much-needed rite of spring that lightens people's moods after the cold days and long nights of winter. Many people are in need of a laugh as the weather starts to get warmer.

Write an essay about one of the topics listed below (or the topic your teacher assigns). You will have 50 minutes.

1 Explain what people in a particular occupation do and why their work is important.
2 Explain why getting a college or university degree is important.
3 Explain why including art or athletics in one's education is important.

Editing Checklist

Are the grammar, sentence structure, mechanics, and punctuation correct?

Is the vocabulary appropriate? Are the words spelled correctly?

Is the essay well organized, well developed, and clear?

_____

_____

_____

Comparing and Contrasting

Model Essay (block pattern)

Yoga Practices in India and the U.S.

Yoga is an ancient tradition that began in India more than 5,000 years ago. It came to the United States in the early 20th century but was not popular in the West until very recently. Now, yoga is a part of mainstream culture. You can find yoga classes at work, in community centers, and in the gym. While there are some similarities between the yoga practices in India and the United States, there are also a number of differences.

Yoga practices in both places include two types of activities. First, there is a series of poses called *asanas*. These are positions people hold for one to three minutes at a time. The second type of exercise involves a special kind of breathing called *pranayama*. These breathing exercises help people focus and calm down. In both countries, teachers lead students through a series of asanas in yoga classes. A yoga practice in both places will usually begin or conclude with pranayama.

People in India and the United States practice yoga for different reasons. Yoga began in India thousands of years ago as a spiritual practice. In the United States, it has only recently become popular as a type of exercise. In India, yoga is a part of the Hindu spiritual tradition. People there believe that yoga prepares the body and the mind for spiritual practice. The practice helps people calm down so that they can sit for long periods of time during meditation. In contrast, people in the United States see yoga as exercise. Many Americans feel that yoga is a good defense against health problems, such as depression and heart disease. Unlike in India, yoga in the United States is often practiced faster and more athletically than in India. This kind of practice raises the heart rate and tones muscles. Breathing exercises focus more on relaxing and removing stress.

In conclusion, it's clear that yoga has become popular in both countries for different reasons. However, the practice is becoming increasingly more popular, because it has many benefits.

Model Essay (point-by-point)

The Difference between Books and Movies

I began reading the Harry Potter books because my daughter wanted me to read them with her. I quickly became obsessed with the stories. I made other adult friends who were also "Potterphiles." We would meet to discuss the books. We couldn't wait for the movies to come out. However, unlike my friends, to my surprise, I was quite disappointed with the movies. I learned that books and movies may share many similarities, but they differ in some important ways.

One of the main differences between reading a book and watching a movie is sensory. When you watch a movie, you can see the characters and hear how they sound. Many people prefer movies because they are more vivid and life-like. However, when you read a book, you rely on the written description to picture the story. People who like reading books prefer to use their own imaginations to re-create what they read.

Another difference between a book and a movie is the amount of detail. Movies tend to have less plot detail because they have to tell the story in two or three hours. Oftentimes, movies leave out important information about characters and previous events. This can make the story inconsistent and leave viewers with questions. Books, on the other hand, are designed to be read over a long period of time, and they therefore contain a lot of information about the characters and the events that preceded the plot.

A final difference between books and movies is the use of language. In movies, there does not have to be a narrator or person to tell the story. Most of the communication happens in the dialogue and interaction between characters. By contrast, books have greater access to different narrative modes. There is often a third-person narrator who describes the scene or explains what people are thinking and feeling. Depending on the person, reading a book can be more or less exciting than watching a movie.

Differences in the experience, the amount of detail, and the use of language can affect people's preferences for reading books or watching movies. As I discovered, with my Harry Potter experience, my preference is to read the book and not watch the movie.

Write an essay about one of the topics listed below (or the topic your teacher assigns). You will have 50 minutes.

1   Compare and contrast two cities.

2   Compare and contrast two people you know well.

3   Compare and contrast two types of animals from the same family (for example, lions and tigers).

Editing Checklist

Are the grammar, sentence structure, mechanics, and punctuation correct?

Is the vocabulary appropriate? Are the words spelled correctly?

Is the essay well organized, well developed, and clear?

_____

_____

_____

_____

_____

_____

_____

_____

_____

_____

Describing Causes and Effects

Copyright © 2017 by Pearson Education, Inc. Duplication is not permitted.

Presentation

Model Essay (causes)

Why People Don't Vote

One of the features of democratic life is the average citizen's right to vote for officials and laws. However, even in the United States, a country known for its democratic practices, only 50–60 percent of people who can vote exercise this right. Research has shown that socioeconomic status and convenience are factors that influence whether people vote or not.

Socioeconomic status influences voter turnout in a few ways. Studies show that more educated people vote more often than less educated people. There could be several reasons for this. Education is linked to social status and class in the United States. People with more education tend to have better paying jobs and more satisfying lives. Perhaps due to their success, people with more education have more positive attitudes about the role of government in their lives. Highly educated citizens are also more likely to follow the news. They are probably better informed than less educated citizens. Therefore, they are probably more aware of the issues and more interested in doing their part.

Another reason people don't vote has to do with convenience. People who live in rural areas vote less often than people who live in more urban areas. There are probably fewer voting stations in these areas. Thus, it would take more time and effort for these citizens to vote. States that give citizens the choice to mail in ballots have higher voter turnout than states that don't. This suggests that people would be more likely to vote if the process were more convenient and took less time.

It is clear that education and convenience play major roles in voter turnout. An understanding of why people make time to vote can have clear implications for countries that are interested in increasing how many citizens choose to vote.

Model Essay (effects)

The Effects of Facebook on Modern Society

Only a couple of decades ago, people communicated primarily in person or by telephone. The technology of today, such as video chatting, was considered by many to be science fiction. All of this has changed. Now, we have many ways to maintain relationships with others, regardless of distance. We can post messages, pictures, and email to people all over the globe with ease using social networking sites, such as Facebook. As a result, Facebook has had several effects on people's social behavior.

With millions of users, Facebook has made it possible for people to maintain relationships in an unprecedented way. Before social networking, psychologists agreed that people were more likely to socialize with a lot more people in their late teens and early 20s than in later years. Maintaining a large network requires a lot of effort. Therefore, there is less time to build close relationships. As people start families and begin to age, they maintain fewer intimate relationships.

With social networking, people are able to connect with all types of people from different times in their life. A potential community is now much larger than ever. However, these relationships might not be as satisfying as non-digital ones. People have to spend a lot of time on the computer to maintain these relationships. Thus, they spend less time with people in person. In addition, Facebook has changed the way people communicate. When people post messages to Facebook, they are more motivated to entertain others than to convey information. People share information that would be considered antisocial and awkward in a face-to-face conversation.

Since posts are available to everyone in your network, there is no privacy. Facebook invites people into our homes, on our vacations, and into our thoughts. Even if we choose to opt out, our friends, family, and acquaintances can post information about us. Social networking has definitely made our lives more open to scrutiny. For example, I was recently at a dinner where a friend asked us to wait while she took a photograph of us. When she was asked why, she said she wanted to post it to Facebook. What might have been an intimate dinner with friends became a performance broadcast to millions.

To conclude, social networking has unexpectedly changed attitudes and practices in some beneficial and in some harmful ways. While it has expanded the range of our friends and acquaintances, social networking makes it difficult to be very close to people. In addition, social networking can have unintended consequences because our worlds are more transparent now than they were. In this way, technology is changing our ideas about community and privacy.

Write an essay about one of the topics listed below (or the topic your teacher assigns). You will have 50 minutes.

1 Describe the various causes of pollution and the effects they have on the environment.

2 Describe the causes of a particular disease and the effects the disease has on people's lives.

3 Describe the causes of marital problems and the effects marital problems have on families.

Editing Checklist

Are the grammar, sentence structure, mechanics, and punctuation correct?

Is the vocabulary appropriate? Are the words spelled correctly?

Is the essay well organized, well developed, and clear?

Describing a Process

Model Essay

How to Become a U.S. Citizen

Every year at least one million immigrants come to live in the United States. There are many reasons people from around the world want to settle here. People leave their home countries for the United States to, among other things, study, work, and reunite with their families. Many of these new immigrants hope for a better future in this new country, but the process to citizenship can be long and confusing. If you are interested in becoming a citizen, you should be aware of the requirements before you apply, for otherwise you may not meet them when you become eligible. There are a number of procedures you should follow if you are interested in becoming an American citizen.

At the beginning of the process, it is important to understand what makes you eligible. For example, you cannot apply for citizenship unless you are at least 18 years old. You also must either have a green card or be married to a U.S. citizen in order to begin the process. At the time you apply, you will have to prove that the United States has been your primary residence for a certain number of years. This means you will have to be physically present in the country for the required number of years.

After you have started to establish your eligibility, you should get prepared for the citizenship tests. There are two required tests that you will take as a part of the citizenship process. The first one tests your English language skills. If you are from a country that is not English speaking, you may need to improve your English. If that's the case, you may want to enroll in a low-cost or free ESL class. You can find these classes at local colleges, in community centers, or at your neighborhood library. The second one is a civics test and examines your knowledge of U.S. history, the government, and citizen rights and responsibilities. There are many books, websites, and free civics classes available to help you prepare for this test.

Finally, the government will not grant citizenship to people who don't obey the law. You must be of "good moral character" to become a citizen. That is, you cannot have committed serious crimes, you must have paid taxes if you are working, and, above all, you must not lie in any part of your application. In addition, if you are a man between the ages of 18 and 25, you may be required to register with the Selective Service System.

To sum up, the process of becoming a U.S. citizen can take many years. If you are aware of the requirements beforehand, you will be prepared to complete your application when the time comes.

Write an essay about one of the topics listed below (or the topic your teacher assigns). You will have 50 minutes.

1   Describe how to play a game that you are familiar with.

2   Describe how to make a special food or drink from your country.

3   Describe how to drive a car or ride a bicycle.

Editing Checklist

Are the grammar, sentence structure, mechanics, and punctuation correct?

Is the vocabulary appropriate? Are the words spelled correctly?

Is the essay well organized, well developed, and clear?

_____

_____

_____

_____

_____

_____

_____

_____

_____

_____

_____

_____

_____

_____

_____

_____

_____

_____

_____

_____

_____

_____

Writing a Persuasive Essay

Presentation

Model Essay

Mandatory Parenting Classes?

Raising children is a huge responsibility. Parents have a big impact on who their children become as adults. Good parents raise children who are secure, well-educated citizens. In contrast, bad parents can raise children who have a number of social problems. Children with difficult home lives often have difficulties in school. They act out and get in trouble with teachers. This can have detrimental effects on their future. Since parenting is so important, I believe all parents should be required to attend a parenting class once a year.

First, parents often make mistakes because they are not well informed. Ongoing classes can give parents important information about the latest theories in child and adolescent psychology. New ideas can really have a positive impact on parenting practices. Every stage in a child's life is different, which means parents will need new information every year.

A second reason for requiring these classes is to help parents discuss their values with an expert and develop a parenting plan. Often, couples decide to have children without ever discussing such important issues as education, punishment, and appropriate pastimes for their children. Parents need to make decisions about these issues using expert advice.

The final reason parents should be required to attend classes is to provide them with resources and community. Families manage better when they have strong ties to a supportive community. Parents need to talk with other parents to discuss their challenges. They also need access to resources when they are having a hard time. Potential parenting problems could then be addressed before they get out of control.

All in all, mandatory ongoing parenting classes would have positive effects on families and the community at large. Some people might say that the government does not have the right to require classes for parents. They might argue that mandatory classes would interfere with a family's freedom and privacy. Nevertheless, many social problems can be traced back to family life. If the government wants to reduce crime, drug addiction, and other social problems, it can start by helping parents raise their children.

Write an essay about one of the topics listed below (or the topic your teacher assigns). You will have 50 minutes.

1 Should young people have tattoos and other body art? Support your opinion with reasons and examples.

2 Is violence in movies dangerous for young people? Support your opinion with reasons and examples.

3 Are people too cruel to animals? Support your opinion with reasons and examples.

Editing Checklist

Are the grammar, sentence structure, mechanics, and punctuation correct?

Is the vocabulary appropriate? Are the words spelled correctly?

Is the essay well organized, well developed, and clear?

_____

_____

_____

_____

_____

_____

_____

_____

_____

_____

_____

_____

_____

_____

_____

_____

_____

_____

_____

_____

_____

_____

_____

Division and Classification

Model Essay

Types of Intelligence

Scientists once believed that some people were born with intelligence, and some people were born without it. Intelligence had to do with luck, not work. Modern thinking about intelligence is slowly changing. In the past, if you could reason logically or if you were a good communicator, you were considered smart. These skills are valued in our educational system. Thus, those who can think logically and express themselves clearly tend to be more successful in school. In the 1980s, Howard Gardner developed a theory to classify different types of intelligence. He called it the Multiple Intelligences model. This theory was meant to debunk the notion that some types of thinking were inferior to others. He also wanted to help learners become more aware about how they think in order to help them succeed in school. In Gardner's model, intelligence can be classified into three main categories: social, sensory, and cognitive.

First, Gardner identified types of social intelligence. People who are socially intelligent tend to be keenly interested in themselves and others. This category of thinking Gardner further divided into two distinct types: interpersonal and intrapersonal. People who have interpersonal intelligence are great with people. They tend to learn better in groups and understand the world through their relationships. People who have intrapersonal intelligence are primarily interested in themselves and their own motivations. They are more self-directed. They tend to learn better when the material at hand is personally meaningful.

The second category of intelligence is sensory. People with sensory intelligence perceive the world through their senses. Some are oriented to visual intelligence. They have a strong sense of physical space and the environment. Others have physical intelligence; that is, they learn through hands-on activities and movement. People who are verbally intelligent are great with language and words. They are good readers but can learn through listening, as well. The final type of sensory intelligence involves sensitivity to sound, music, and rhythm. People who have musical intelligence remember and work better with music. Musical learners can use rhymes to memorize information or play music when they are studying.

The final category of intelligence is cognitive intelligence. People with cognitive intelligence are logical. They find it easy to think critically about concepts and abstract ideas. They are also usually quite good at mathematics. They learn better when they can see the big picture.

Gardner theorized that every person has an orientation to one of these seven types of intelligence. These seven types can be classed under social, sensory, and cognitive intelligence. It is important for people to become aware of their own dominant type of intelligence, because this information can help them direct their learning strategies effectively to succeed.

Write an essay about one of the topics listed below (or the topic your teacher assigns). You will have 50 minutes.

1 Describe the different types of personalities required for a successful family life.

2 Describe the different types of foods and flavors that are important to planning a good meal.

3 Describe the different types of vacations that might appeal to people with different interests and income levels.

Editing Checklist

Are the grammar, sentence structure, mechanics, and punctuation correct?

Is the vocabulary appropriate? Are the words spelled correctly?

Is the essay well organized, well developed, and clear?

_____

_____

_____

_____

_____

_____

_____

_____

_____

_____

_____

_____

_____

_____

_____

_____

_____

_____

_____

_____

_____

_____

_____

Presenting Problems and Solutions

Model Essay 1

Protecting Your Privacy

The Internet has completely changed society. People now have access to information, services, and resources anytime and almost anywhere. The Internet has made privacy almost impossible for many people. Nonetheless, there are some very effective actions anyone can take to protect his or her privacy.

There can be serious consequences to having your personal information online. Every time you go on the Internet, your preferences are saved. Companies track your online activity in order to sell you products. For example, Facebook looks at what you write and share with your friends and family. Then, it changes the ads on your page. Your private information is not just available to companies. It is also available to the average person. Anybody can search and find your address, phone number, and photos. Some people have been fired because of compromising photographs on social networking sites. Many others have experienced harassment or even identity theft.

Lack of privacy online can be scary, but there are a few solutions to this problem. First, people should regularly review what information about them is online. If you want to see what companies and other people can see about you, try Googling yourself. It is a good idea to use your full name and even the cities you have lived in to see what there is about you. If you are uncomfortable with the information you find, you can ask the site's webmaster to remove it. Also, you can contact Reputation Defender (www.reputationdefender.org) for help. Next, you can take security measures. Most of your private information online comes from your email and social networking accounts. However, it is easy to protect your privacy when you use these accounts. Facebook, Gmail, and Yahoo! allow you to change your account settings to keep your information private and safe. For instance, on Facebook you can set up your account so that only your friends can see your information. Remember that the default setting allows everyone, including strangers, to see your information. You therefore have to take the time to make your online presence secure.

The Internet can be an amazing tool. In contrast, unwanted advertising, identity theft, and harassment can make being online unsettling or even dangerous. There are two ways to protect your privacy online. Check your information regularly and take action to ensure safety. If you are careful, you can enjoy the Internet without worrying about the safety of you or your family.

Model Essay 2

Protecting Your Privacy

The Internet has completely changed modern society. People now have access to information, services, and resources anytime and almost anywhere. Every time you go on the Internet, your preferences are saved. Companies track your online activity in order to sell you products. Your private information is not just available to companies. It is also available to the average person. Anybody can search and find your address, phone number, and photos. Some people have been fired because of compromising photographs on social networking sites. Many others have experienced harassment or even identity theft. The Internet has made privacy almost impossible for many people. Nonetheless, there are some very effective actions anyone can take to protect his or her privacy.

Lack of privacy online can be scary, but there are a few solutions to this problem. First, people should regularly review what information about them is online. If you want to see what companies and other people can see about you, try Googling yourself. It is a good idea to use your full name and even the cities you have lived in to see what there is about you. If you are uncomfortable with the information you find, you can ask the site's webmaster to remove it. Also, you can contact Reputation Defender (www.reputationdefender.org) for help.

Next, you can take security measures. Most of your private information online comes from your email and social networking accounts. However, it is easy to protect your privacy when you use these accounts. Facebook, Gmail, and Yahoo! allow you to change your account settings to keep your information private and safe. For instance, on Facebook you can set up your account so that only your friends can see your information. Remember that the default setting allows everyone, including strangers, to see your information. You therefore have to take the time to make your online presence secure.

The Internet can be an amazing tool. In contrast, unwanted advertising, identity theft, and harassment can make being online unsettling or even dangerous. There are two ways to protect your privacy online. Check your information regularly and take action to ensure safety. If you are careful, you can enjoy the Internet without worrying about the safety of you or your family.

Write an essay about one of the topics listed below (or the topic your teacher assigns). You will have 50 minutes.

1 Describe the problems faced by parents raising children today. Suggest some solutions for parents.

2 Describe the problems faced by new students of the English language. Suggest some solutions to these problems.

3 Describe the problems faced by people living in big cities. Suggest some solutions for dealing with these problems.

Editing Checklist

Are the grammar, sentence structure, mechanics, and punctuation correct?

Is the vocabulary appropriate? Are the words spelled correctly?

Is the essay well organized, well developed, and clear?

_____

_____

_____

_____

_____

_____

Writing a Character Analysis

Presentation

Model Essay

Pride in "A Sound of Thunder"

They say that "pride comes before the fall." This cliché is proven true in "A Sound of Thunder," a well-known short story by American writer Ray Bradbury. This story, set in 2055 BCE, follows an experienced hunter named Eckels as he travels back in time to hunt a Tyrannosaurus Rex. When he sees the dinosaur, Eckels is frightened. Though he was warned about the dangers of his journey, he stumbles off a raised path and kills a butterfly. Upon returning to the year 2055, the hunters discover a world that has been altered because of Eckels's mistake. Eckels's excessive pride, or what the ancient Greeks called *hubris*, causes him to misjudge how afraid he'd be of the Tyrannosaurus Rex, and this fear leads to a fatal mistake.

At the beginning of the story, Eckels is presented as an experienced and avid hunter. He's hunted the biggest animals and is now after even bigger quarry. So he travels through time to confront a dinosaur. He believes that hunting proves his bravery. He comments that this trip will make a previous trip to Africa " … seem like Illinois." He is too proud of his abilities. When his guide tries to warn him about staying on the raised path so that he does not do anything to change the future, Eckels ignores him. He treats the hunt like a game.

However, when Eckels first sees the dinosaur, he is afraid and loses his confidence. He remarks that "[they] were fools to come." The dinosaur is so big, he feels guns won't kill it. He doesn't think he will live through the experience. In his fear, he stops listening to the guide and steps off the path. He accidentally kills a butterfly and alters the future.

The tragedy that befalls Eckels springs from his arrogance. He wants to test his courage, and he believes he cannot fail in his mission. However, his pride prevents him from acknowledging danger, and he makes a fatal mistake. This story illustrates the importance of humility and the dangers of excessive pride.

Bradbury, Ray. "A Sound of Thunder." *R Is for Rocket*. New York: Doubleday, 1952.

Write an essay about one of the topics listed below (or the topic your teacher assigns). You will have 50 minutes.

1 Choose a character you are familiar with from a movie. Describe the character's personality and what motivates that character in the movie.

2 Choose a character you are familiar with from a TV show. Describe the character's personality and what motivates that character in the show.

3 Describe the personality of a friend, family member, or colleague. Explain what motivates this person in his or her everyday life.

Editing Checklist

Are the grammar, sentence structure, mechanics, and punctuation correct?

Is the vocabulary appropriate? Are the words spelled correctly?

Is the essay well organized, well developed, and clear?

_____

_____

_____

_____

_____

_____

_____

_____

_____

_____

_____

_____

_____

_____

_____

_____

_____

_____

Special Writing Skills

Writing a Journal

Presentation

Model Journal Entry

My Trip to India

Day One:

Today is my first proper day in Delhi, India. The flight took us more than 22 hours, so we did not arrive until late Tuesday night. Our stopover in Seoul was interesting. Incheon International Airport has been completely remodeled, and it is like a mini shopping mall. It has stores like Gucci and Sephora. You know me, I couldn't care less about the shopping, but it had a hotel that offered massage and spa services. I had to get a massage to pass the time. Anyway, back to Delhi. When we arrived, we drove to the Likir House, a Buddhist monastery. There is a huge altar in the lobby. I was so tired that I could not wait to get to my room, take a shower, and go to bed.

In the morning, we went to the University of Delhi for a tour and lunch. We met the president of the college and a bunch of professors. They were all so friendly and happy to meet us. I talked for hours with an MBA graduate student about Hinduism. After lunch, we went to Lal Qila (the Red Fort), built in the 16th century by Shah Jahan, one of the Mughal rulers. I took a lot of pictures, but I cannot upload them until I get new batteries. My batteries died while I was taking pictures of some Indian schoolchildren on vacation. I am now off to dinner. I'll write more tomorrow.

Write a journal entry about one of the topics listed below (or the topic your teacher assigns). You will have 40 minutes.

1 Write a short journal entry about your experiences earlier today or about your plans.
2 Write a short journal entry about your feelings and thoughts today.

Editing Checklist

Are the grammar, sentence structure, mechanics, and punctuation correct?

Is the vocabulary appropriate? Are the words spelled correctly?

Is the journal entry well organized, well developed, and clear?

_____

_____

_____

_____

_____

_____

Writing a College Essay

Presentation

Model Essay

Winning the Lottery

Dreams really can come true. If it happened to me, it can happen to anybody. I am originally from Addis Ababa, the capital city of Ethiopia. Ethiopia is a country located in East Africa between Sudan and Somalia. My country is poor, and there are not a lot of job opportunities. It was difficult for me to make enough money to take care of my wife and my two little children, Mesfin and Hirut. My wife and I both wanted something better. Thus, in 2005, my wife and I entered the United States diversity visa lottery. Every year, the United States holds an annual lottery in certain countries to boost diversity. The people who win this lottery receive a Green Card to live and work in the United States. Millions of people enter the diversity visa lottery, but only about 50,000 are selected. When my wife won, we were so surprised and happy. We didn't think it could happen to us. In 2006, my family made the move to the United States. Winning the lottery transformed the lives of my family and me in a number of ways.

At first, we confronted many challenges. It was difficult to be in a new country with a different language. My wife and I quickly realized that we didn't speak enough English to get the kind of jobs we wanted. We both had to take low-paying jobs. I believe in the value of education, so, in addition to work, I enrolled in ESL classes at our local community college. I knew that I needed to improve my English to get a college degree so that I could get a better paying job. I studied English for three years at that community college and completed an ESL certificate in 2010. It was difficult to balance my work, family, and school responsibilities. I learned a lot about discipline in those years.

Living in the United States has opened my eyes to different cultures, religions, and customs. There are so many different types of people here. Before living in the United States, I used to think people who had different ideas from me were wrong. Since coming to the United States, I have met different people in my neighborhood and at work. Though I don't always like their ideas, I have adopted an American attitude toward diversity. Americans value the ideals of freedom and respect for everyone. I now believe that all people have the right to follow their dreams.

Finally, living in the United States has given me new goals and aspirations. In my ESL program, I explored the college system and different careers. I was amazed at the wealth of opportunities available to me. I feel so lucky to be in a country where you can accomplish your goals with a little hard work. After my research, I concluded that I would like to be a financial advisor. I like mathematics, and I would particularly like to help people grow their wealth and prepare for their futures. I think many people struggle with money because they do not know how to budget it. That is why I am applying to the accounting program at your university. I have already completed my associate degree in accounting at my community college, and I am ready to transfer to a four-year institution to get a bachelor's degree. After I complete my bachelor's degree, I plan to work for a non-profit agency and help people get out of debt and save.

> I could not have imagined how that lottery back in 2005 would change my life. I am a very different person now. I am more hopeful about my family's future, and I believe that anything can happen if I put a little effort into it. Though I am not a typical student, I know I would be a great addition to your campus.

Write an essay about one of the topics listed below (or the topic your teacher assigns). You will have 50 minutes.

1 Write an essay about a person who has had a strong influence in your life.

2 Write an essay about the greatest challenge you have faced in your life.

Editing Checklist

Are the grammar, sentence structure, mechanics, and punctuation correct?

Is the vocabulary appropriate? Are the words spelled correctly?

Is the essay well organized, well developed, and clear?

_____

_____

_____

_____

_____

_____

_____

_____

_____

_____

_____

_____

_____

_____

Writing a Formal Letter

Copyright © 2017 by Pearson Education, Inc. Duplication is not permitted.

Presentation

Model Formal Letter

Winnie Song
341 NW Main St., Apt. 214
Seattle, WA 98103

September 14, 2013

Natalie Hearn, Manager
Mountain Trails Apartments
341 NW Main St.
Seattle, WA 98103

Dear Ms. Hearn:

I am a tenant in Apartment 214 in Mountain Trails, and I am writing to express my concern about my new neighbors, the tenants in 212.

Since they have moved in a week ago, the tenants in the apartment next door have been extremely disruptive and unpleasant. First, the husband and wife have been arguing loudly at all hours. Last night, I could hear their voices until 3 A.M., for example. In addition, the older children leave their garbage in the hallway. They also hang out in front of the building after school and play loud music with their friends. I find their behavior really upsetting. I am embarrassed when I have guests over.

Please discuss these issues with this family as soon as possible. I have been a member of this community for five years now, and I have enjoyed living in this building. However, I will be forced to look for new housing if this situation continues. Thank you in advance for your prompt handling of this matter.

Sincerely,

Winnie Song, Tenant (214)

Write a formal letter about one of the topics listed below (or the topic your teacher assigns). You will have 40 minutes.

1 Write a formal letter to apply for a job. Describe your qualifications and experience.
2 Write a formal letter to apply to a college or university. Explain why you have chosen that school and what your academic plans and qualifications are.

Editing Checklist

Are the grammar, sentence structure, mechanics, and punctuation correct?

Is the vocabulary appropriate? Are the words spelled correctly?

Is the letter well organized, well developed, and clear?

_____

_____

_____

_____

_____

_____

_____

_____

_____

_____

_____

_____

_____

_____

_____

_____

_____

APPENDICES

Appendix 1
Irregular Verbs

Base Form	Simple Past	Past Participle	Base Form	Simple Past	Past Participle
arise	arose	arisen	leave	left	left
be	was/were	been	lend	lent	lent
bear	bore	born	let	let	let
become	became	become	lie (to be at rest)	lay	lain
begin	began	begun	lose	lost	lost
bend	bent	bent	make	made	made
bet	bet	bet	mean	meant	meant
bid	bid	bid	meet	met	met
bite	bit	bitten	mistake	mistook	mistaken
bleed	bled	bled	overtake	overtook	overtaken
blow	blew	blown	pay	paid	paid
break	broke	broken	prove	proved	proved/proven
bring	brought	brought	put	put	put
broadcast	broadcast	broadcast	quit	quit	quit
build	built	built	read	read	read
burn	burned/burnt	burned/burnt	ride	rode	ridden
buy	bought	bought	ring	rang	rung
catch	caught	caught	run	ran	run
choose	chose	chosen	say	said	said
cling	clung	clung	see	saw	seen
come	came	come	seek	sought	sought
cost	cost	cost	sell	sold	sold
cut	cut	cut	send	sent	sent
deal	dealt	dealt	shake	shook	shaken
do	did	done	shine	shone/shined	shone/shined
draw	drew	drawn	shoot	shot	shot
dream	dreamed/dreamt	dreamed/dreamt	shrink	shrank	shrunk
drink	drank	drunk	shut	shut	shut
drive	drove	driven	sing	sang	sung
eat	ate	eaten	sit	sat	sat
fall	fell	fallen	sleep	slept	slept
feed	fed	fed	sneak	snuck/sneaked	snuck/sneaked
feel	felt	felt	speak	spoke	spoken
fight	fought	fought	spell	spelled/spelt	spelled/spelt
find	found	found	spend	spent	spent
flee	fled	fled	spill	spilled	spilled
fling	flung	flung	spoil	spoilt/spoiled	spoilt/spoiled
fly	flew	flown	spread	spread	spread
forbid	forbade	forbidden	spring	sprang	sprung
forecast	forecast	forecast	stand	stood	stood
forego	forewent	forgone	steal	stole	stolen
foretell	foretold	foretold	strike	struck	struck
forget	forgot	forgotten	sweep	swept	swept
forgive	forgave	forgiven	swim	swam	swum
forsake	forsook	forsaken	take	took	taken
get	got	gotten	teach	taught	taught
give	gave	given	tear	tore	torn
go	went	gone	tell	told	told
grow	grew	grown	think	thought	thought
hang (to put up)	hung	hung	throw	threw	thrown
hang (to kill by hanging)	hanged	hanged	undergo	underwent	undergone
			understand	understood	understood
have	had	had	undertake	undertook	undertaken
hear	heard	heard	wake up	woke up	woken up
hide	hid	hidden	wear	wore	worn
hold	held	held	weep	wept	wept
hurt	hurt	hurt	win	won	won
keep	kept	kept	wind	wound	wound
know	knew	known	withdraw	withdrew	withdrawn
lay	laid	laid	write	wrote	written
learn	learned/learnt	learned/learnt			

Appendix 2
Spelling Rules

Spellings of Plural Nouns	
Rules	**Examples**
Add -s to form the plural of most count nouns.	pencil > pencil**s**
	cat > cat**s**
Add -es to form the plural of nouns that end in a consonant + o.	tomato > tomato**es**
Add -es to form the plural of nouns that end in ch, sh, x, or ss.	kiss > kiss**es**
	box > box**es**
	witch > witch**es**
	wish > wish**es**
To form the plural of words that end in consonant + y, change the y to i and add -es.	party > par**ties**
To form the plural of words that end in vowel + y, add -s.	boy > boy**s**
Some plural nouns have an irregular plural form.	child > children
	foot > feet
	man > men
	person > people
	tooth > teeth
	woman > women
Some nouns have the same form for singular and plural.	pants > pants
	clothes > clothes
	deer > deer
	fish > fish
	sheep > sheep
Some nouns have only a singular or plural form.	economics (is)
	news (is)
	the United Arab Emirates (is)
	clothes (are)
	glasses (are)
	scissors (are)

Nouns with Greek or Latin roots take irregular plural endings that must be learned.	appendix > appendices	
	cactus > cacti	
	datum > data	
	medium > media	
	thesis > theses	
Add -s to the first noun in a compound noun	father-in-law > fathers-in-law	
	attorney general > attorneys general	
Add -'s to form plurals for letters	p and q	p's and q's

Spelling of Third-Person Simple Present Verbs	
Rules	**Examples**
Add -s to form the third-person singular of most verbs.	to cook > cook**s**
Add -es to verbs ending in s, z, x, sh, and ch.	kiss > kiss**es**
	buzz > buzz**es**
	fix > fix**es**
	push > push**es**
	watch > watch**es**
If a verb ends in consonant + y, change the y to i and add -es.	try > tr**ies**
If a verb ends in vowel + y, do not change the ending.	pay > pa**ys**
The verbs have, do, and be take irregular third-person singular forms.	be > is
	do > does
	have > has

Spelling of Present Participles	
Rules	**Examples**
Add -ing to the base form of most verbs.	walk > walk**ing**
If a verb ends in e, drop the e and add -ing.	come > com**ing**
If a one-syllable verb ends in consonant + vowel + consonant (CVC), double the last consonant and add -ing.	sit > sitt**ing**
Do not double the last consonant if a word ends in w, x, or y.	flow > flow**ing**
	fix > fix**ing**
	play > play**ing**
In words of more than one syllable that end in consonant + vowel + consonant (CVC), double the last consonant if the syllable is stressed.	permit > permi**tting**

Spelling of Regular Past Participles	
Rules	**Examples**
If a verb ends in a consonant, add -*ed*.	jump > jump**ed**
If a verb ends in e, add -*d*.	like > lik**ed**
If a verb ends in consonant + *y*, change the *y* to *i* and add -*ed*.	carry > carr**ied**
If the verb ends in vowel + *y*, do not change the *y* to *i*. Just add -*ed*.	play > play**ed**
If a one-syllable verb ends in consonant + vowel + consonant (CVC), double the last consonant and add -*ed*.	jog > jog**ged**
Do not double the last consonant if a word ends in *w, x*, or *y*.	fix > fix**ed**
In words of more than one syllable that end in consonant + vowel + consonant (CVC), double the last consonant if the syllable is stressed.	permit > permi**tted**
British and American Spelling Differences	
Common American Spelling	fulfill, fulfillment, traveled, traveling, center, color, connection, defense, encyclopedia, burned, judgment, realize, realization
Common British Spelling	fulfil, fulfilment, travelled, travelling, centre, colour, connexion, defence, encyclopaedia, burnt, judgement, realise, realisation

Appendix 3

Confusing Words

These are words that students sometimes confuse. They sound similar, but they have different meanings. You can always check the meanings of words in your dictionary.

Accept / Except

Accept is a verb. It means "to receive something offered with gladness."

He **accepted** the job.

Except is a preposition. It is used to show things or people that are not included in a statement. It means "other than."

Everybody came to the party **except** Ellen.

Advice / Advise

Advice is a noun. It means "a suggestion about what should be done about a situation."

My brother gave me good **advice**.

Advise is a verb. It means "to tell someone what you think he or she should do." When you advise, you offer advice.

I'm confused. What do you **advise** me to do?

Affect / Effect

Affect is a verb. It means "to have an influence on."

The medicine **affected** her badly.

Effect is a noun. It is a result produced by a cause.

The medicine did not have any **effect** on her.

Effect can also be used as a verb meaning "to bring about", "to cause", or "to achieve."

We will **effect** these changes on Monday morning.

Every day / Everyday

Every day is an adverbial phrase. It means "each day."

I brush my teeth twice **every day**.

Everyday is an adjective. It means usual or ordinary.

For most people, stress is a part of **everyda**y life.

For / Four

For is a preposition. It has many meanings. For example, it indicates the purpose of something.

This machine is **for** blending fruit.

Four is a number.

I have **four** sisters.

Hard / Hardly

Hard can be an adjective or an adverb. As an adjective, it can mean "resistant to pressure."

She is so strong. Her arms are **hard** like steel.

As an adverb, it means "doing something with effort or energy."

I worked **hard** all day long.

Hardly is an adverb. It means "barely or almost not."

There is **hardly** any milk left in the bottle.

Its / It's

Its is a possessive adjective. It means "belonging to something."

The tree lost all **its** leaves.

It's is a contraction. It means "it is."

It's a nice day. Let's go to the beach.

Lie / Lay

Lie is a verb meaning "to be at rest in a horizontal position" or "to occupy a position." It is conjugated *lie, lay, lain*.

The treasure **lies** between the palm trees and the river.

Lay means "to put or place something or someone in a particular position." It is conjugated *lay, laid, laid*.

Lay the baby in the crib.

Loose / Lose

Loose is an adjective. It refers to something that is movable or not fixed.

I lost weight, so these pants are **loose** on me.

Lose is a verb. It means "to come to be without."

I **lost** my cell phone.

Lose can also mean "to fail to keep."

We **lost** a game.

Quite / Quiet

Quite is an adverb meaning "to a certain extent or degree." *Rather* is a synonym of it.

The movie was **quite** good.

Quiet is an adjective meaning "silent or not noisy."

The girl was so **quiet** that I didn't know she was there.

Right / Write

Right is an adjective. It means "correct."

Your answer is **right**.

Write is a verb. It means "to produce symbols on a surface."

I need to **write** a paper for my history class.

Sight / Site

Sight is a noun. It means "the ability to see."

He lost his **sight** in a car accident, and now he is blind.

Site is also a noun. It is a place or location of something.

There are several possible **sites** for the new museum.

Suppose / Be Supposed to

Suppose is a verb that means "to guess or assume."

The committee **supposed** that she would make a good candidate.

Be supposed to is a modal verb phrase meaning "something is expected or required."

You **are supposed to** file your taxes today.

Their / There / They're

Their is a possessive adjective. It means "belonging to them."

Where is **their** house?

There is an adverb. It means "in or near a particular location."

Please put the books **there**.

They're is a contraction. It means "they are."

They're too tired to go to the party.

To / Too / Two

To is a preposition. It has many meanings. For example, it means "in the direction of."

We drove **to** the store.

Too is an adverb. It means "also."

Joe has blond hair, and his sister does, **too**.

Two is a number.

The family owns **two** cars.

Use / Used / Used to / Be Used to

The verb **use** means "to practice or operate."

Can we **use** your phone?

Used is the past form of the verb *use*.

John **used** a hammer to break the ice.

Used to is a verb phrase to talk about past habits.

When they were children, they **used to** play with each other.

Be used to is a verb phrase to talk about what is familiar or customary.

I don't know if I can move to a smaller apartment. I **am used to** having a lot of space.

Weather / Whether

Weather is a noun. It refers to the state of the atmosphere at a certain time and place.

In good **weather**, Jane likes to walk to work.

Whether is a conjunction. It means "if."

I don't know **whether** I will go to the party (or not).

Who's / Whose

Who's is a contraction. It means "who is."

Who's that man talking with our teacher?

Whose is a possessive adjective. It's used to ask which person or thing something belongs to.

Whose phone is this?

You're / Your

You're is a contraction. It means "you are."

You're late.

Your is a possessive pronoun. It means "something belongs to you."

Is that **your** dog?

Appendix 4
Coordinating Conjunctions

Coordinating conjunctions connect equal parts of a sentence. When they connect clauses, they form compound sentences. Here are the coordinating conjunctions and their meanings.

Meaning	Examples
Addition *and, nor*	Gary has lived in Spain, **and** Joanne has lived in Japan. *(similar ideas)*
	Gary hasn't lived in France, **nor** has he lived in China. *(similar negative ideas)* (Nor *has a negative meaning. Don't use a negative verb phrase in the second clause. Use a question word order.)*
Contrast *but, yet*	I was working a lot, **but** I was still able to pay the rent. *(contrasting ideas)* I didn't study at all, **yet** I passed the test. *(surprising contrast in light of first clause)*
Cause/Effect *so, for*	John didn't have any eggs left for breakfast, so he went to the store. *(The first clause is the reason for the second.)*
	I couldn't eat lunch, **for** I had left my wallet at home. *(The first clause is the result of the second.)*
Choice *or*	After the movie, we can go for a walk, or we can drive to my friend's party. *(The sentence presents two choices.)*

Appendix 5
Subordinating Conjunctions

Subordinating conjunctions begin an adverb clause. Adverb clauses connect to a main clause in order to give more information. Here are some common subordinating conjunctions and their meanings.

Meaning	Examples
Time Order *after, as soon as, since, until, when, whenever, while*	The students met at the library **after** they finished their test. (*The event in the second clause comes first*).
	As soon as I finish reading this book, I'll call her back. (*The event in the second clause comes immediately after the first.*)
	They haven't seen each other **since** Susan had that party. (*past to present*)
	We waited at the coffee shop **until** it was 5:30 p.m. (*The event in the first clause happened to the time in the second clause and no more.*)
	When we ran out of gas, we were almost home. (*The event in the first clause happened, and then the event in the second clause happened.*)
	I like to get a coffee **whenever** I go to Java Hut. (*habits and routines*)
	While the children were walking, it began to snow. (*Both events happened at the same time.*)
Location *where, wherever*	They prefer to study in the library **where** there are a lot of books. (*location*)
	Wherever my daughter goes, she gets a lot of attention. (*anywhere*)
Reason *because, since, as*	She's going to the party, **because** she wants to dance.
Condition *if, unless*	**If** it rains, I will go home. (*The event in the first clause is a condition for the event in the second clause to happen.*)
	I'll stay at the picnic **unless** it rains. (*The event in the first clause will happen except under the conditions in the second clause.*)
Contrast *even though, although, though*	**Even though** it was noisy, we had a good time. Mary let her daughter go to the beach, **although/though** she was not happy about it. (*Although and* though *introduce contrast. Even though* is like although, *but more emphatic.*)
Opposites *whereas, while*	**While** I am a good singer, my sister is not.
	My sister is not a good singer, **whereas** I am.
	(*Use a comma in both positions with these subordinating conjunctions. Both mean "in contrast to the fact that."*)
Result *so that*	I had to go home early **so that** I could work in the morning. (*indicates purpose*)

Appendix 6

Transition Signals

Transition signals are words or phrases that connect ideas. These signals connect your sentences and paragraphs together to make your writing more coherent. Review the chart of common transition signals organized by their relationship and meanings.

Relationship	Coordinating and Paired Conjunctions	Subordinating Conjunctions	Conjunctive Adverbs	Phrases
Addition	and, nor, neither . . . nor		also, in addition, moreover, furthermore	
Contrast	but, yet, not . . . but	although, while, whereas	nevertheless, however, by contrast, on the other hand	instead of, in spite of, despite, unlike
Reason	for	because, since	for this reason	due to, because of, as a result of
Result	so	so that, in order that	therefore, as a result, consequently, thus	the cause of, the reason for, provided that
Choice	or, either . . . or		on the other hand, otherwise	
Condition		if, unless		
Time or Logical Order		before, after, when, while, since, as soon as	first of all, next, subsequently, then, after that, above all, more importantly	
Examples			for example, for instance	such as, an example of
Comparison	and, both . . . and, not only . . . but also	as	similarly, likewise	the same as, just like, similar to
Conclusion			finally, in conclusion, to conclude, for these reasons, last of all, in summary, in conclusion	it is clear that, you can see that, these examples show that

Appendix 7
Common Phrases for Introducing an Opinion

Here are some helpful phrases to express your opinion:

I think/believe/feel that

In my opinion

In my experience

I suppose that

In my view

It is my belief that

It seems to me

From my point of view

I am certain that

Personally,

Here are some helpful phrases to introduce other points of view:

According to (this source)

Some/Many people say that

The author believes/thinks/feels that

Appendix 8
Common Participial Adjectives

Present participles end in *–ing*. They describe the people or things that result in the feelings:

This is a confusing problem. (The problem confuses the speaker.)
The teacher is so interesting. (The teacher interests the speaker.)

Past participles end in *–ed*. They describe how people feel.

They are confused students. (The students feel this way because of the problem.)
I am really interested in what the teacher has to say. (The speaker feels this way because of what the teacher says.)

Present participle: *amazing, boring, convincing, depressing, embarrassing*
Past participle: *amazed, bored, convinced, depressed, embarrassed*

Appendix 9

Noncount Nouns

Noncount nouns have no plural form, because you can't count them. They are considered whole and cannot be divided into parts.

*I drank some **water**.* (not *waters*)
*We took three pieces of **luggage** on our trip.* (not *three luggages*)

Type of Noncount Noun	Examples
Names for a whole group	equipment, furniture, jewelry, luggage, mail, meat, software
Fluids	blood, gasoline, juice, milk, oil, water, wine
Solids	beef, butter, cheese, ice, paper, pork, poultry
Gases	air, carbon dioxide, exhaust, fire, fog, smoke, steam
Particles or Small Pieces	cereal, corn, flour, rice, salt, sugar, wheat
Material	brick, chalk, dirt, gold, steel, wood, wool
Abstract Ideas	advice, beauty, grammar, information, love, peace, war
Languages	Amharic, Arabic, Chinese, English, French, Korean, Spanish
Fields of Study	biology, geography, history, literature, math, physics, psychology
Recreation/Sports	baseball, football, singing, swimming, tennis, walking, work
Natural Phenomena	fire, heat, lightning, rain, snow, thunder, weather

Appendix 10
Modals

Modals, or modal verbs, are different from regular verbs:

- They have only one form and do not take an –s or –ed ending.
- They are followed by the base form of the main verb.
- They have different meanings that modify the main verb.

Rules	Modals	Examples
Use *can*, *could*, and *be able to* to talk about ability.	*can* = ability in the present and the future	John **can** swim. Betsy **can't** (cannot) cook.
		Can Andrew sing at the wedding tomorrow?
	could = general ability in the past	When I was a child, I **could** speak Korean.
		I **couldn't** drive a car.
	be able to = completed task in the past; ability in all tenses	They **were able to** get the tickets after all.
		Have you **been able** to reach her?
Use *have to* and *must* to talk about necessity.	*have to* = what is required in statements and questions; what is not required	Why does she **have to** get her driver's license?
		She **has to** commute 20 miles to work.
		They **don't have to** study for that test.
	must = law or necessity in statements; what is not allowed	International students **must** apply for a visa.
		You **must not** smoke in public.
Use *can't*, *could*, *may*, *might*, and *must* to talk about possibility.	*can't* = no possibility	Jill **can't** be in the house. She called from the school.
	could = no or a small possibility	It's not likely, but the boys **could** finish cleaning their room on time.
	might = no or a fair possibility	There **might** not be any way to reach them.
	may = no or a good possibility	My friends **may** come if they have time.
	must/must not = no or very strong possibility	The line is really long for the movie. It **must** be excellent.
		The line for the restaurant is short. It **must not** be very good.

Use *should*, *ought to*, and *had better* to give advice or make suggestions.	*should / should not* = suggestion or some advice; intentions, duty, or obligation in questions	Katie **should** break up with her boyfriend. He's not very nice.
		What **should** Kevin do after school?
		He **shouldn't** play video games. He does that all the time.
	ought to = suggestion or some advice in a more formal manner; not frequently used in negative statements	The medical group **ought to** evaluate their procedures.
	had better / had better not = strong suggestion for or against doing something in statements, not questions	You **had better** clean your room, or you can't go out to play!
		She **had better not** leave the house by herself. It's too dangerous.
Use *used* and *would* to talk about past habits and routines.	*used to / would* = past habits and routines that we no longer have; frequently used in negative and affirmative statements and questions.	My sister **used to play** the piano when we were kids.
		My brother and I **didn't use to play** the piano.
		When I was in college, I **would stay up** all night studying.
		My roommate **wouldn't stay up** late. She worked in the morning.
		Would you stay up all night to work in college?

POST-TEST

Post-Test

Post-Test 1

In the timed Post-Test 1, you will demonstrate how well you understand sentence structure, grammar, punctuation, mechanics, and organization. You have 50 minutes to complete the test. To mark your answer, circle the letter of the correct choice.

1 They decided that the highway would be safer during the snowstorm, because street roads are usually _____ .

  a icer
  b icier
  c more icy
  d most icy

2 Do you know which school is _____ away from us?

  a the furthest
  b the farthest
  c the most far
  d the farther

3 My boss says that if I _____ coming to work on time, she _____ me.

  a don't start / may fire
  b didn't start / fires
  c won't start / might fires
  d couldn't start / fired

4 My daughter's school is peanut-free. This means that children are not allowed _____ food with peanuts in it.

  a bring
  b bringing
  c to bring
  d brough

5 The wedding is in two months. When _____ send out the invitations?

  a will you
  b you will
  c are you going to
  d you are going to

6 My husband forgot to call his mom on her birthday. He _____ a good excuse ready when he speaks to her again.

  a should think of
  b had better have
  c ought not to have
  d had better not have

7 That beef was so tender. How _____ it?
   a are you cooking
   b did you cook
   c were you cooking
   d will you cook

8 Tell me, _____ so much about fashion?
   a have you always cared
   b were you always caring
   c are you always caring
   d you always cared

9 The price of houses is really low right now. If I _____ the money for a down payment, I _____ a new one.
   a have / buy
   b should have / bought
   c will have / will buy
   d had / would buy

10 Teachers are typically required to have a college degree. _____ must also have completed one year of supervised teaching before a class is assigned to _____ .
   a He or she / them
   b They / him or her
   c He or she / him or her
   d They / them

11 My youngest daughter is demanding and requires _____ attention.
   a several
   b a lot of
   c so many
   d a few

12 My grandmother's rocking chair is made of _____ wood from _____ Appalachian Mountains.
   a the / the
   b the / Ø
   c a / the
   d Ø / the

13 I can't decide which sheets to buy. The ones at Roland's are _____ the ones at Cleiborn's.
   a so beautiful as
   b more beautiful as
   c too beautiful as
   d as beautiful as

14 Her husband has quit _____ . That's why he's so jittery.
   a smoked
   b to smoke
   c smoke
   d smoking

15 Mario _____ the information about the test, because he _____ .

    a missed / doesn't listen

    b was missing / didn't listen

    c missed / wasn't listening

    d has missed / hasn't listened

16 My coworkers and I _____ to three conferences in the last month.

    a go

    b going

    c have gone

    d were going

17 Many state highways have a carpool lane. People _____ in that lane if they don't have two or more people in the car.

    a do not have to drive

    b mustn't drive

    c don't have to drive

    d must not to drive

18 Circle the letter of the correct report for the original quote.

    Yesterday, Sara said, "I'm going to the gym for a workout and a massage tomorrow."

    a Yesterday, Sara said that she was going to the gym for a workout and a massage the next day.

    b Yesterday, Sara said that she will go to the gym for a workout and a massage tomorrow.

    c Yesterday, Sara said that she is going to the gym for a workout and a massage the next day.

    d Yesterday, Sara said that she was going to the gym for a workout and a massage tomorrow.

19 That book has been out of print for some time. Where _____ that copy?

    a you can find

    b could you find

    c you are able to find

    d were you able to find

20 No one who _____ the time to help others _____ it.

    a take / regret

    b takes / regrets

    c takes / regret

    d take / regrets

21 Amber _____ the person who stole your wallet. She wasn't even here.

    a could not be

    b won't be

    c ought not to be

    d had not to be

22 Which sentence is written correctly?

a Many of the religious holidays in the eastern orthodox church fall on a different date every year because of their relationship with Easter.

b Many of the Religious Holidays in the Eastern Orthodox Church fall on a different date every year because of their relationship with Easter.

c Many of the religious holidays in the Eastern Orthodox Church fall on a different date every year because of their relationship to Easter.

d Many of the religious holidays in the eastern orthodox church fall on a different date every year because of their relationship with easter.

23 Lucy, the famous human skeleton found in Ethiopia in 1974, was named after the Beatles song _____

a "Lucy in the Sky with Diamonds."

b "Lucy in the Sky With Diamonds".

c ", Lucy In the Sky with Diamonds."

d Lucy in the Sky with Diamonds.

24 Which sentence is written correctly?

a Because of the stormy weather, the picnic, was canceled.

b The picnic was canceled because of the stormy weather.

c The picnic was canceled, because of the stormy weather.

d Because of the stormy weather the picnic was canceled.

25 My favorite novel is *Little Women* _____ published in 1868.

a , when was

b , that was

c , which was

d which was

26 The couple _____ live next door painted their house bright green.

a whom

b which

c whose

d that

27 My first cat was solemn and dignified _____ my new cat is playful and frisky.

a while

b wherever

c , though

d , whereas

28 What kind of phrase or clause is the underlined part of this sentence?

When I get married, I hope to buy a house and plant a garden.

a Prepositional phrase

b Adjective (dependent) clause

c Adverb (dependent) clause

d Independent or main clause

29 George can't find the keys to his house, _____ he'll have to call his wife again.

   a because

   b thus

   c for

   d so

30 Which label describes the following?

She plans to finish her degree now that her husband has found a job.

   a Fragment

   b Run-on

   c Comma Splice

   d Correct

31 Which label describes the following?

The letter came in the mail I opened it.

   a Fragment

   b Run-on

   c Comma Splice

   d Correct

32 Which sentence is incorrectly written?

   a We hired an installer, in order to fix a broken window in our house.

   b We hired an installer so that he could fix a broken window in our house.

   c We hired an installer, for we needed someone to fix a broken window in our house.

   d We hired an installer in order to have a broken window in our house fixed.

33 What is the pattern for the sentence?

The U.S. House of Representatives with 435 members and one of two parts of the legislative branch.

   a Subject Verb Phrase

   b Compound Subject Verb Phrase

   c Subject Compound Verb Phrase

   d This is not a sentence.

34 We will never finish this project on time without everyone's _____ .

   a cooperate

   b cooperation

   c cooperating

   d cooperatively

35 During the 1920s and 1930s, alcohol was _____ in the United States.

   a prohibit

   b prohibitive

   c prohibition

   d prohibited

36 Which part of the sentence is an appositive phrase?

In 1892, the women of Washington State chose the state flower, the rhododendron, before they had the right to vote.

a In 1892
b of Washington State
c the state flower
d the rhododendron

37 My husband talks to himself _____ he is working _____ it helps him think.

a until / since
b while / because
c whereas / if
d whenever / though

38 What kind of phrase or clause is the underlined part of this sentence?

Washington Mutual, the bank where I have kept my savings for more than 20 years, has been bought by J.P. Morgan Chase.

a Prepositional phrase
b Adjective (dependent) clause
c Adverb (dependent) clause
d Independent or main clause

39 The summer weather was hot and sticky, _____ Betsy never missed her morning jog.

a yet
b and
c nor
d or

40 Chicago was named "the Windy City" because of the breezes that blow off Lake Michigan _____ one could argue that Cleveland is just as windy.

a but,
b ; however,
c , though
d , nevertheless

41 Which option is written incorrectly?

a The family can't decide where to vacation. On the one hand they could go back east to visit relatives, they could drive down the coast and explore.
b The family can't decide where to vacation. They could go back east to visit relatives. On the other hand, they could drive down the coast and explore.
c The family can't decide where to vacation. They could go back east to visit relatives; on the other hand, they could drive down the coast and explore.
d The family can't decide where to vacation. Either they could go back east to visit relatives, or they could drive down the coast and explore.

Circle the letter of the correct answer.

42 Some higher education is helpful in order to get a good job. It is very difficult to earn a decent wage without at least one year of college education. There are a number of ways adults can get a college education. Both community colleges and universities provide good options. Before planning your college education,

- **a** there are a number of steps you should follow.
- **b** it is important to note the differences between community colleges and universities.
- **c** it is helpful to determine the problems you will face.
- **d** you should learn about the similarities between community colleges and universities.

The community college system

- **a** provides an education to many people and is not as selective as a university.
- **b** has many programs, is cheaper, and is more flexible.
- **c** has many choices.

Community colleges offer degree programs

- **a** such as
- **b** specifically
- **c** for instance

two-year degrees, professional certificates, high school classes for adults, and ESL classes. The students at community colleges are an incredibly diverse group. Because they are committed to providing affordable education, community colleges have

- **a** much lower tuition than
- **b** as much tuition as
- **c** not as many tuition as

universities. Also, community colleges are more flexible. Classes are offered during the day and evening. Therefore, students can work while attending school.

- **a** Yet
- **b** While
- **c** In contrast,

universities tend to be more selective. Universities are focused on academics and research, so acceptance is based on your abilities and achievements. For these reasons, universities are less diverse. Nevertheless, students are more academically prepared. A university offers

- **a** its
- **b** it's
- **c** their

students four-year and graduate degrees. Classes can be more difficult, so students have to study more. Also, classes are usually offered during the day only. For these reasons, most university students find it challenging to balance work, family, and school responsibilities. University students may pay higher tuition fees, and they may have to live on campus if the university is

- **a** near to
- **b** far from
- **c** further

home.

In conclusion,

a Community colleges and universities differ in terms of access, costs, and education.

b there are some similarities and differences between community colleges and universities.

c the differences between a community college and a university can affect a person's choice about which to attend.

d community colleges and universities share more similarities than differences.

While community colleges are more flexible and cheaper, universities generally provide a better education and more opportunities. It is important to consider all the factors before deciding what type of college to attend. The choice really depends on your current living circumstances and goals.

Which outline best describes the overall organization of the previous essay? Circle the letter of the correct answer.

43 a Differences between Community Colleges and Universities

Community College

1. not selective

2. cheaper

3. more flexible

University

1. very selective

2. more difficult

3. more expensive

4. less flexible

b Similarities between Community Colleges and Universities

Who attends

1. Community College

2. University

Tuition

1. Community College

2. University

Student life

1. Community College

2. University

c Similarities and Differences for Community Colleges and Universities

University

1. Access

2. Cost

3. Student responsibilities

Community College

1. Access

2. Cost

3. Student responsibilities

POST-TEST 2

Paragraph

In the timed Paragraph Post-Test 2, you will demonstrate how well you can write about a topic. Pay attention to sentence structure, grammar, punctuation, mechanics, organization, and vocabulary.

Write about the following topic or the topic your teacher assigns.

You have 30 minutes to complete the test.

Write a paragraph to express your opinion on the following topic: What are the qualities of a good teacher? Support your ideas with specific reasons and examples. Include a topic sentence, supporting sentences, and a concluding sentence.

_____

_____

_____

_____

_____

_____

_____

_____

_____

_____

_____

_____

_____

_____

_____

_____

_____

_____

Essay

In the timed Essay Post-Test 2, you will demonstrate how well you can write about a topic. Pay attention to sentence structure, grammar, punctuation, mechanics, organization, and vocabulary.

Write about the following topic or the topic your teacher assigns. You have 50 minutes to complete the test.

Write an essay to express your opinion on the following topic: What are the qualities of a good teacher? Support your ideas with specific reasons and examples. Include an introductory paragraph, two or three body paragraphs, and a concluding paragraph.

_____

_____

_____

_____

_____

_____

_____

_____

_____

_____

_____

_____

_____

_____

_____

_____

_____

_____

_____

_____

ANSWER KEY

PRE-TEST

Pre-Test 1 pp. 1–7

1. d, 2. a, 3. a, 4. b, 5. c, 6. a, 7. b, 8. c, 9. d,
10. a, 11. d, 12. c, 13. b, 14. a, 15. d, 16. b,
17. c, 18. a, 19. c, 20. d, 21. c, 22. d, 23. a,
24. b, 25. c, 26. b, 27. a, 28. a, 29. d, 30. a,
31. c, 32. c, 33. c, 34. a, 35. c, 36. c, 37. c,
38. c, 39. b, 40. c, 41. a, 42. c

Pre-Test 2 pp. 7–8

Answers will vary.

PUNCTUATION AND MECHANICS

Periods and Question Marks

Practice 1 p. 10

1. a	5. b	9. a
2. a	6. b	10. b
3. b	7. a	
4. a	8. a	

Practice 2 p. 11

April 10, 2014

Ms. Karen Ruiz, Manager
ABC Electric Co.
100 W. Bolton St.
Des Moines, IA 50302

Dear Ms. Ruiz:
I am interested in working with your company and would like to know if you have any positions available. I have been working as a certified electrician for two years. I completed my apprenticeship in Washington, DC, in September of 2011, and I received my certification from the National Association of Electricians the following year.

I have attached a résumé for your review. May I call you to discuss job opportunities and to answer any questions you may have about my skills and experience? If so, what would be a convenient time for me to call?

Thank you for your consideration.

Sincerely,
John Nguyen, Jr.

Apostrophes

Practice 1 p. 13

1. The politicians' speeches
2. The mother and father's room
3. The table's surface
4. The children's play area
5. My sister-in-law's husband
6. The Earth's diameter
7. Mrs. Allen's and Mrs. Ellis's schedules
8. The UN's policy
9. The Queen of England's home
10. Nobody's responsibility
11. The actresses' roles

Practice 2 p. 14

1. b, 2. a, 3. a, 4. b, 5. a, 6. a, 7. a, 8. a, 9. b,
10. b

Capitalization

Practice 1 p. 16

1. Dear Ms. Andres,

Last Friday, I dropped off my application for employment, but, unfortunately, it contained an error. Attached is the corrected copy. Please replace the old copy with this one. Thank you.
Sincerely,
Lorena Cardozo

2. *The Old Man and the Sea* is one of Ernest Hemingway's more famous novels. The story is about Santiago, a fisherman who hasn't caught any fish in months. When he goes out to fish, he has a desperate struggle to bring a giant fish home. He wants to sell the fish and make money for his village.

Practice 2 p. 16

Lorena Cardozo

401 Second Avenue North

Hollywood, California 90049

Objective:

To obtain a position as a Teaching Intern

Experience:

Teaching Assistant, Psychology 101, 2012

Spanish Tutor, 2008 to Present

Camp Counselor, Roxbury Park 2006–2008

Education:

University of California, Riverside: MA, Education, 2014

California State University, Northridge: BA, Spanish, 2012

Skills:

Spanish (fluent), Computers, Typing (50 WPM)

References:

Available Upon Request

Colons

Practice 1 pp. 17–18

1. c, 2. a, 3. c, 4. b, 5. b, 6. b, 7. c, 8. a, 9. a, 10. a, 11. c

Practice 2 p. 19

1. b, 2. b, 3. a, 4. b, 5. a, 6. b, 7. a, 8. a

Parentheses

Practice 1 pp. 20–21

1. As we read, we often come across words we don't understand. Here's a useful strategy to help you figure out the meaning of unfamiliar words: a read the sentence the word appears in; b decide what part of speech the word is noun, verb, adjective, etc.; c determine if the word contains any letters before it or after it that give hints to its meaning prefixes, suffixes; d look for important words, phrases, and sentences around the unfamiliar word that might also give hints to its meaning context clues; e think of other words or phrases that could be used in place of the word synonyms.

2. Dear Azhar,

   I can't wait to see you and your family at the company's annual picnic next Sunday afternoon. Your husband and son will be attending, too, I hope! My daughters, Leah and Yameena, are so big now eight and ten years old. I'm sure your son, Nabil, has grown a lot, too. My girls are looking forward to the picnic and to seeing and playing with him again.

   It's been a long time since we've seen each other. When I moved to our office in the East something I wasn't happy about at first, I didn't think we'd lose touch for so long time flies, though. You still live in Venice Beach, right? I was wondering if you'd like to carpool to the picnic? We've got plenty of room in our car. I rented an SUV that seats seven comfortably! Give me a call at (205)555–6573.

   See you on Sunday,

   Jamie

Practice 2 pp. 21–22

1. Jerusalem is a holy city for three major religions (Judaism, Christianity, and Islam).

2. The famous actor owned a Porsche, a Mercedes, and a 1968 Volkswagen Beetle. (It was a gift from his father when he was 18 years old.)

3. Danny–Please remember to take care of the dog before you leave (i.e., put water in his bowl, give him food, and take him for a walk).

4. Some fruits (peaches, avocados, plums, apricots, etc.) will ripen faster if you keep them inside a paper bag.

5. My grandparents are celebrating their 50th wedding anniversary (August 10, 1962) this year.

6. The child picked up the box of toys and dumped it on the floor. (He was having a temper tantrum.)

7. The insurance company paid us three thousand dollars ($3,000.00) after the car accident.

8. Abraham Lincoln (1809–1865) was the 16th president of the United States.

9. We spent all day Saturday (8:00 A.M. to 6:00 P.M.) working in the garden.

10. Every year, hikers head to one of the many national parks (Mt. Rainier, Olympic National Forest, North Cascades) near Seattle to enjoy nature.

11. To use the copier in this office, it is important to (1) enter your code and (2) choose copying options.

Semicolons

Practice 1 p. 24

An eclectic room tells a lot about a person; in fact, it tells more about a person than any other type of decor. Take, for example, my living room. It has an old Victorian sofa and armchair, which my grandmother gave me; a Turkish carpet I bought on a trip to Istanbul last year; a coffee table crafted from recycled wood; and a modern floor lamp, which I found for five dollars at a yard sale last week! My living room tells you a lot about me; it tells you that I cherish family heirlooms, enjoy traveling, care for the environment, and love a good bargain!

Practice 2 p. 24

1. a, 2. a, 3. a, 4. b, 5. a, 6. a, 7. b

Commas

Practice 1 pp. 26–27

1. b, 2. a, 3. c, 4. b, 5. b, 6. b, 7. b, 8. b, 9. b

Practice 2 p. 27

1. United States,
   country, especially
   wetlands, and swamps

2. China, alligators
   However, they
   extinct, and fewer
   world, where
   Florida, for example,
   alligators and has released

3. Smith, Ron
   May 7, 1975
   Beverly Hills, CA 90210
   $55,000.00

Quotations

Practice 1 pp. 28–29

1. a, 2. a, 3. b, 4. a, 5. b, 6. b

Practice 2 p. 29

1. "Where are you going?"
2. "To Portland,"
3. "Me, too."
4. lives there,"
5. this weekend."
6. a wedding, too."
7. Kindra Ramsay,"
8. "and she's marrying
9. Bill Mason."
10. "We're going
11. Bill is my brother!"

Paragraph Format

Practice 1 p. 31

1. Heading

2. Title

3. Indent

4. Even left margin

5. Uneven right margin

Practice 2 p. 32

1. Upper left-hand corner

2. Heading

3. 8½ by 11 (white or lined)

4. Month, Day, Year

5. Center on the line after the heading

6. 2.0 or every other line

7. 1 inch on all sides

8. Times New Roman

9. 10–12 points

10. ½ inch or 5 spaces

GRAMMAR

Simple Future

Practice 1 p. 34

1. b, 2. a, 3. a, 4. b, 5. a, 6. b, 7. a, 8. b, 9. b,
10. a

Practice 2 p. 35

1. 's going to get

2. 'll walk

3. will probably vote

4. are going to travel

5. isn't going to apply

6. will be

7. won't raise

8. 's going to miss

9. will pay

10. won't give

Articles

Practice 1 pp. 37–39

1. a, 2. d, 3. b, 4. d, 5. d, 6. d, 7. a, 8. b, 9. c,
10. a, 11. c

Practice 2 p. 39

Last week, I had <u>an</u> amusing experience. There was <u>a</u> group of basketball players on my flight to Chicago. <u>The</u> players were all young, lean, and tall. <u>The</u> tallest was nearly 7 feet; <u>the</u> shortest was at least 6 feet 2. I am only 5 feet 8, and <u>the</u> amusing thing was that I had <u>a</u> seat on <u>the</u> aisle, while two of the players had the middle seat and the window seat next to me. Unfortunately, <u>the</u> plane was full, and there were no empty aisle seats for them to move to. I decided to offer my seat to one of the players. But which one? Both were equally uncomfortable. They discussed <u>the</u> situation and decided that <u>the</u> only fair solution was to flip <u>a</u> coin. <u>The</u> player with the window seat lost the toss. His friend moved to the aisle, I sat in <u>the</u> middle, and the player who had the window seat spent most of <u>the</u> flight to Chicago standing and walking up and down <u>the</u> aisle.

Comparative and Superlative Adjectives

Practice 1 p. 42

subtler	the subtlest
farther	the farthest
cleverer	the cleverest
softer	the softest
sadder	the saddest
dirtier	the dirtiest
more athletic	the most athletic

Practice 2 p. 42

1. older

   the youngest

2. roomier

   least attractive

   the most beautiful

   more open

   narrower

   less spacious

   taller

more panoramic

the best

the farthest

Comparisons with as . . . as

Practice 1 p. 44

1. as naughty as

2. the same state as

   not as tall as

   not as old as

   just as majestic as

   just as scenic as

3. not as active as

   as much attention as

   just as many visitors as

   not as far south as

   not as accessible as

Practice 2 p. 44

1. as many passengers as

2. as noisy as

   as comfortable as

   not as cheap as

3. as many points as

   as safe as

   as much gas mileage as

   not as aerodynamic as

4. the same number of options as

   not as quiet as

   as well as

Conditional

FUTURE REAL CONDITIONAL

Practice 1 pp. 45–46

1. c, 2. d, 3. a, 4. b, 5. a, 6. a, 7. a, 8. a, 9. a

Practice 2 p. 46

MOTHER: don't hurry

           you'll miss

JOSH: don't find

           I won't be able to leave

MOTHER: miss

           I won't drive

JOSH: I'll be

MOTHER: she'll lock

JOSH: take

           I'll do

MOTHER: don't wake up

           I'll dump

PRESENT UNREAL CONDITIONAL

Practice 1 pp. 47–49

1. a, 2. a, 3. a, 4. d, 5. c, 6. d, 7. d, 8. b, 9. c, 10. c, 11. a

Practice 2 p. 49

1. gave

   I'd be

2. wasn't

   could take

   were

   I'd be

   would be

   had

   might not be able to pay

   if you lost

   If I won

   wouldn't have to find

Direct and Indirect Objects

Practice 1 p. 51

1. a, 2. a, 3. a, 4. a, 5. a, 6. a, 7. a, 8. a, 9. a, 10. a, 11. a, 12. a

Practice 2

Part 1 p. 52

1. me

   me

   me

   you

Part 2 p. 52

1. clothes
2. lights
3. piano
4. teeth

Gerunds and Infinitives

Practice 1 p. 55

1. to travel / traveling
2. packing
3. not taking
4. looking
5. staying / to stay
6. waiting / to wait
7. to speak
8. writing
9. going
10. to come
11. to pay
12. to return

Practice 2 p. 56

1. allowed him to play / allowed Tim to play
2. ordered me to slow down
3. enjoy going
4. love to drink / love drinking
5. happy to meet
6. ask my teacher to help / ask the teacher to help
7. don't feel like going out / do not feel like going out
8. promised to help
9. encouraged me not to drive
10. began swimming
11. can't wait to see

Modals

ABILITY

Practice 1 p. 58

1. c, 2. a, 3. b, 4. c, 5. a, 6. b, 7. b, 8. a, 9. c, 10. b, 11. c

Practice 2 pp. 58–59

A: be able to watch

can't watch / isn't able to watch / cannot watch / is not able to watch / 's not able to watch

B: could keep up / was able to keep up

A: be able to take care of

B: Maybe. What do you plan to do about the band in the meantime?

A: can play / is able to play

can't sing / cannot sing / can not sing / isn't able to sing / is not able to sing / 's not able to sing

B: can't play / am not able to play / cannot play / can not play / 'm not able to play

can sing / am able to sing / 'm able to sing

A: What a great idea!

NECESSITY

Practice 1 p. 60

has had to develop

must behave

will have to

have to leave

must sign

must be

has to report

must not

will have to follow

have to cite

does not have to cite

Practice 2 pp. 60–61

1. has to have / must have
2. must not speed / mustn't speed
3. have to use / must use
4. must not be / mustn't be
5. Does

   have to be
6. had to install
7. doesn't have to take / does not have to take
8. will have to eat / is going to have to eat / 'll have to eat / 's going to have to eat / has to eat
9. doesn't have to be / does not have to be
10. must not litter / mustn't litter
11. did

    have to go

POSSIBILITY

Practice 1 pp. 62–63

1. c, 2. a, 3. a, 4. c, 5. a, 6. c, 7. a, 8. b, 9. a, 10. c

Practice 2 pp. 63–64

1. c, 2. b, 3. a, 4. a, 5. a, 6. c, 7. b, 8. b, 9. b, 10. b

ADVISABILITY

Practice 1 pp. 66–67

1. c, 2. b, 3. a, 4. c, 5. b, 6. c, 7. a, 8. b, 9. c, 10. a

Practice 2 p. 67

1. had better get out
   ought to be / should be
   should tell
   had better not bother / 'd better not bother
   should I do
2. should not give up / shouldn't give up
   should write / ought to write
   had better get out / 'd better get out
   should end / ought to end
   had better think / 'd better think

Phrasal Verbs

Practice 1 pp. 69–70

1. up
2. off
3. back
4. out
5. after
6. over
7. off on
8. over
9. out
10. on
11. back

Practice 2 p. 70

1. take their hats off / take off their hats
   keep them on
2. dress up
3. try her wedding dress on / try on her wedding dress
4. drop in on each other
   call on somebody

5. throw anything old, broken, or useless away / throw away anything old, broken, or useless
   stay up
   get together
6. show up
7. take it back

The Past

THE SIMPLE PAST

Practice 1 p. 72

1. came
   attended
   wanted
   learned
   didn't get / did not get
   decided
2. called
   didn't answer / did not answer
   wasn't / was not
   left
   wanted

Practice 2 pp. 72–73

1. happened
   yawned
   flew
   was
   swallowed
2. sat
   read
   heard
   got
   looked
   were

THE PAST PROGRESSIVE

Practice 1 p. 74

1. were you doing
2. was looking
3. was smiling

4. wasn't paying / was not paying

   was taking

5. weren't fixing / were not fixing

   were cleaning

6. was finishing

7. were playing

   were you doing

   were you shouting

Practice 2 p. 74

1. The students in Ms. Baker's English grammar class <u>were waiting</u> for almost ten minutes when she finally <u>arrived</u>. They asked her, "Where have you been? What <u>were you doing</u>?

   Ms. Baker <u>apologized</u> and <u>explained</u> that she <u>was</u> in a car accident while she <u>was driving</u> to work. She <u>was waiting</u> at a red light when a car <u>hit</u> her from behind. Fortunately, she <u>wasn't</u> hurt, but the other driver <u>had</u> some injuries.

The Present Perfect

Practice 1 p. 76

1. haven't called / have not called

2. have sighted

   has increased

   have poured

   have reported

   have investigated

   haven't been able / have not been able / 've not been able

   haven't completed / have not completed

   haven't solved / have not solved

   have inspected / 've inspected

   have had

Practice 2 p. 77

got

has already planned / 's already planned

has helped

haven't had / have not had

hasn't found / has not found

have visited

decided

have planned / 've planned

responded

Have I ever enjoyed

have dreamed / 've dreamed

Subject–Verb Agreement

Practice 1 pp. 79–80

1. a, 2. a, 3. b, 4. a, 5. a, 6. a, 7. b, 8. b, 9. b, 10. b

Practice 2 p. 80

1. are

2. is

3. come

4. keeps, has kept

5. hasn't been / has not been

6. Was / Is

7. has

8. call

9. have been

10. makes, has made

11. doesn't grow / does not grow

The Passive Voice

Practice 1 p. 82

1. is adjourned

2. were destroyed

3. is remodeled

4. is being remodelled / 's being remodeled

5. was hired

6. was started

7. the old carpeting had been removed

8. was being painted

9. will be delivered

10. will be finished

11. has to be dealt with

Practice 2 p. 82

1. is spoken

   uses

2. was bitten

   was wearing

   was seen

   was picked up

   reported

   has recently been identified / was recently identified

   was frequently chased / had frequently been chased

   wanted, had wanted

   was charged / has been charged

   is suing / has sued

Reported Speech

Practice 1 p. 85

1. she had a stomachache
2. he might have to work
3. if the boys were going to eat at that restaurant / whether the boys were going to eat at that restaurant
4. to get down
5. the ocean looks blue because it reflects
6. if the study group met / whether the study group met
7. marriages ended in divorce / marriages end in divorce
8. to call her / to please call her
9. if he could have the rest of my popcorn / whether he could have the rest of my popcorn
10. I ought to call my
11. patient information was / patient information is

Practice 2 pp. 85–86

I was talking on the phone last week when the doorbell rang. I went to the door and asked who it was. The person told me he was my / it was my / that he was my / that it was my Uncle David. I was surprised. I explained that I didn't have / I did not have an Uncle David. Then he inquired what my name was and who lived there. I told him that my name was Andrew. He thought that he had the wrong house. I wanted to know who he was looking for so I could help him. He answered that he was looking for his niece, Yolanda. According to him, she had moved to / she had recently moved to / Yolanda had moved to / Yolanda had recently moved to the neighborhood, but he didn't know where. I knew Yolanda, so I told him to just go to the yellow house at the end of the block. He thanked me and left.

Pronoun Agreement

Practice 1 p. 88

1. He
2. She
3. They
4. it
5. They
6. They them
7. She them
8. We it
9. them her

Practice 2 p. 88

These days, security at airports is very strict. Now, all departing passengers are required to come to the airport three hours before their flights. Upon arrival, each passenger is required to have his / her / his or her / her or his luggage checked before he / she / he or she / she or he is allowed to enter the boarding area. If someone is carrying a gun or any kind of sharp object, security officers will question and possibly even arrest him / her / him or her / her or him. In addition, passengers must pass through a metal detector and have their carry-on bags X-rayed. At this point, they must say good-bye to family and friends, because no one except passengers with tickets is allowed past the metal detectors. There is also a new procedure for picking up arriving passengers. It has changed. In the past, people could meet a passenger at the gate as soon as he / she / he or she / she or he got off the plane. Nowadays, they must meet passengers in the baggage-claim area. The new security measures are time-consuming and inconvenient. Nevertheless, most people cooperate with them, because everybody understands that these measures could save their life.

Quantifiers

Practice 1 p. 90

1. each
   some of
2. one of the
   both of
3. a little
   a few
4. plenty of, a great deal of / a great deal of, plenty of
   a number
5. much
   many

Practice 2 p. 90

1. a couple of
   a number of
2. any
   a few
   much

3. several
   a lot of
4. a few
   every
   plenty of
   a great deal of

SENTENCE STRUCTURE

Simple Sentences

Practice 1 pp. 91–93

1. a, 2. a, 3. a, 4. b, 5. d, 6. c, 7. b, 8. a, 9. b, 10. d, 11. c

Practice 2 p. 93

1. Subject: Wisconsin; Verb: is known
2. Subject: The cat; Verb: sat
3. Subject: All plants and animals; Verb: need
4. Subject: Paul, Verb: went and bought
5. Subject; My friends and I; Verb: decided OR decided to go
6. Subject: Gun violence; Verb: has risen
7. Subject: My grandparents; Verb: get up and take
8. Subject: Trinidad and Barbados; Verb: are
9. Subject: The recession; Verb: has increased
10. Subject: Susana and Jack; Verb: like to drink and listen
11. Subject: Experts on environmental pollution; Verb: are studying

Compound Sentences and Coordinating Conjunctions

Practice 1 p. 95

1. so
2. My sister asked me to babysit my two nieces last Monday from 1:00 P.M. to 4:00 P.M., but I wasn't sure I wanted to (or could!) watch the girls for three hours. I love my nieces, but they're very close in age (4 and 2), and they're also very active! I knew I'd have to find a fun activity for us to do for those three hours. We had two choices—we could stay home and watch videos, or we could go to the park and play on the slide and swings. It wasn't a very nice day, nor was the sun shining. I knew the girls loved books, so I decided we'd go to the library. I'm glad we did, for the storyteller arrived ten minutes after we did. She amused the children for the next hour and a half, and she amused me, too! I didn't want to babysit, yet I had fun. I can't wait until the next time!

Practice 2 p. 96

1. so / and
2. or / and
3. for
4. for / and
5. so / and
6. so / and
7. but / yet
8. but / yet
9. nor
10. yet / but

Complex Sentences

INDEPENDENT AND DEPENDENT CLAUSES

Practice 1 p. 98

1. b, 2. a, 3. c, 4. b, 5. c, 6. a, 7. b, 8. a, 9. b, 10. c, 11. b

Practice 2 p. 99

SHARON: Jack's 21st birthday is on Saturday, and we're planning a surprise party for him. Let's decide how we're going to divide up the work.

MAX: What are the things that need to be done?

SHARON: We need to clean the apartment, send out invitations, buy food, and get the drinks.
Oh, and we need to find someone who will bring Jack to the party.

MARTA: I can do that. I'm taking Jack to a movie that afternoon, and afterward, we're going to have dinner. While we're eating, the guests can come over and help set everything up. After eating, I'll say that I need to stop by your apartment to get my guitar. Then everybody will shout, "Surprise!"

SHARON: That's a great plan. OK, now let's decide what we're going to eat and drink. Of course, we need a cake.

MAX: I'll get that if you tell me where to buy it.

SHARON: Go to Sophie's mom's bakery. But go early in the morning so that you can find a parking place.

MAX: What about the drinks and food?

SHARON: I'll ask Sophie to bring juice and soft drinks. When I call the guests, I'll ask each of them to bring something. If people want anything else to drink, they can bring their own.

SUBORDINATING CONJUNCTIONS

Practice 1 p. 101

John and his best friend, Thomas, have been friends since they started elementary school. Now, because they will both be graduating from high school next spring, they will be going separate ways. Although both of them are excellent students, they have very different plans when they graduate. John wants to be an engineer, whereas Thomas wants to join the army. As soon as John graduates, he plans to leave for a summer science program. Right after he finishes his summer science program, he plans to start college in New York. John wants to finish college as quickly as possible so that he can start working at his father's engineering firm. Thomas, on the other hand, isn't as sure about his long-term plans. He thinks that if he serves in the army first, he can learn useful skills and figure out what he wants to study in college. He doesn't plan to start college until he is finished with basic training.

Practice 2 pp. 101–102

1. As soon as the handyman moves the furniture from the wall, we can hang the picture.
2. My friend Tomoko is creative and outgoing, whereas her twin, Yutaka, is quiet and business-minded.
3. Berhan plans to accept the marriage proposal if her father approves.
4. Scientists send probes into space so that they can study other planets.
5. Since everybody loves coffee, Starbucks is very successful.
6. My favorite pianist won't be able to play for my recital unless he finds a babysitter for his daughter.
7. Since Ann was twelve years old, she has been going to visit her family in Houston every year.

8. Although the lock was rusty, the door opened with one turn of the key.

9. The boys stayed up all night packing before they left for Europe.

10. While Mike was mowing the lawn, his wife was doing the dishes.

11. Companies hire temporary workers when they get too busy.

ADJECTIVE CLAUSES AND RELATIVE PRONOUNS

Practice 1 pp. 104–105

1. b, 2. a, 3. c, 4. c, 5. a, 6. b, 7. b, 8. a, 9. a, 10. c, 11. c

Practice 2 p. 105

1. , whose house is near the beach,

2. whose parents you just met

3. who don't speak English / that don't speak English

4. , who lives by herself and never talks to anyone,

5. , who has a wonderful sense of humor,

6. , which was a famous center for music

7. whose names were called

8. who explained the homework to me / that explained the homework to me

9. that we had never seen / which we had never seen / we had never seen

10. where they're taking Bob / that they're taking Bob / which they're taking Bob

11. when I do my best work / that I do my best work

Word Forms

Practice 1 p. 106

Column 1. revolt, predict, motivate

Column 2. commitment, tradition, identification, presumption, motivation, interpretation

Column 3. accurate, revolutionary, predictable, philosophical

Column 4. accurately, traditionally, identically, presumably, philosophically

Practice 2 p. 107

1. natural
2. Canadian
3. variation
4. relatively
5. typically
6. complaints
7. difficulty
8. adaptation
9. accessible
10. easily
11. entertainment

Appositives

Practice 1 p. 108

Example: Wolfgang Amadeus Mozart

Mozart was born in 1756 in the Austrian town of Salzburg, a stunningly beautiful city with a long musical history. Mozart's musical gifts became obvious almost immediately. By the age of four, he could already play the piano. He published his first compositions, four pieces for violin and harpsichord, before his eighth birthday.

Mozart's father, Leopold, had been a music teacher. However, he quit teaching to manage young Wolfgang's career. When Mozart was six, he began playing concerts with his sister, Nanerl, who was also a gifted musician. At the age of seven, Mozart was invited to Vienna, the capital of Austria, to play for the royal family. From there, his reputation as a genius spread all over Europe.

Mozart's first public performance took place in Munich, a city in southern Germany. In 1984, a mostly fictional account of Mozart's life was told in the film *Amadeus*. Much of the film focuses on Mozart's rivalry with another composer, Salieri. At the end of the movie, Salieri, who was jealous of Mozart's genius, poisons Mozart. In fact, the cause of Mozart's death at age 35 is not certain. It may have been a medical condition called uremia, a result of advanced kidney disease. Mozart died before completing his last masterpiece, his unforgettable "Requiem."

Practice 2 p. 109

1. *, one of the most expensive U.S. movies,*
2. *, injera,*
3. teammates
4. *, blue*
5. , a popular print newspaper in Seattle,
6. , one of the bestselling cookies in the U.S.,
7. , an attorney
8. , a reliable Korean car
9. , the capital of the United States
10. , an excellent biologist,

Fragments

Practice 1 p. 110

Los Angeles is a multinational city with immigrants from all over the world. Many of these immigrants live in "ethnic" neighborhoods. <u>For example, Chinatown. Is a unique community of approximately 14,000 people.</u> Chinese culture dominates the area. <u>Have Chinese restaurants, clothing stores, bakeries, banks, bookstores, gift shops, jewelers, markets, beauty salons, and more.</u> Some of Chinatown's residents have lived there for 40 or 50 years, and they have never learned much English. <u>Because they haven't needed it. Is possible to get almost any Chinese product or service in Chinatown. Without traveling to China.</u>

Los Angeles is an enjoyable city to visit. <u>If you have a car.</u> If not, you will need to depend on public transportation. <u>Which is neither fast nor convenient.</u> Los Angeles has a new subway, but it does not travel to most of the popular tourist attractions. There is no system of elevated trains or streetcars. <u>Only buses, and they can take a long time to go anywhere. Because traffic is very heavy. Especially in the early morning and late afternoon, when people are traveling to and from work.</u>

Practice 2 p. 111

1. b, 2. a, 3. a, 4. c, 5. c, 6. a, 7. b, 8. b, 9. a, 10. b, 11. b

Run-on Sentences and Comma Splices

Practice 1 pp. 113–114

1. b, 2. b, 3. a, 4. a, 5. c, 6. b, 7. c, 8. b, 9. a, 10. a

Practice 2 p. 115

1. b, 2. a, 3. c, 4. a, 5. b, 6. b, 7. c, 8. a, 9. a, 10. b

Transition Signals

Practice 1 pp. 117–118

1. a, 2. c, 3. c, 4. b, 5. b, 6. a, 7. c, 8. b, 9. a, 10. c

Practice 2 p. 118

Many adults find it difficult to balance work, family, and school when they return to college. <u>Therefore,</u> it is important for these students to develop good time-management skills <u>so that</u> they can have an enjoyable and successful experience. <u>First of all,</u> students must be aware of the important dates for each class, such as those for assignments, quizzes, and tests, <u>for</u> they will need to take these into account when scheduling family and work-related events. <u>In addition,</u> college students must count on approximately two hours of study time for every hour of class time they have, <u>and</u> they need to include these study hours into their weekly schedules; <u>otherwise,</u> the hours will easily be taken up by activities that are not school-related. <u>It is clear that</u> adult students can, <u>because of</u> their responsibilities, face difficulties, <u>but</u> good time management skills will help them overcome these difficulties. <u>Moreover,</u> they will have fun in the process!

PARAGRAPH ORGANIZATION

Paragraph Structure

Practice 1 pp. 119–120

Topic Sentence: [1]

Concluding Sentence: [11]

1st sub-point: [2]

2nd sub-point: [5]

3rd sub-point: [8]

Supporting Details for the 1st sub-point: [3, 4] and [4, 3]

Supporting Details for the 2nd sub-point: [6, 7] and [7, 6]

Supporting Details for the 3rd sub-point: [9, 10] and [10, 9]

Practice 2 p. 120

[6] College can be an important place to network and talk to people about the kind of job you might want to do when you are finished with school.

[9] Children of college-educated parents are more likely to see the value of a college education.

[5] An additional reason to go back to college is to meet people in the field you are interested in.

[2] The number one reason to return to college is that people with a college education make more money.

[4] In addition, it is almost impossible to take care of a family with a very low wage.

[8] The final reason for attending college is to set an important example for your children.

[3] Jobs that only require a high school education often pay the lowest wage.

[7] Also, teachers and other students will become valuable resources.

[10] As you can see, going back to school will contribute to your success in a number of ways.

Topic Sentence and Controlling Idea

Practice 1 pp. 122–123

1. d, 2. a, 3. c, 4. b, 5. d, 6. a, 7. b, 8. b

Practice 2 pp. 123–124

1. c, 2. b, 3. a

Concluding Sentences

Practice 1 pp. 125–126

1. b, 2. c, 3. a

Practice 2 pp. 126–127

1. b, 2. a, 3. c

Supporting Sentences

COMPARISON SIGNALS

Practice 1 p. 129

A comparison of the Harry Potter stories and the King Arthur legend reveals a number of common events and characters. First, not only Harry Potter but also young King Arthur are hidden after their parents die to protect them. Similarly, neither Harry Potter nor Arthur is aware of his special heritage because both are adopted by new families. Both boys, in addition, are rescued from these families by events that mark them as special. Harry Potter discovers he is a wizard when he talks to a snake, and King Arthur discovers he is meant to be king when he pulls a sword out of a stone. Once Arthur is marked as king, he goes to study with a teacher named Merlin, an old white-haired man with a beard. Harry Potter has a similar teacher named Dumbledore. Both popular stories explore heroic themes that have been popular in literature throughout centuries.

Practice 2 pp. 129–130

Baseball and cricket have several similarities. Not only cricket but also baseball began in England and later came to the United States.

Both sports are bat and ball games. The games mostly use the same equipment, but the bats are not similar in shape. Cricket bats are flat, and baseball bats are round. However, the balls in baseball are made of the same material as the balls in cricket. The objective in both sports is to win points called runs by batting the ball when the opposing team throws it, similar to other bat and ball games. Likewise, in both sports, the hitting team wins points by hitting the ball and running from one base to another. The opposing team tries to strike out or stop the hitting team so that they can take a turn at hitting. As you can see, the popular sports share many similar features.

CONTRAST SIGNALS

Practice 1   p. 131

The contrast between dogs and cats is not always obvious, yet the two animals are different in many ways. One way they differ is in their behavior. Dogs are far more social than cats. For example, because dogs are eager to please their owners, they can be trained to do tricks and to obey simple commands like come, sit, and fetch. Cats, on the other hand, have no interest in pleasing their owners and cannot be trained in this way. Also, dogs are pack animals, whereas cats are solitary creatures. This means that dogs like (and sometimes need) to travel and be in the company of other dogs. In contrast, cats are loners whose main concern is protecting their territory, not spending time with other cats. Another difference is that cats are good jumpers and climbers, dogs are not. Cats in the wild climb and jump to hunt and escape from danger. However, dogs do not climb and jump well, so they need to travel in packs to hunt effectively, and they fight rather than flee when they feel threatened.

Practice 2   pp. 131–132

Conventional farming differs from organic farming in several ways. First, unlike organic farmers, conventional farmers use many non-natural substances. For example, they use chemical fertilizers to promote plant growth, whereas/while organic farmers use compost or manure to fertilize the soil. Conventional farmers use insecticides to eliminate pests and disease, while/whereas their organic counterparts use insects and birds, traps, and other methods. Conventional farmers use herbicides to control weeds; however, organic farmers control them by rotating crops or removing the weeds by hand. Another key difference is in the food that the animals eat and the conditions in which they live. Conventional animals eat a variety of food, but they are also given antibiotics and growth hormones to prevent disease and make them grow faster. The animals are also housed in small, crowded spaces indoors. In contrast, organic animals eat a strict diet of grass and organic feed, and, living in confined spaces, they are allowed to roam freely outdoors. A final contrast is the impact that farming has on the land. Because organic farming helps to reduce pollution and conserves water and soil, it is better for the environment than conventional farming.

DESCRIPTIVE DETAILS

Practice 1   p. 133

He was not a man given to flowery speeches and long explanations. Personality

He never wasted anything including words. Personality

Every Sunday, he would sit and cut coupons carefully from the Sunday paper to save money. Personality

When he stood still, he was like a tree rooted to the earth. Physical appearance

When he talked, he had a quiet stern voice that rumbled like distant thunder. Personality

At 6 feet 4 inches, he was a tall man with a large bones and a heavy frame. Physical appearance

He had an angular face with high cheekbones, and his skin was the color of reddish-brown clay. Physical appearance

He was all economy and efficiency because of his poor rural upbringing in Oklahoma. Background information /Personality

When he spoke, it was always carefully measured and brief. Personality

Practice 2 p. 134

1. c, 2. a, 3. b, 4. b, 5. d, 6. b

EXAMPLES AND REASONS

Practice 1 pp. 135–136

[4] According to a report from the U.S. Census Bureau, a high school graduate makes about $20,000 less than a college graduate annually.

[6] Second, college tuition is rising, and many students need to take out student loans to pay for their education.

[10] Finally, because high school graduates are no longer able to get good jobs, and many are unable to afford college tuition, the government should prepare citizens for the workforce by offering free college education.

[7] More and more students are leaving college with too much debt.

[1] In my opinion, there are two important reasons to make college education free for anyone who wants to attend.

[8] For example, it is common for a university graduate with a bachelor's degree to leave school with $100,000 or more in student loans.

[2] First, it is no longer possible for a person to make a decent salary with only a high school education.

[5] Thus, it is clear that a college education can prevent the likelihood that someone will be poor.

[9] Therefore, college graduates may struggle financially even with their earning potential because of debt.

[3] For instance, many high school graduates end up in minimum-wage jobs that pay less than $9 an hour.

Practice 2 pp. 136–137

1. More and more people are eating larger amounts of fatty and sugary food.

   For instance, a McDonald's value meal in the United States 20 years ago consisted of a 12-ounce soda, a small side of French fries, and a 3-ounce hamburger; however, the current "super-sized" value meal consists of a 20-ounce soda, a large side of French fries, and an 8-ounce hamburger.

2. According to the Food Research and Action Center, many people spend too much time on sedentary activities.

   The average person spends at least half of the day sitting at a desk, playing video games, surfing the Internet, and driving from one place to another.

3. Grocery stores in low-income neighborhoods do not stock healthy foods like fruit, vegetables, and whole grains because most people cannot afford to buy them.

   It is unacceptable that in many countries an apple costs more than a candy bar.

4. People tend to eat when they are depressed and unhappy about their lives for a number of reasons.

   People with a stressful lifestyle may overeat because they do not have time to prepare healthy food, or because they use food as a way to relax.

SPATIAL ORDER

Practice 1 p. 138

[5] To my right are our parents.

[2] At the far left is my sister, Yolanda, who's holding her oldest child.

[7] We all dressed in black and white outfits for the photo.

[1] The photo was taken by a professional photographer who used sepia tones to get the warm, antique effect.

[4] That's my sister Cerise and me next to Yolanda's husband.

[6] Then at the far right is my eight-year-old nephew, who, as you can see, loves having his picture taken!

[8] The sepia tones and our simple black and white outfits give the photo its old-time look.

[3] Next to Yolanda is her husband, Raul, who's holding their six-month-old baby.

Practice 2 p. 138

[3] Yolanda's husband is standing behind her holding their six-month-old baby.

[7] My mother and father are to the right of Cerise and me.

[5] I am sitting on a stool at the center of the photograph with Cerise behind me.

[2] To the left, my sister, Yolanda, is sitting in a high-backed chair and holding her oldest child in her lap.

[1] The photograph was professionally done using sepia tones that give the picture a warmer appearance than a stark black and white photograph would have.

[9] My father and my sister's husband are dressed simply in plain black suits and white shirts, and my mom, my sisters, and I are all in simple black dresses.

[4] My other sister, Cerise, and I are next to Yolanda and her husband.

[8] My father is sitting next to me, and my mother is on his right side.

[6] Cerise is standing next to Yolanda's husband with her hands on my shoulders.

TIME ORDER SIGNALS

Practice 1 p. 140

Before you start	Next
First	as long as
As soon	Finally
Once	until
After	

Practice 2 p. 140

[5] Meanwhile, my father had decided to coach a women's basketball team to meet girls.

[2] My father, on the other hand, is American.

[10] If it hadn't been for basketball, my parents might never have met 40 years ago.

[6] Both teams played against each other in the spring of 1973.

[3] He moved to Seattle, Washington, when he returned from the Vietnam War in 1969.

[8] At the party, my parents were introduced to one another by a mutual friend.

[1] My mother is from San Juan, Puerto Rico, but she left when she was 18 years old to move to Vancouver, B.C., in Canada.

[7] My father's team lost, but the Canadian team hosted a party for them anyway.

[4] After my mother moved to Vancouver, she began to play on a women's basketball team to make friends.

[9] It was love at first sight.

Coherence

LOGICAL DIVISION OF IDEAS

Practice 1 pp. 142–143

1. Tell them the rules, be consistent about punishment, don't get angry and criticize.
   Solutions to a problem
   Easy to difficult
2. Use an unpleasant solution on your nails, find new ways to release your anxiety, and do things that help you relax.
   Steps
   First to last
3. Copying someone's assignment, not citing a source, using your own work from a different class
   Types
   Most obvious to least obvious

Practice 2 p. 143

First of all	In addition
Furthermore	Finally

NOUNS AND PRONOUNS

Practice 1 p. 144

it	Their
coulrophobia	they
their	them
coulrophobia	the phobia

Practice 2 p. 144

them / it / they / she / him

Unity

Practice 1 pp. 145–146

1. a, 2. b, 3. a, 4. b, 5. a, 6. b, 7. c, 8. c, 9. b, 10. a

Practice 2 pp. 147–148

1. b, 2. c, 3. b, 4. b, 5. a, 6. a, 7. a, 8. a, 9. b, 10. a, 11. b, 12. b, 13. b

Essay Structure

Practice 1 pp. 149–150

1. a, 2. d, 3. b, 4. d, 5 d

Practice 2 pp. 150–151

a. 1

b. 3

c. 2

Conclusion: 4

2 Thesis: 4

a. 2

b. 1

c. 5

Conclusion: 3

INTRODUCTORY PARAGRAPHS AND THESIS STATEMENTS

Practice 1 p. 152

[4] These couples think that divorce will solve their problems and make life easier.

[2] The latest figures say that over 50% of marriages end in divorce.

[5] However, there is evidence that divorce might actually have a number of harmful effects as well.

[1] A surprising number of marriages fail in the United States.

[3] Most couples get divorced because of money problems or because of lack of commitment.

Practice 2 pp. 152–153

a

I was out of a job.

I didn't know what to do.

d

c

e

b

BODY PARAGRAPHS

Practice 1 p. 154

1. b, c, e

2. a, c, d

3. b, d, f

Practice 2 p. 155

Note: No sub-topics and supporting details in the first or last paragraph of the essay.

First, Hurricane Katrina destroyed the social systems in New Orleans and surrounding areas. More than 1,800 people died in the initial days after the storm, and more than one million people were moved to other areas of the United States. Many of these people were never able to return to their original homes. They left the city for good, and the rich cultural roots of New Orleans were weakened. The huge migration of all people devastated by Katrina represents the largest U.S. migration since the Great Depression.

Next, the storm severely damaged the environment in the southern coastal areas. The massive flooding covered more than 215 square miles of beaches, swamps, marshes, and islands in water. Acres of land have been lost forever. A number of oil refineries malfunctioned as well because of the storm. All in all, there were more than 40 oil spills, and a total of seven million gallons of oil leaked into the water.

Economically, the hurricane cost local, state, and federal governments a lot of money. Since the canal levees broke in New Orleans, there was a huge amount of damage to historical buildings. Restoring these buildings is still costing a lot of money. So far, the government has spent more than $100 billion. However, the economic stability completely vanished from the region. People were unable to resume normal economic activities for months after the storm. For instance, the two biggest industries in the area are tourism and oil production. With the city in ruins and oil refineries shut down, it became impossible for many people to resume working.

CONCLUDING PARAGRAPHS

Practice 1 p. 157

2. In addition, adults may find school work and the classroom overwhelming if they been out of school for a while.

4. Since more and more adults are going back to school, colleges need to be more prepared to help these students transition.

3. They have to balance their responsibilities to family and work with their responsibilities at school.

1. To conclude, adult students may find college difficult.

Practice 2 p. 157

3. In order to determine this, people should always seriously consider if a divorce is right for them.

4. Ultimately, only the individual can really determine the best decision for himself or herself.

2. Divorce can be emotionally painful, but in some cases, may lead to a better situation.

1. To sum up, people who get divorced often experience financial, emotional, and or health effects.

Body Paragraph Organization

BLOCK VS. POINT-BY-POINT

Practice 1 pp. 158–159

1. Similarities

8	6	

Android

2	7	4

iPhone

3	5	9

2. b

Practice 2 pp. 160–161

1. Similarities

2	5	6

U.S. education system

4	8	1

Chinese education system

9	7	3

2. a

WRITING ASSIGNMENTS PP. 162–208

Answers will vary.

POST-TEST

Post-Test 1 pp. 224–231

1. b, 2. b, 3. a, 4. c, 5. c, 6. b, 7. b, 8. a, 9. d, 10. d, 11. b, 12. d, 13. d, 14. d, 15. c, 16. c, 17. b, 18. a, 19. d, 20. b, 21. a, 22. c, 23. a, 24. b, 25. c, 26. d, 27. d, 28. d, 29. d, 30. d, 31. b, 32. a, 33. d, 34. b, 35. d, 36. d, 37. b, 38. b, 39. a, 40. b, 41. a, 42. b, a, a, a, c, a, b, c 43. a

Post-Test 2

Paragraph p. 232

Answers will vary.

Essay p. 233

Answers will vary.